D1230602

Fixing the Food System

FIXING THE FOOD SYSTEM

Changing How We Produce and Consume Food

Steve Clapp

Foreword by Marion Nestle

An Imprint of ABC-CLIO, LLC
Santa Barbara, California • Denver, Colorado

Library of Congress Cataloging-in-Publication Data

Names: Clapp, Steve, 1938– author.
Title: Fixing the food system : changing how we produce and consume food / Steve Clapp ; foreword by Marion Nestle.
Description: Santa Barbara, California : Praeger, [2017] | Includes bibliographical references and index.
Identifiers: LCCN 2016029142 (print) | LCCN 2016030914 (ebook) | ISBN 9781440843709 (hard copy : alk. paper) | ISBN 9781440843716 (EISBN)
Subjects: | MESH: Nutrition Policy | Food Industry | Food Safety | Food—economics | United States
Classification: LCC TX359 (print) | LCC TX359 (ebook) | NLM QU 145.7 AA1 | DDC 363.8/561—dc23
LC record available at https://lccn.loc.gov/2016029142

ISBN: 978-1-4408-4370-9
EISBN: 978-1-4408-4371-6

21 20 19 18 17 1 2 3 4 5

This book is also available as an eBook.

Praeger
An Imprint of ABC-CLIO, LLC

ABC-CLIO, LLC
130 Cremona Drive, P.O. Box 1911
Santa Barbara, California 93116-1911
www.abc-clio.com

This book is printed on acid-free paper ∞

Manufactured in the United States of America

Contents

Foreword

In this welcome addition to my library of books about food policy and politics, Steve Clapp's *Fixing the Food System* reviews the past and current history of calls for a national food policy, the most contentious controversies over food and nutrition issues that have impeded development of such a policy, and the work of advocates to achieve one. As this book makes clear, this history began decades ago.

I first became aware of the importance of federal food policies in the early 1980s when I was teaching nutrition to medical students at the University of California–San Francisco (UCSF). First-year students were eager to learn about nutrition, but for personal more than for professional reasons. They wanted to know what they—and the patients whose health problems they were learning to treat—should eat. But by the time they were residents, I could see their dietary concerns vanish under the daily demands of patient care. Trying to advise about diets was too difficult, time-consuming, and financially unrewarding to be worth the trouble. It seemed unreasonable to expect doctors to take the time needed to counsel individual patients about the prevention of diet-related conditions—heart disease, type 2 diabetes, cancer, and the like. If nutritionists like me wanted to focus on disease prevention rather than treatment, we would have to advocate to change the food environment to make healthful food choices the easy choices—even better, the preferred choices. This meant we would have to advocate for food and nutrition policies aimed at promoting public health.

In 1983, I coauthored an article with UCSF colleagues on the need for such policies.[1] It began, "The U.S. government helps to assure an adequate food supply for Americans by sponsoring a wide variety of food, nutrition, and agricultural support programs. These federal activities were developed in the absence of a clearly articulated national policy, a situation that has resulted in the fragmentation of government programs and their wide disbursement among numerous agencies and departments."

Our article quoted the earliest calls we could find for a national policy to address these problems. In 1974, long before the term "food system" came into common use, the National Nutrition Consortium of four leading nutrition and food science societies[2] argued for a national nutrition policy that would

- Assure an adequate, wholesome food supply, at reasonable cost, to meet the needs of all segments of the population;
- Maintain food resources sufficient to meet emergency needs and to fulfill a responsible role as a nation in meeting world food needs;
- Develop a level of sound public knowledge and responsible understanding of nutrition and foods that will promote maximal nutritional health;
- Maintain a system of quality and safety control that justifies public confidence in its food supply;
- Support research and education in foods and nutrition with adequate resources and reasoned priorities to solve important current problems and to permit exploratory basic research.

Whether offered as nutrition or food policies, these were and remain highly appropriate goals for an abundant, healthy, safe, and effective food system.

My coauthors and I went on to identify the constraints that then limited government action to achieve such goals. Despite an emerging consensus on the basic elements of healthful diets—fruits and vegetables, balanced calories, not too much junk food (as Michael Pollan put it more recently, "eat food, not too much, mostly plants"[3])—the greatest impediment to policy development was the controversy over the science of diet and health. As our article understated this issue, "The effect on the nation's health of food processing and other changes in the U.S. diet is controversial. Salt, sugar, fiber, saturated fats, alcohol, caffeine, calories, vitamins, and food additives all elicit vigorous debate."

Today, more than 30 years later, we are still arguing about that science and the scientific arguments still impede policy development. In *Fixing the Food System*, Steve Clapp brings us up to the minute on federal progress (or the lack thereof) toward achieving a clearly articulated national food policy. He begins and ends his book with the most recent policy proposals from leading food advocates Michael Pollan, Mark Bittman, Olivier de Schutter, and Ricardo Salvador. Their recent suggestions for improving our current food system reflect the many changes in agricultural production and food consumption that have taken place since 1974 but retain the basic elements of those earlier proposals. *Fixing the Food System* explains why a national food policy is so badly needed and matters so much.

Steve is in a unique position to comment on food policy issues. He's been at the policy game for a long time. I don't remember when I first met him, but I have been reading his work since he reported for the Community Nutrition Institute's newsletter, *Nutrition Week*. For those of us outside the Beltway in those pre-Internet days, *Nutrition Week* was a lifeline to the ins and outs of food politics in Washington, D.C. Later, when Steve moved to *Food Chemical News*, also—and still—a lifeline, I continued to read his reporting. I often ran across him at meetings and hearings in Washington, D.C., and found it instructive to read what he wrote about those deliberations, not least because he got it right.

I say all this because he has been a keen observer of the food politics scene in Washington for decades, and I can't think of anyone who ought to know it better. *Fixing the Food System* reviews the major debates he has witnessed—the Dietary Guidelines, of course, but also attempts to set policy for food safety, marketing to children, hunger in America, and humane treatment of farm animals, among others.

Over the years, he also has observed the work of policy advocates, and this book includes profiles of many individuals engaged in this work, some likely to be familiar to readers, whereas others may not. Impossible as it is for me to judge whatever impact my own writing and advocacy might have, I am honored to be included among those whose work he presents.

Fixing the Food System describes political arguments over the kind of food system we ought to have and what an ideal system should accomplish. But it is also about the importance of personal and political advocacy for better food policies, those aimed squarely at promoting public health and environmental sustainability.

Advocacy makes a difference. Advocates are scoring successes in improving one after another aspect of the food system. In comparison to the 1970s or 1980s, we now have better food in supermarkets, more organic foods, more farmers' markets, more nutritious food in schools, and impressive declines in consumption of sugary drinks. My personal favorite among indicators of advocacy success—the change that makes me most optimistic—is the increasing number of college students who care deeply about food issues. They are demanding local, seasonal, organic, and sustainably produced food in their cafeterias, and campus vegetable gardens. And they are demanding and getting food studies courses and programs like the ones we started at New York University in 1996 that teach about how food is produced and consumed and the practical and symbolic meanings of food in modern culture and societies. Today's students are tomorrow's advocates for healthier and more sustainable diets for everyone, everywhere, and for fixing what needs fixing in our food systems. This book is a great starting place for this work.

—Marion Nestle, Paulette Goddard Professor of Nutrition, Food Studies, and Public Health at New York University, June 2016

Preface

Not long ago, in answer to a question at a dinner party, I remarked that I covered the politics of food.

"What's political about food?" I was asked.

"Everything," I replied, and the other dinner guests laughed.

In the second decade of the 21st century, I don't have to go into a lengthy treatise to explain my answer. A sophisticated listener knows that food policy involves everything from animal welfare to nutrition labeling.

It wasn't always so. In the 1960s and 1970s, food was pretty much taken for granted, and a healthy diet was personal responsibility. My career in food policy journalism dates back to 1971, when Rodney Leonard, executive director of the Community Nutrition Institute, asked me to edit his weekly newsletter. I remember asking myself, "Do I really want to get stuck in a journalistic backwater like food?" How little I knew!

I went on to edit *CNI Weekly Report/Nutrition Week* for a dozen years and then became communications coordinator for Interfaith Action for Economic Justice, an antipoverty lobby funded by religious denominations and agencies.

I ended up at *Food Chemical News*, a weekly newsletter greatly valued by the food industry, federal regulators, and consumer advocates. I covered countless meetings in North America and Europe, spent two years as a foreign correspondent in Brussels, and retired as senior editor in 2013.

The 1970s were a time of ferment in food advocacy. At CNI we hired Bob Greenstein, who went on to run the USDA's Food and Nutrition Service and found the think tank Center on Budget and Policy Priorities. Ellen Haas was recruited to form CNI's consumer division, from which she launched Voice for Food and Health Policy and became a USDA undersecretary who sought to improve school meals.

I also came to know and admire other food advocacy pioneers: Carol Tucker-Foreman, a USDA assistant secretary who fought for food safety and Dietary Guidelines; Michael Jacobson, who founded the influential Center for Science in the Public Interest; Ron Pollack, founder of the antihunger Food Research and Action Center; Marian Burros, a reporter who created a food policy beat in newspapers and television; Joan Dye Gussow, who revolutionized nutrition education at Columbia Teachers College; and Marion Nestle, a New York University professor who gave birth to food studies and wrote a landmark book, *Food Politics: How the Food Industry Influences Nutrition and Health*.

All these pioneers, including Nick Kotz, a Pulitzer Prize–winning journalist, and Art Simon, founder of Bread for the World, are profiled in this book.

Today's influential food advocates include best-selling author Michael Pollan; former *New York Times* columnist Mark Bittman; Ricardo Salvador, director of the food and environment program at the Union of Concerned Scientists; and Olivier De Schutter, a former high-ranking official at the UN Food and Agriculture Organization (FAO). Their manifesto for a national food policy, published in *The Washington Post* in 2014, provided an outline for this book.

I owe a debt of gratitude to Hilary Claggett, a senior editor at ABC-CLIO who shepherded me through book publication. I'm also grateful to a string of editors at *Food Chemical News*, especially Ray Galant, Jason Huffman, Declan Conroy, and the late Lou Rothschild, who founded the newsletter.

My daughter Melissa Clapp Johnson, a freelance editor, and my wife Bette Hileman, a journalist who retired from the American Chemical Society, helped edit my manuscript with numerous valuable suggestions. My older daughter Emilia Clapp Kelly, a graduate of Columbia Teachers College, was also helpful. Other supportive family members include my brother-in-law Steven Channing, a southern historian, author, and video producer; my sister Nancy Clapp-Channing, a retired clinical research manager at Duke Medical Center; my brother David Clapp, a retired world history teacher at Lincoln-Sudbury (Mass.) High School; and my sister-in-law Diane Clapp, a retired nurse specializing in infertility.

But enough of the thank-yous. Let's fix the food system!

Acronyms

ABA	American Beverage Association
AHI	Animal Health Institute
AMS	Agricultural Marketing Service
CAFO	Concentrated Animal Feeding Operation
CBPP	Center on Budget and Policy Priorities
CDC	Centers for Disease Control and Prevention
CFA	Consumer Federation of America
CFBAI	Children's Food and Beverage Advertising Initiative
CFS	Center for Food Safety
CFSAN	FDA Center for Food Safety and Applied Nutrition
CNI	Community Nutrition Institute
CSPI	Center for Science in the Public Interest
CVM	FDA Center for Veterinary Medicine
DGAC	Dietary Guidelines Advisory Committee
EDF	Environmental Defense Fund
EITC	Earned Income Tax Credit
EPA	Environmental Protection Agency
ERS	Economic Research Service
EWG	Environmental Working Group
F&WW	Food & Water Watch
FAO	UN Food and Agriculture Organization
FDA	Food and Drug Administration

FNS	USDA Food and Nutrition Service
FRAC	Food Research and Action Center
FSIS	USDA Food Safety and Inspection Service
FSMA	Food Safety Modernization Act
FTC	Federal Trade Commission
GAO	Government Accountability Office
GMA	Grocery Manufacturers Association
GRAS	Generally Recognized as Safe
HEW	Health, Education, and Welfare
HHS	Health and Human Services Department
NAMI	North American Meat Institute
NCC	National Chicken Council
SNA	School Nutrition Association
SNAP	Supplemental Nutrition Assistance Program
UCS	Union of Concerned Scientists
USDA	U.S. Department of Agriculture
WHO	UN World Health Organization
WIC	Women, Infants, and Children supplemental nutrition program

PART I

A Broken Food System

CHAPTER ONE

Toward a National Food Policy

In newspapers, television, and social media, we are constantly confronted with clashes between the food system we know and an emerging movement that wants to change the way we produce and consume our food. For example, beverage companies advertise sodas they say will make us feel loved and happy. Coca-Cola in 1971 famously ran a TV ad showing young people singing, "I'd like to buy the world a Coke and keep it company."

For their part, consumer advocates want to limit the size of sodas, tax them, and print health warnings on their labels. New England Patriots quarterback Tom Brady called Coca-Cola "poison for kids."[1]

On the food policy front, there are fierce battles over ensuring food safety, establishing dietary guidelines, marketing to children, setting school meal standards, cutting food stamps, encouraging sustainability in food production, raising wages and reducing injuries among food workers, and treating food animals kindly before slaughter.

This book sorts out the messages on both sides of the conflict. What changes are needed? Who is advocating them? Who is opposing them and why? Can there be solutions? What would a new food system look like?

On November 18, 2013, four leaders of the emerging food movement met in the living room of Michael Pollan, best-selling author of *The Omnivore's Dilemma* and journalism professor at the University of California in Berkeley.[2] The other three leaders in Pollan's Berkeley living room were Mark Bittman, a *New York Times* food columnist; Ricardo Salvador, director of the Union of Concerned Scientists' (UCS) food and environment program in Washington, D.C.; and Olivier De Schutter, a visiting fellow at the Berkeley Food Institute who formerly served as special rapporteur for right to food at the UN Food and Agriculture Organization (FAO).

The four participants knew one another by reputation and meeting here and there, where they recognized their compatible views. The opening question they asked one another was "Where to press?" It was clear to them that food issues weren't on the agenda of the nation's elected officials, and the dysfunction of the U.S. political system wasn't conducive to changing the food system.

The Farm Bill, which authorizes federal agriculture and nutrition policies, was again in its five-year cycle after much delay, and there was no prospect for that legislative leviathan to achieve anything but "gilding the status quo in favor of Big Ag and Big Food," the four leaders recall. In fact, the final 2014 Farm Bill cut billions from food stamps. In the past, rural and urban lawmakers agreed to help one another's constituents through the Farm Bill. This time conservatives wanted to separate nutrition provisions into a separate bill and make deep cuts to food stamps.

After discussing a long list of issues ripe for attention, the Berkeley group said it reached three conclusions:

- The United States needs to consider a series of related policy issues in coordination: fair wages, immigration, healthy food access, public health, the economic viability and livelihood of family farms, conservation practices in agriculture, animal welfare, climate change, democratic process, and the public interest.
- Advancement of the changes through the Farm Bill was very unlikely. The Obama administration surprisingly gave lip service to food and health issues through First Lady Michelle Obama, yet it was ignoring any real political power in the emerging food movement.
- The most viable recourse might be to influence the administration, through a combination of direct advocacy and public pressure, to develop a coordinated policy for food, health, and well-being. This Berkeley group's small, impromptu "think tank" was composed of four academics and writers. The best the partners could do was to write about their ideas.

One year later, on November 7, 2014, the leaders published a widely circulated manifesto in *The Washington Post's* Sunday Outlook section, "How a National Food Policy Could Save Millions of American Lives." They proposed that President Obama announce, in his 2015 State of the Union address, an executive order establishing a national policy for food, health, and well-being.[3]

Though the Obama administration never responded directly, the advocates' appeal generated public conversation and interest. It inspired follow-up writing, speaking requests, and background conversations with current and prospective officeholders at all levels of government. It also galvanized the various quarters of the food movement around the idea of a coherent, coordinated national food policy, a certain sign of an idea whose time has come, the advocates concluded.[4]

Fallout from Unhealthy Diets

Like the rest of us, the four food movement leaders have witnessed the fallout from unhealthy diets. Overweight and obesity have become the new normal, resulting in thousands of deaths and millions of health care dollars spent on preventable chronic diseases, such as diabetes, hypertension, and atherosclerosis.

At a USDA Agriculture Outlook Forum, Pamela Hess, executive director at the Alexandria, Virginia–based Arcadia Center for Sustainable Food and Agriculture, urged Agriculture Secretary Vilsack to "create health as an important part of agriculture policy." She noted that low-income people don't eat the right food and suffer obesity and diabetes.[5] Hess, whose center attracts military veterans for farming careers, said low-income people with diabetes have more foot amputations than war veterans whose feet were blown off by improvised explosive devices (IEDs) in Iraq and Afghanistan. She cited some 70,000 amputations annually for diabetics.

The 20th century witnessed public health achievements extending people's lives. Now today's children can expect to live shorter lives than their parents because of preventable diseases.

Stressing that the food industry touches everything from health to the environment, climate change, and economic inequality, the food movement leaders lamented, "We have no food policy—no plan or agreed-upon principles—for managing American agriculture or the food system as a whole."

The movement leaders urged investing resources to guarantee that

- All Americans have access to healthful food;
- Farm policies are designed to support our public health and environmental objectives;
- Our food supply is free of pathogens, toxic chemicals, and drugs;
- Production and marketing of our food are done transparently;
- The food industry pays a fair wage to those it employs;
- Food marketing sets children up for healthful lives by instilling in them a habit of eating real food;
- Animals are treated with compassion and attention to their well-being;
- The food system's carbon footprint is reduced, and the amount of carbon sequestered on farmland is increased; and
- The food system is sufficiently resilient to withstand the effects of climate change.

"Only those with a vested interest in the status quo would argue against creating public policies with these goals," they declared.

National Food Policy Isn't New

The food movement leaders cited precedents for a U.S. food policy. Already a handful of states have developed food charters, and scores of U.S. cities have established food policy councils to expand access to healthful food.

Elsewhere, Brazil and Mexico have already developed national food policies. Mexico's recognition of food as a key driver of public health led to passage in 2013 of a national tax on junk food and soda, which in the first year reduced consumption of sugary beverages by 10 percent and increased consumption of water.

Brazil has implemented a national food policy since 2004. In the city of Belo Horizonte, that policy—coupled with an investment of 2 percent of the local budget in food access and farmer support programs—has reduced poverty by 25 percent and child mortality by 60 percent, and provided access to credit for two million farmers, all within a decade.

Canada moved toward a national food policy following the election of Justin Trudeau as prime minister in October 2015. He and his party advocated:

- New restrictions on the commercial marketing of unhealthy food and beverages to children, similar to those now in place in Quebec;
- Tougher regulations to eliminate *trans* fats, similar to those in the United States, and to reduce salt in processed foods;
- Improved food labels to give more information on added sugars and artificial dyes in processed foods; and
- Additional investments of $40 million for Nutrition North and $80 million for the Canadian Food Inspection Agency.[6]

The four movement leaders in Berkeley weren't the first to propose a national food policy. In the heyday of emerging consumer food groups in the 1970s, advocates proposed policies to achieve healthy outcomes. There were calls for a national nutrition policy emerging from antihunger programs.

In 1977, the Community Nutrition Institute organized a National Food Policy Conference, in Washington, D.C., that brought together consumer advocates and representatives of government and the food industry. That annual conference was later sponsored by Public Voice for Food and Health Policy, and it continued to thrive every year, thanks to the Consumer Federation of America.[7]

The healthful food policy concept caught fire at the Federal Trade Commission (FTC), which sought to impose major restrictions on television advertisements aimed at young children. That proposal ran into an unlikely buzz saw, the liberal *Washington Post*, whose editorial board, in 1978, called the idea "a preposterous intervention that would turn the agency into a great national nanny."[8]

The food and broadcasting industries, and their congressional allies, seized the "national nanny" insult to criticize any further efforts to curb junk food marketing to children. In a November 1981 lecture to the University of California's Business School titled "Stoning the National Nanny: Congress and the FTC in the Late '70s," former FTC chair Mark Pertshuck described the agency's failure to extend "an inescapable and conservative extension of the common law's ancient strictures against the exploitation of minors."[9]

The dream of a national food policy largely evaporated with the arrival of the Reagan administration. In a 1988 report titled "Empty Calories: The Reagan Record on Food Policy," the Public Voice for Food and Health Policy said there are "promises, rhetoric and gestures toward consumers but little real substance" in the areas of food safety, diet and health, and food assistance to poor people.[10]

More recently, consumer advocates, members of Congress, and the Government Accountability Office (GAO) have argued for the creation of a single food safety agency. However, they have met strong resistance from existing agencies and entrenched congressional committees on Capitol Hill.

The food movement leaders also conceded that "reforming the food system will ultimately depend on a Congress that for decades has been beholden to agribusiness, one of the most powerful lobbies on Capitol Hill. As long as food-related issues are treated as discrete rather than systemic problems, congressional committees in thrall to special interests will be able to block change."

To the leaders' disappointment, President Obama's 2015 State of the Union address made no mention of food policy. However, the UCS launched a petition drive on the national food policy proposal that quickly garnered nearly 20,000 signatures. A Twitter chat by the authors potentially reached three million users with the hashtag #NFPtalk.[11]

Pushback from Wide Range of Critics

Any discussion of food policy strikes a raw nerve in the public. Everyone has to eat, and no one likes others making food choices for him or her. Once the food movement leaders' op-ed piece was published on *The Washington Post*'s website, 788 comments flooded in over the next week before the comment period closed. Many comments were vitriolic in nature, calling the writers Big Brother, "comrades," "commissars," and "fascists." Comments from the other side dismissed the opponents as ignorant.

"This is part-and-parcel of how progressives will take a good idea like 'healthy eating' and make it into a leftist referendum of liberal tyranny," wrote commenter Kirk Rende. "This isn't about healthy eating—this is about controlling people and forcing society to conform to liberal agendas. It's not even a subtle manifesto."

"This is leftists' attempts to control our lives under some sort of 'benevolent' guise. Look at all the liberal talking points they hit in their faux concern about our health: state-control, organic foods, animal treatment leading to vegetarianism, more regulations, 'fair wages,' 'global warming' indoctrination, 'carbon footprint,' etc."

A commenter identified as *jurynullification* added, "Nations that have instituted national 'food policies' usually end up starving large segments of their populations to death. In the grand scheme of things, we have plentiful food, cheaper than most of the rest of the world. We choose what and how much we eat. WE chose to buy our food or raise it ourselves. We're free to choose wisely or poorly, depending upon our whims and inclinations.

"In other words, there is NOTHING wrong, except some people think we are too stupid to choose the way they want us to choose. Coercive utopians, intent on taking away your choices, your options, and treating you like a pet dog—fed only what they want to feed you, when they want to feed you."

On the other side, a commenter identified as *Mark75* said, "The folks who feel these ideas are socialist are perhaps missing the point that the government is already engaged in central planning by subsidizing sugar, corn, wheat and soybeans. It's your tax dollars being redistributed right now to make Doritos and ice cream so cheap. And you are also paying for the insulin shots needed by people who choose to (or due to budget) subsist on this food.

"The current situation is the worst kind of central planning gone awry one could imagine. The authors are suggesting that we discontinue this practice. Are you speaking in favor of it?"

Dialogue about a National Food Policy

The Washington Post manifesto did start a public dialogue about a national food policy. For example, David Festa, vice president of ecosystem programs at the Environmental Defense Fund (EDF), offered thoughtful analysis on an EDF food blog titled *Growing Returns*. He questioned the food movement leaders' suggestion that Obama unveil the national food policy initiative in his State of the Union address.[12]

Festa explained that the only time a presidential announcement of a "national policy" reliably works is when the elements of a national policy already exist but people haven't yet realized it. "Think Wizard of Oz: he made all the difference to the lion, tin man and scarecrow by recognizing and elevating what they already had," he suggested.

Festa said big policy announcements work when all but a few key ingredients have been assembled. "In other words, presidential action can be immensely powerful when there's some consensus on viable solutions," he said. "Unfortunately, we aren't there yet in the food debate. Having the president put a stake in the ground on food policy in today's political reality is more likely to elicit swift and strong statements in opposition. That will slow down progress at a time when there isn't a moment to lose."

Elsewhere, on Capitol Hill, Sen. Cory Booker (D-N.J.) and Reps. Rosa DeLauro (D-Conn.) and Chellie Pingree (R-Maine) all joined in on a Twitter chat following *The Washington Post* article by the food movement leaders. DeLauro commented, "Long past time for a National Food Policy. Thanks to all who joined #NFP talk and made your voices heard."[13]

A Model for Political Action

Asked about *The Washington Post* manifesto, David Acheson, a former high-level FDA official who now runs his own consulting firm, said he supports policies that bring down barriers and leverage resources. However, he acknowledged the entrenchment of current systems. Whenever anyone wants to change government policy, fiefdoms seek protection.[14] Government is unlike business, where new leadership can undertake mergers or "clean house" of dead wood, he said. In government, all workers are protected, and they can undercut change as quiet agitators or passive saboteurs.

Another barrier confronting food policy change is the need to address all sectors at once: public health, regulation, legal aspects, and consumer benefits, said Acheson. It's imperative to take the private sector into account. Leadership must get private groups to buy in to make the change successful.

A third barrier is resources, said Acheson. The change process requires resources, such as new technology for data handling, and they must be used efficiently. "There may ultimately be cost savings, but there needs to be investment up front," he said.

Acheson played an important role in passage of the FDA Food Safety Modernization Act, a major piece of legislation known as FSMA. After joining FDA in 2002, he became associate commissioner for foods, which provided him an agency-wide leadership role for all food and feed issues. He was given responsibility for the development of the 2007 Food Protection Plan, which served as the basis for many of the authorities granted to the agency by FSMA.

After the 9/11 terrorist attack in 2001, increasing concern over bioterrorism and major outbreaks of foodborne illness forced the FDA to rethink its food safety mission. A major outbreak of salmonellosis in 2008 and 2009 was linked to tainted peanuts processed by the Peanut Corporation of America, whose customers ranged from small, family-owned businesses to multinational companies.

In 2009 and 2010, Congress debated several food safety proposals that directly and indirectly affected farms and on-farm processing. These proposals extended regulatory authorities to farms and made some on-farm safety standards mandatory. Concurrently, the Obama administration created an interagency Food Safety Working Group through which the FDA and USDA started adopting new food safety standards and oversight.

Signed into law in January 2011, the FSMA overhauled the nation's food safety practices for the first time since 1938 and became a model for other legislative action. FDA officials recognized the need for change, as did consumer advocates and the food industry. The obvious need for reform overcame the inertia that normally resists major changes in government.

Both the Grocery Manufacturers Association, an umbrella food trade association, and the Center for Science in the Public Interest, a leading consumer advocacy group, lobbied for passage of the FSMA. "Consumers had one agenda and the industry had another, but they were both shooting at the same target," said Acheson. "But there must be common pain somewhere to force action."[15]

Examining Elements of National Food Policy

The four food movement leaders were disappointed that the Obama administration didn't immediately embrace their national food policy concept. But they didn't give up. "Think of the food system as something that works for us rather than exploits us, something that encourages health rather than undermines it. That is the food system the people of the United States deserve," the four leaders quote from their *Washington Post* manifesto. They conclude, "This concept remains available as a winning political hand for some future visionary President or group of legislators to deliver. [We] continue to work in support of a movement-based strategy to insert food issues into the highest levels of the nation's political discourse and policy setting."[16]

Jenn Yates, campaign strategist at the UCS, noted that earlier the UCS had published reports on concentrated animal feeding operations (CAFOs), antibiotic resistance, and investment in fruits and vegetables. "All of these reports point to a need for a unified food policy or strategy," she said. "We're starting to make progress on how to execute such a strategy. Critics complain we gave no specifics, but we're not naïve about how the government works. We're laying out our vision.[17]

"The notion that our food system is based on a free market is pretty far from the truth. There are lots of political forces at work. We think a safety net for farmers is appropriate, but making increased productivity the prime objective no longer makes sense.

"Our vision should be attractive to political conservatives, because it saves money needed for environmental cleanup and medical bills from bad diets. These should be compelling arguments for conservatives. We're not telling consumers what to eat or telling farmers what to produce."

In the chapters to follow, we examine the various elements of the national food policy proposed by the food movement leaders: true food costs, food safety, dietary guidelines, marketing to children, hunger, sustainability, fair wages for food workers, and animal welfare. Each of the proposals has its advocates and its opponents, and each problem can be solved.

CHAPTER TWO

The Real Cost of Food

Americans are fortunate to have an abundant food supply with products that cost relatively little in supermarkets and restaurants compared with the cost in other countries.

We take pride in buying cheap, high-quality food. In annual consumer expenditures, we spend on average 6.7 percent for food at home, according to the USDA's Economic Research Service. That percentage is less than all of the 92 other countries for which ERS tracks data. Even high-income countries, such as Norway (13 percent) and Japan (13.6 percent), spend a larger percentage of their annual consumer expenditures on food than Americans do.[1]

However, the true cost of food is something else. A realistic accounting of the price of food would include: short- and long-term medical problems from foodborne illness and occupational injuries to food and agriculture workers; medical bills generated by obesity, diabetes, and other diet-related chronic diseases; and environmental problems created by concentrated animal feeding operations (CAFOs) and other agricultural pollution.

Solving all these problems could save millions of dollars. Ignoring the problems costs millions of dollars.

"Imagine if the price you paid for a hamburger included factors such as heart disease, the number one cause of death worldwide; or the runoff of manure spread on fields from [CAFOs]; or injuries to workers in slaughterhouses and processing plants; or the poor animal welfare practices in livestock operations," asked Danielle Nierenberg, president of the Washington, D.C.–based Food (think) Tank. "It would certainly be more than US$0.99 and would not be part of the value menu."[2]

Trouble with Salmonellosis Ignored for Many Years

A dramatic example of true cost accounting occurred at the Consumer Federation of America's National Food Policy Conference, in Washington, D.C., in April 2015. Foodborne diseases in general are very costly to America. The Centers for Disease Control and Prevention (CDC) estimates that each year roughly one in six Americans (48 million people) suffers foodborne illness, 128,000 are hospitalized, and 3,000 die. The annual cost to society is an estimated $78 billion, including medical costs, productivity losses, and long-term pain, suffering, disability, and death.[3]

Salmonella each year cause approximately 1.2 million illnesses in the United States, with 19,000 hospitalizations and 380 deaths, according to the CDC. Salmonellosis may occur in small, contained outbreaks in the general population or large outbreaks in hospitals, restaurants, or institutions for children or the elderly. Symptoms include diarrhea, fever, abdominal cramps, and headache along with possible nausea, loss of appetite, and vomiting.

Children are the most likely to contract salmonellosis, according to the National Institute of Allergy and Infectious Diseases. Noah Craten, an 18-month-old boy in Phoenix, developed a severe infection in September 2013 that led to bacteria pooling on his brain. Surgeons opened his skull to ease the pressure. He survived, but his mother reports his left eyebrow sags and his left eye blinks rapidly. He also developed cysts on his brain that must be removed if they grow.[4]

The elderly, infants, and individuals with compromised immune systems are more likely to experience a severe illness than the general population. People with AIDS are particularly vulnerable, often suffering from recurring episodes.

While most people recover successfully from salmonellosis, a few develop Reiter's syndrome, a chronic condition that can last for months or years and can lead to arthritis, according to the NIH. Symptoms include painful joints, irritated eyes, and painful urination. Unless treated properly, *Salmonella* bacteria can escape from the intestine and spread by blood to other organs, sometimes leading to death.

The USDA's Economic Research Service in May 2015 estimated the cost of nontyphoidal salmonellosis in the year 2013 at $3.7 billion, calculating medical costs, productivity loss, and deaths. *Salmonella* accounted for 24 percent of the $15.5 billion in costs caused by the 15 leading foodborne pathogens, including *Campylobacter*, *Norovirus*, *Listeria monocytogenes*, and *Toxoplasma gondii*.[5]

As the final speaker at the 2015 National Food Policy Conference's breakout session on *Salmonella*, Anna de Klauman, minister counselor for food and agriculture at the Danish embassy, described Denmark's success in eliminating salmonellosis in an agricultural country with "more pigs than people." She said salmonellosis was a major problem in Denmark in the 1990s before a *Salmonella* action plan effectively eliminated the disease.[6]

Denmark in 1988 experienced roughly 3,600 cases of salmonellosis related to broiler chickens, she reported. Thanks to the action plan, in 2015 there had been no cases linked to broilers in the past three years, and the same was true regarding table eggs. Denmark now has zero tolerance for *Salmonella*, even on the farm. De Klauman acknowledged that Denmark's program is expensive because it relies on destruction of feeder flocks contaminated with *Salmonella*. Farmers are compensated for destruction of such flocks, "but the cost of illness is much greater." Denmark calculated that the cost of salmonellosis outweighed the cost of reimbursing farmers for destruction of contaminated flocks. The government turned its anti-*Salmonella* program over to industry in 2002 and continues to monitor its success.

Better Late Than Never

Unlike Denmark, the United States only recently paid serious attention to salmonellosis. The USDA's Food Safety and Inspection Service (FSIS) didn't create a *Salmonella* Action Plan until December 2013. Before 2015, the FSIS tested for *Salmonella* only on whole-chicken carcasses, ignoring chicken parts, such as legs and breasts, which are most popular with consumers.

In January 2015, the FSIS proposed new performance standards to reduce *Salmonella* and *Campylobacter* contamination in raw chicken breasts, legs, and wings, as well as in ground chicken and turkey products. The agency's risk assessment estimated that implementation of these standards would lead to an average of 50,000 prevented illnesses annually.

However, the new standards aren't enforceable, and plants that fail to achieve them can't be shut down. Rep. Rosa DeLauro (D-Conn.), a long-time food safety advocate on Capitol Hill, complained that "voluntary standards are not sufficient to protect American families from two of the most common foodborne pathogens. Time and again we have seen that when we trust industry to police themselves, public health suffers. I fear this time will be no different."[7]

The public face of salmonellosis is the giant chicken processing firm Foster Farms, based in Livingston, California, which was linked to nearly 1,000 cases in four separate outbreaks over a decade beginning in 2004 and ending in 2014. "About 300 of those cases occurred in Oregon and Washington," an investigative team reported in the Portland *Oregonian* newspaper in a series headlined 'A Game of Chicken.' "The overall toll was possibly much higher. The CDC estimates that for every confirmed *Salmonella* infection, more than 29 go unreported. . . . Oregon investigators became so familiar with the culprit they gave it a name: the Foster Farms strain."[8]

The *Oregonian* team reported that hundreds of people were "struck by bouts of food poisoning so severe they fled to their doctors or emergency rooms for treatment." The salmonellosis victims had no idea where their illness came from, but federal regulators did. Oregon and Washington public health officials repeatedly told the USDA they had linked salmonellosis outbreaks in 2004, 2009, and 2012 to Foster Farms chicken. "State officials pushed federal regulators to act, but *Salmonella*-tainted chicken flowed into grocery stores, first in the Northwest, then across the country," the newspaper reported.[9]

The *Oregonian* team says it reviewed thousands of pages of government records related to Foster Farms and interviewed dozens of health officials, inspectors, food safety experts, and federal managers. "The records and interviews reveal for the first time an agency [the FSIS] that over a 10-year span had repeatedly failed to protect consumers when confronting one of the nation's largest poultry processors.

"During that time, FSIS issued hundreds of citations at the company's sprawling plant in Kelso, Wash. But the agency allowed the plant to operate even though people kept getting sick."

The Foster Farms debacle was also thoroughly investigated for a widely watched *Frontline* hour-long documentary, "The Trouble with Chicken," which was aired on PBS stations in May 2015.[10]

Nine Months before a Recall Took Effect

FSIS officials recommended recalling Foster Farms poultry products tainted with *Salmonella Heidelberg* as early as October 25, 2013, almost nine months before the recall went into effect, according to documents released June 4, 2015, by the advocacy group Food & Water Watch. The documents were obtained through a Freedom of Information Act (FOIA) request filed on October 17, 2013.

"Why it took so long for FSIS and Foster Farms to take action to prevent further illnesses is still baffling to us," commented Wenonah Hauter, F&WW executive director. "These documents show that some staff at FSIS wanted to protect consumers from further exposure to potentially dangerous chicken, but their bosses were too timid to do so. The federal government needs to close the loophole in FSIS's statutory authority so the agency can do its job to protect the public and finally act without ambiguity."[11]

Foster Farms Sees the Light

To its credit, Foster Farms sought to repair its reputation with a major overhaul of its efforts to control *Salmonella* contamination. The company developed a multihurdle *Salmonella* control program across breeder stock, grow-out, and processing plant facilities. Foster Farms said it has consistently achieved a 5 percent or lower level of *Salmonella* contamination in raw chicken parts, one-third of the 15.4 percent parts contamination standard proposed by the USDA in January 2015.[12]

Foster Farms worked closely with the USDA, the CDC, the poultry industry, and retailers to share its lessons in controlling *Salmonella* to help create a safer food supply system nationwide. The company says it "continues to draw on the best food safety advice in and outside of the poultry industry" through its Food Safety Advisory Board.[13]

Foster Farms in 2013 implemented a $75 million food safety program that it said "effectively reduced *Salmonella* system-wide from the breeder level, to the farms where the birds are raised and to the plants where the chicken is processed and packaged. This included improvements to equipment and processes, the implementation of a continuous testing program and food safety education."[14]

Robert O'Connor, the company's senior vice president for technical services, led a National Chicken Council committee on *Salmonella* reduction at the parts level and assisted retailers in their development of vendor protocols. In recognition of his efforts, he received a 2015 Food Safety Innovation Award at the Food Safety Summit in April 2015.[15]

The United States has a long way to go to eliminate the costly disease salmonellosis. The USDA is caught between its public health obligations and the politically powerful meat and poultry industry, which often pushes Congress or the courts against food safety measures it dislikes.

Contamination often starts on the farm, but the USDA's FSIS isn't authorized to visit farms. Contaminated birds then proceed to the slaughterhouse, where bacteria can spread to other carcasses. When the FSIS finds solid evidence of an outbreak, it first alerts the company, not the public. In the Foster Farms cases, the agency didn't notify consumers throughout the first three outbreaks. As a rule, the agency waits for evidence it believes would stand up to a potential court challenge before taking significant enforcement action.

The Cost of Diet-Related Diseases

It's difficult to measure precisely the cost of food related to chronic diseases such as diabetes, hypertension, atherosclerosis, and cancer, but the most convenient way is to measure the astonishing increase in overweight and obesity in the United States since 1980. The estimated annual health care cost of obesity-related illness is a staggering $190.2 billion, or nearly 21 percent of annual medical spending in the United States.[16]

Diet and exercise are intertwined when it comes to weight gain. The food industry often blames the obesity epidemic on lack of "personal responsibility" among adult men and women. A study by researchers at the Stanford University School of Medicine, published in the August 2014 issue of the *American Journal of Medicine*, supports this argument.[17]

Analyzing 20 years of data from the National Health and Nutrition Examination Survey (NHANES), the Stanford researchers found a sharp decrease in physical exercise and an increase in average body mass index (BMI) while calorie intake remained the same. According to the NHANES data, the number of U.S. adult women who reported no physical activity jumped from 19.1 percent in 1994 to 51.7 percent in 2010. For men, the number increased from 11.4 percent in 1994 to 43.5 percent in 2010. During that period, average BMI increased across the board, with the most dramatic rise found among women 18–39 years old.[18]

"These changes have occurred in the context of substantial increases in the proportion of adults reporting no leisure-time physical activity, but in the absence of any significant population-level changes in average daily caloric intake," explained lead investigator Uri Ladabaum, a Stanford medical professor. The study was financed by the NIH.[19]

Coca-Cola in 2015 embraced the lack-of-exercise argument to create a Global Energy Balance Network aiming to convince the public that the secret for combating obesity is to exercise more, not to eat or drink fewer calories. But *The New York Times* reported that Coca-Cola had financially supported the researchers who came up with scientific evidence underpinning the Global Energy Balance Network. "The beverage giant has teamed up with influential scientists who are advancing this message in medical journals, at conferences and through social media," the newspaper reported.[20]

"The soda industry would love you to believe that the principal cause of obesity is lack of physical activity, and they put tons of money into research to discourage other ideas," commented Marion Nestle, a New York University nutrition professor in her *Food Politics* blog. "They much prefer you to believe that all of their products can be part of an active, healthy lifestyle that includes balanced diets, proper hydration and regular physical activity. I call the idea the 'physical activity diversion.' It deflects attention from what really counts in obesity prevention: not eating huge amounts of junk foods, snack foods and sodas."[21]

The University of Colorado announced that it was giving back the $1 million Coca-Cola had donated to fund the Global Energy Balance Network. Coke said it would donate the returned money to the Boys & Girls Clubs of America. "Both deserve congratulations for making a difficult but necessary decision," Nestle told *The New York Times*. "Let's hope other groups also decide to do the right thing and end such financial relationships."

The Global Energy Balance Network folded, and Rhona Applebaum, Coke's chief science and health officer who had orchestrated the project, announced her retirement on November 24, 2015. Blaming lack of exercise for obesity turned out to be a public relations disaster for the company.[22]

Whether or not lack of exercise is to blame, obesity and related diseases have real economic costs affecting all of us, according to the National League of Cities (NLC), which sponsors the Let's Move! project. The United States has the highest diabetes prevalence among developed nations, reported a new International Diabetes Federation atlas released in November 2015.[23] Some 11 percent of the U.S. adult population aged 20–79—an estimated 30 million persons—suffer from the disease. Americans count for about one-third of the 83 million cases among all the 37 developed countries.

Childhood obesity alone is responsible for $14 billion in direct medical costs, said the NLC. Obesity-related medical costs in general are expected to rise significantly, especially because today's obese children are likely to become tomorrow's obese adults. If obesity rates remained at 2010 levels, the projected savings for medical expenditures would be $549.5 billion over the next two decades.[24]

The direct and additional hidden costs of obesity are stifling businesses and organizations that stimulate jobs and growth in U.S. cities, the NLC reported. In the 10 cities with the highest obesity rates, the direct costs connected with obesity and obesity-related diseases are roughly $50 million per 100,000 residents. If these 10 cities cut their obesity rates down to the national average, the combined savings to their communities would be $500 million in health care costs each year.

According to a Gallup-Healthways survey in 2012–2013, the 10 most obese cities by percentage were Huntington-Ashland, Ohio (39.5 percent); McCallen, Texas (38.3 percent); Hagerstown, Maryland (36.7 percent); Yakima, Washington (35.7 percent); Little Rock, Arkansas (35.1 percent);

Charlestown, West Virginia (34.6 percent); Toledo, Ohio (34.2 percent); Clarksville, Tennessee (33.8 percent); Jackson, Mississippi (33.8 percent); and Green Bay, Wisconsin (33.0 percent).[25]

Over the past four decades, childhood obesity rates in America have quadrupled, and today more than 23.5 million children and youth in America—nearly one in three—are overweight or obese. Moreover, significant disparities exist. For example, more than 39 percent of Hispanic youth and African American youth aged 2–19 are overweight or obese, compared with about 28 percent of white youth.[26]

Overweight and obese children are at higher risk than their healthy-weight peers for a host of serious illnesses, including heart disease, stroke, asthma, and certain types of cancer. Obese children are being diagnosed with health conditions historically only seen in adults, such as type 2 diabetes, high blood pressure, and cardiovascular disease (CVD). In a sample of youth aged 5–17, some 60 percent of obese children had at least one CVD risk factor.

"If we don't reverse the obesity epidemic, our children are in danger of becoming the first generation of Americans who live sicker and die younger than their parents' generation," the NLC forecast. Furthermore, one-third of all boys and two out of every five girls born in 2000 or later will suffer from type 2 diabetes at some point in their lives. That number is even higher among Hispanic and African American children.[27]

The NLC noted that access to unhealthy food has increased in the past few decades. Some 30 years ago, kids ate just one snack per day, whereas now they are trending toward three snacks, resulting in an additional 200 calories per day. One in five school-aged children consumes up to six snacks per day. In total, we are now eating 31 percent more calories than we were 40 years ago—including 56 percent more fats and oils and 14 percent more sugars and sweeteners. The average American now eats about 30 more pounds of sugar per year than in 1970.[28]

"If trends continue, we will see a 42 percent obesity rate in this country among adults, and future trends in childhood obesity prevalence will have a major impact on adult obesity prevalence and obesity-related costs," warned the NLC.[29]

In addition to growing health care costs attributed to obesity, the United States will incur higher costs for disability and unemployment benefits, according to "The State of Obesity," a project of the Trust for America's Health and the Robert Wood Johnson Foundation. Obesity-related job absenteeism costs $4.3 billion annually. Obesity is also associated with lower productivity while at work ("presenteeism"), which costs employers $506 per obese worker per year. As a person's body mass index (BMI) increases, so do the number of his or her sick days, medical claims, and health care costs.[30]

The Environmental Cost of Agriculture

Meat is cheap at the supermarket, at least compared with similar prices in Europe and elsewhere. But American shoppers rarely consider what keeps prices down. In addition to foodborne illness and chronic diseases, the real cost should be measured by the meat industry's use of CAFOs, which the Environmental Protection Agency (EPA) defines as feeding operations with a relatively large number of food animals and a significant amount of pollutants.

Federal law and policy disproportionately favor large meat producers that operate CAFOs, said Foscolo & Hanel PLLC, a food law firm based in Sag Harbor, New York, adding, "Federal law helps other big producers to distort the cost of their agricultural production by allowing them to sequester lakes of animal waste on their land, which are absolutely inevitable byproducts of CAFO production."[31] This regulatory policy allows CAFO operators to hide some of their production costs. "For a multitude of reasons, small scale farmers and ranchers do not share these economic benefits and are therefore held hostage to inelastic costs of production which they must reflect in their retail pricing," said the law firm.[32]

Foscolo & Hanel acknowledged that CAFOs "definitely create efficiencies in agriculture. Cramming many animals in a small lot most obviously saves acreage, and land is expensive. Putting all the animals in one place allows ranchers to stuff cattle full of cheap, subsidized commodity crops like soybeans and corn. It is easier to apply veterinary care to CAFO animals, and they require less labor to oversee during their development."[33]

However, to achieve these efficiencies, CAFOs must contend with the stubborn problem of waste concentration. "Thousands of cattle confined to a small lot produce a volume of waste that overloads the ability of the natural environment to recuperate on its own," said the law firm. "CAFO operators need to scoop it all up and put it someplace. Federal law allows for these waste products to be sequestered into lagoons adjacent to farms and fields. But for these lakes of animal waste, all of the other efficiencies created by CAFO production would be obviated."[34]

In contrast, cattle raised mostly on grass and moved frequently don't require collection of their waste, which fertilizes fields naturally.

The regulators intend to make the sticker price of commodity meat *seem* as low as possible without regard to production costs. Most commodity farmers may view CAFO policy as completely benign, said the law firm.

"The vast majority of supermarket consumers may be supremely indifferent to it, even if made aware of its deleterious environmental consequences or its dishonesty as an agricultural ethic."

The size of CAFOs grew significantly larger from 1997 to 2012, according to five-year USDA census data released May 27, 2015. The advocacy group F&WW created a map that displayed the location of CAFOs by size and species and provided interactive 15-year changes and county-level geographic locations.[35] Key findings from the F&WW analysis include the following:

- The total number of livestock on the largest factory farms rose by 20 percent between 2002 and 2012. The total number of livestock units on factory farms increased from 23.7 million in 2002 to 28.5 million in 2012. "Livestock units" is a way to measure different kinds of animals on the same scale based on their weight—one head of beef cattle is the equivalent of approximately two-thirds of a dairy cow, eight hogs, or 400 chickens.
- These factory-farmed livestock produced 369 million tons of manure in 2012, about 13 times as much as the sewage produced by the entire U.S. population. These 13.8 billion cubic feet of manure would fill the Dallas Cowboys stadium 133 times. Unlike sewage produced in cities, the manure on factory farms doesn't undergo any treatment.
- The number of dairy cows on factory farms doubled, and the average-sized dairy factory farm increased by half, between 1997 and 2012. The number of dairy cows on factory farms with more than 500-head rose 120.9 percent from 2.5 million cows in 1997 to 5.6 million in 2012. The average size of dairy factory farms grew by half (49.1 percent), from 1,114 cows in 1997 to 1,661 in 2012. In nine states—Kansas, Oklahoma, New Mexico, Arizona, Idaho, Texas, Indiana, Missouri, and Nevada—the average size was more than 2,000 cows in 2012.
- The number of hogs on factory farms increased by more than one-third, and the average farm size swelled nearly 70 percent from 1997 to 2012. The number of hogs on factory farms with more than 1,000 head grew by 37.1 percent—from 46.1 million in 1997 to 63.2 million in 2012. The average size of a hog factory farm increased 68.4 percent, from 3,600 hogs in 1997 to nearly 6,100 in 2012.
- The number of broiler chickens on factory farms rose nearly 80 percent from 1997 to 2012, to more than 1 billion. The number of broiler chickens raised on factory farms that marketed more than 500,000 chickens annually rose 79.9 percent, from 583.3 million in 1997 to 1.05 billion in 2012—about three birds for every person in the United States. The average size of U.S. broiler chicken operations rose by 5.9 percent, from 157,000 in 1997 to 166,000 birds in 2012. The average size in California and Nebraska exceeded 500,000 birds in 2012.
- The number of egg-laying hens on factory farms increased by nearly one-quarter from 1997 to 2012, to 269 million. The number of egg-producing layer hens on factory farms with more than 100,000 hens increased 24.8 percent, from

215.7 million in 1997 to 269.3 million in 2012. Nearly half (49.3 percent) of the egg-laying hens in 2012 were in the top five egg-producing states: Iowa, Ohio, Indiana, California, and Texas. The average size of egg operations has grown by 74.2 percent over 15 years, rising from 399,000 in 1997 to more than 695,000 in 2012.

- The number of beef cattle on feedlots rose 5 percent from 2002 to 2012. Feedlot size grew even as the 2012 drought reduced total cattle numbers. The number of beef cattle on operations with at least 500 head grew from 11.6 million in 2002 to 12.1 million in 2012. Texas, Nebraska, and Kansas each had more than 2 million beef cattle on feedlots in 2012. The 2012 drought reduced the total number of beef cattle on feedlots nationwide, but the average feedlot size increased by 13.7 percent over five years, from 3,800 in 2007 to more than 4,300 in 2012.

F&WW said the growth of factory farms can be attributed to several factors: "Unchecked food company mergers and corporate acquisitions have contributed to increased consolidation that allows giant agribusinesses to exert influence over livestock markets and production. Lax environmental rules and enforcement have allowed factory farms to balloon in size without being held accountable for the tremendous amounts of waste they create."[36]

Nationwide, animals produce 130 times more waste than humans—roughly five tons for every U.S. citizen, according to the GAO. Some operations with hundreds of thousands of animals produce as much waste as a town or a city.[37]

"These large volumes of waste threaten surface water and groundwater quality in the event of waste spills, leakage from waste storage facilities, and runoff from fields on which an excessive amount of waste has been applied as fertilizer," the GAO reported.

"Furthermore, as animal production is increasingly concentrated in larger operations and in certain regions of the country, commonly used animal waste management practices may no longer be adequate for preventing water pollution. Consequently, new waste management practices may be needed, including alternative uses for waste, new means of treating waste, and improved methods of moving waste to cropland where it can be used as fertilizer."

In 2015, the poultry industry in the Midwest experienced outbreaks of highly pathogenic avian influenza (HPAI) that forced the slaughter of 48 million birds, caused egg prices to soar, and required the USDA to provide $191 million in indemnification to farmers for killing diseased poultry. The economic loss to the United States was "conservatively estimated at nearly $3.3 billion."[38]

Surveying the damage, Michael Osterholm, director of the University of Minnesota's Center for Infectious Disease Research and Policy, questioned the egg industry's huge "layer operations," which house millions of birds in one location. When a virus pierces biosecurity defenses or when defenses lapse, the result is devastating, he told *Fortune*.[39]

Other Environmental Costs Need to Be Considered

Among the many environmental costs that need to be considered in a full-cost accounting of industrial agriculture, the Union of Concerned Scientists listed the following:

- Damage to fisheries from oxygen-depleting microorganisms fed by fertilizer runoff
- Increased health risks borne by agricultural workers, farmers, and rural communities exposed to pesticides and antibiotic-resistant bacteria
- Enormous indirect costs implicit in the high energy requirements of industrial agriculture. "This form of agriculture uses fossil fuels at many points: to run huge combines and harvesters, to produce and transport pesticides and fertilizers, and to refrigerate and transport perishable produce cross country and around the world. The use of fossil fuels contributes to ozone pollution and global warming, which could exact a high price on agriculture and the rest of society through increased violent weather events, droughts and floods, and rising oceans."[40]

In short, those "value meals" at restaurants and in your own home cost far more than you have to pay at the cash register. Think carefully about the real cost of your food.

CHAPTER THREE

The Unfinished Business of Food Safety

Nearly a century after Upton Sinclair's muckraking novel, *The Jungle*, which revealed stomach-turning practices in slaughterhouses, the American public in 1993 woke to another scandal that put food safety again at the forefront of national attention.

Undercooked hamburgers sold at the Jack in the Box fast-food chain caused hundreds of people in Northwest states to become ill and four children to die. The culprit was *E. coli* O157:H7, a pathogen found in cattle feces that can enter the food supply through meat or contaminated vegetables. Jack in the Box had cut corners by failing to follow new state health standards for cooking hamburgers.

In worst cases, *E. coli* infection can cause hemolytic uremic syndrome, which results from abnormal premature destruction of red blood cells. The damaged red blood cells clog the kidneys' filtering system, which may cause life-threatening kidney failure. Typical symptoms include swelling of the face and hands, bruises throughout the body, and blood leaking from the nose.

The *E. coli* scandal created four fierce food safety advocates. Bill Marler, a Seattle lawyer who took on the case of a friend's ill daughter, won a settlement of more than $50 million. The settlement included a $15.6 million award for a 10-year-old girl who spent 40 days in a coma. "It was the largest individual food poisoning claim in American history," noted the *New Yorker* in a profile of Marler, who went on to devote his career to fighting foodborne illness.[1]

Marler is fond of saying he wishes food safety officials preventing illness would put him out of business as a plaintiff's lawyer, but he continues suing food companies and makes tons of money. Instead of buying a sailboat as a rich man's plaything, he launched a free daily electronic newsletter, *Food Safety News*, which costs him about $250,000 each year to publish.

Three other noteworthy food safety advocates are two mothers and a grandmother who witnessed the deaths of beloved children from *E. coli* infection. Nancy Donley, a real estate broker in the Chicago area, experienced a life change when her only son Alex died in 1993 at age six after eating an undercooked hamburger at a family picnic.

Donley founded Safe Tables Our Priority (STOP), an organization determined to create a safer food system. Like her, many STOP members are parents of children who died of *E. coli* infection. STOP looks for food safety gaps or loopholes that need to be filled and measures to prevent illness from happening again. "STOP's mission is straightforward: to prevent illness and death from foodborne pathogens," she said.[2]

Two active STOP members were Barbara Kowalcyk and Patricia Buck, the mother and grandmother, respectively, of Kevin, a two-year-old boy who died in 2001 of complications from an *E. coli* infection. His illness was never legally traced to its source, although his O157:H7 strain matched the strain in meat recalled 16 days later.

Kowalcyk and Buck eventually left STOP in 2006 to form their own organization, the Center for Foodborne Illness Research and Prevention (CFI). Based in Raleigh, North Carolina, the center seeks to complement STOP by tackling different foodborne illness issues. Kowalcyk has a master's degree in applied statistics from the University of Pittsburgh and a PhD in environmental health from the University of Cincinnati, specializing in epidemiology and biostatistics. Her mother has a master's degree in English and is a skilled writer and communicator.

In 2002, Kowalcyk and Buck supported legislation to grant the USDA the authority to shut down plants that repeatedly produce meat and poultry products contaminated with *Salmonella*. Introduced by then-senators Tom Harkin (D-S.D.), Dick Durbin (D-Ill.), and Hillary Clinton (D-N.Y.), the Meat and Poultry Pathogen Reduction Act would have required the USDA to work with the Centers for Disease Control and Prevention (CDC) to identify foodborne pathogens that affect human health, set limits for those pathogens in meat and poultry products, and then shut down plants that repeatedly fail to meet those limits. The bill, renamed "Kevin's Law" in memory of Kowalcyk's late son, was introduced three times but failed to pass Congress.[3]

More recently, Tanya Roberts, the center's board chair and a former senior economist at the USDA's Economic Research Service, submitted a paper in 2015 to the International Association for Food Protection, charging that "bad companies are getting a free ride" for lack of a pathogen database that would link 99 percent of acute foodborne illness cases to specific companies and plants.[4]

"Why haven't scientific innovations to test and control pathogens from farm to fork been uniformly adopted by companies?" she asked. "Currently, weak regulations and the voluntary nature of the private marketplace only offer weak economic incentives to provide food safety."

Roberts said private market incentives for food safety are weak because the causative pathogen and the food company are rarely linked to the 47.8 million U.S. acute foodborne illnesses each year. Only 0.05 percent of all acute foodborne illnesses can be linked to the food and its company.

"This is a *very* small percentage of cases and provides minimal economic incentives, except where the rare large company can be identified," she said. "Even when a company can be identified, USDA has shown its reluctance to take action, as in the Foster Farms salmonellosis outbreak that lasted for over a year."

Roberts said, "Bad-actor companies that cause foodborne illness are given a 'free ride,' as these companies are *not* held accountable for the damage they inflict on U.S. consumers. This 'free ride' hurts companies that are good actors and do invest in superior pathogen control.

"As an economist, I look at things differently," she said. "Information is so central for markets to work well. The food industry doesn't want food safety to be a competitive matter. But look at Foster Farms! They got religion [after salmonellosis outbreaks damaged its reputation]. I think it's just a matter of getting your mind right.

"Sweden and Denmark have solved their problems, and it's not impossible for us," she continued. "The *Salmonella* contamination situation isn't changing here, and *Campylobacter* is a worse problem, with the possibility of [paralytic] Guillain-Barré syndrome. It's inexcusable."

In September 2015, the American Association for Justice (AAJ, formerly the Association of Trial Lawyers of America) claimed that the civil justice system is better than government regulations in protecting consumers against unsafe food. Federal regulators have been unable to keep pace with an "ever-changing industry," said AAJ in a report, "Food Safety and the Civil Justice System."[5]

The trial lawyers noted that the FDA lacks funding to make frequent inspections, and the USDA's Food Safety and Inspection Service (FSIS) lacks authority to order companies to recall products. Because 80 percent of foodborne illness cases are never traced to their origins, there are no consistent repercussions on food companies and no economic incentives to keep the promise of safe food.

"With food companies not adequately monitored by regulators or themselves, consumer lawsuits have proven to be the most effective, and sometimes the only, mechanism for deterring negligent behavior," the trial lawyers stated. "Knowing they could be held accountable in court provides significant incentive for manufacturers to improve food safety and end dangerous practices."

Marion Nestle, author of *Safe Food: The Politics of Food Safety*, lamented that the USDA "is caught between Congress, the industry and the courts; and each component of the meat and poultry chain—producers, processors, retailers and consumers—believes that responsibility belongs elsewhere. If nothing else, the legal battles . . . make it clear that nothing less than a complete overhaul of the existing food safety system can fix the problems and provide adequate oversight."[6]

E. coli O157:H7 Declared an Adulterant

In October 1994, FSIS administrator Michael Taylor classified *E. coli* O157:H7 as an "adulterant" that triggers an automatic recall whenever found in raw ground beef.

The FSIS began a sampling program to test for *E. coli* O157:H7 in raw ground beef prepared in federally inspected plants and in retail stores. The agency notified the public that raw ground beef products contaminated with *E. coli* O157:H7 are adulterated under the Federal Meat Inspection Act unless the ground beef is further processed to destroy this pathogen.

The FSIS's action in declaring *E. coli* O157:H7 an adulterant met a legal challenge from meat producers and retailers, but a federal court upheld the decision in December 1994. Pressured by Bill Marler and other food safety advocates, the agency has since taken further steps to prevent *E. coli* infections, declaring in 2012 six additional strains of *E. coli* as adulterants—026, 045, 01013, 0111, 0121, and 0145—and testing for them in beef.[7]

In another victory for food safety advocates, the FSIS now requires labeling of mechanically tenderized beef products. Advocates have argued for years that mechanically tenderized beef presents an increased risk to consumers because use of needles or blades can push *E. coli* from the outside to the inside of the meat.[8]

Under the new rule, which took effect in May 2016, tenderized beef products must include the designation "mechanically tenderized," "blade tenderized," or "needle tenderized" and an accurate description of the product. The designation and the product name must be in a single easy-to-read type style and color and appear on a single-color contrasting background.

The instructions must specify minimum internal temperatures and any hold or "dwell" times for the products to ensure that they are fully cooked.

The mechanically tenderized beef products labeling rule was strongly opposed by the meat industry. Robert Hibbert, a partner in the Washington, D.C., law firm Morgan, Lewis & Bockius, said the industry resisted the tenderized beef rule because companies viewed it as a warning label. "Is there a problem?" he asked, describing the meat industry's point of view. "If there is, is this a reasonable solution? My sense is that this is a world where consumers don't like processing. Few products are identified that way. It becomes a difficult road to go down."[9]

Another important step in keeping pathogenic *E. coli* under control is a rule issued on December 14, 2015, requiring all makers of raw ground beef products, including small retail outlets, to keep records that ensure traceability in case of illness. Noting that retail outlets regularly make ground beef by mixing cuts of beef from various sources, the FSIS requires them to keep clear records identifying the source, supplier, and names of all materials used in the preparation of raw ground beef products.[10]

Failure to Cope with *Salmonella*

In the food safety world, *E. coli* seems easier to deal with than *Salmonella*, although more deaths from *E. coli* continue from undercooked beef or transmission to fruits and vegetables. David Goldman, assistant administrator of the FSIS Office of Public Health Science, lamented that *Salmonella* is found everywhere in nearly every food, not just meat and poultry, and causes the most hospitalizations and deaths from foodborne illness.

"I think the key is virulence rather than the size of the dose," he told the National Food Policy Conference in April 2015. "Whole gene sequencing may be critical" to preventing disease.[11]

Goldman noted that *Salmonella* is expressed in about 2,500 serotypes, some 60 percent of which cause illness. The CDC discovers new serotypes almost every week.

Scott Eilert, vice president for food safety at Cargill Turkey and Cooked Meats, told the conference, "There's more that we don't know than what we do. We learn from outbreaks, especially from ground beef and turkey." Keeping meat clean can prevent *E. coli* outbreaks, he said, but with *Salmonella* "it's not enough to keep the carcass clean. There's internalization of *Salmonella* in the carcass.

"*Salmonella* is a battle fought from farm to table," he added. "We need to prevent colonization and migration into inner tissues. What more could we do? The infective dose is higher in salmonellosis [than in *E. coli*]. Look for products with higher rates of *Salmonella*."[12]

William James, a retired FSIS chief veterinarian, questioned reports of an encouraging decline in salmonellosis. Noting that *Salmonella* performance standards have been fully in place since 2000, he said in a blog, "That's 15 years of futility trying to bring down levels of salmonellosis despite changes in sampling, tightening of standards, and addition of products. But FSIS has political masters just like every other federal agency. The agency doesn't always get to do what it wants to do when it wants to do it. Even if FSIS wanted to do something different so it could report solid accomplishments next year, it couldn't. Politically it's just too late in this [Obama] administration to admit failure after all the 'rah-rah' associated with the rollout of the *Salmonella* Action Plan a couple of years ago [in 2013]."[13]

In a report released in April 2015, the Consumer Federation of America (CFA) analyzed how a 1999 court case (*Supreme Beef v. USDA*), won by a beef company, limited the department's ability to enforce its meat and poultry regulations, effectively barring the USDA from shutting down a processing plant that fails to meet *Salmonella* performance standards. Consumer advocates argue that Congress should provide the USDA with explicit authority to set and enforce food safety performance standards.

The CFA report charged that too often plants failed to develop effective food safety plans, while the USDA failed to adequately identify problems with those plans, and plants are repeatedly cited for recurring food safety violations with little consequence. The CFA said these gaps "have continued to occur and have often been identified in the wake of large, nationwide foodborne illness outbreaks, yet the problems have not been adequately addressed."[14]

Another consumer advocacy organization, the Center for Science in the Public Interest (CSPI), asked the FSIS to declare four antibiotic-resistant strains of *Salmonella* as adulterants in meat and poultry, stressing that antibiotic-resistant strains on meat and poultry have been linked to at least 2,358 illnesses, 424 hospitalizations, and 8 deaths. The CSPI also asked the FSIS to institute a sampling and testing program to detect the presence of the Heidelberg, Typhimurium, Newport, and Hadar strains of antibiotic-resistant *Salmonella*, to enable the agency to get tainted meat and poultry products out of the marketplace before they cause illnesses.[15]

However, the National Chicken Council said the poultry industry "will continue to oppose declaring any *Salmonella* as an adulterant in meat and poultry products. While eradicating *Salmonella* is always the goal of the chicken industry, the ubiquitous nature of the bacteria makes it impossible to get rid of it completely. This is why the industry relies on a multi-hurdle approach to minimize the prevalence of *Salmonella* through the process, even before the egg is hatched.[16]

"Even with very low levels of *Salmonella*, there is still the possibility of illness if a raw product is improperly handled or cooked," the chicken lobby warned. "All pathogens found on raw poultry, regardless of strain or resistance profile, are controlled during processing under existing standards and will be destroyed by cooking the product to an internal temperature of 165°F."

Instructions on chicken product labels, in small print, to "Cook thoroughly" are easily ignored. Also, *Salmonella* bacteria in chicken juice left on cutting boards can find their way to other foods, such as vegetables.

The poultry industry likes to remind us that chicken handled and cooked properly is 100 percent safe to eat. In 2015, the National Chicken Council boasted that processors reduced *Salmonella* on whole chickens by 63 percent over the previous five years, and 98.9 percent of USDA tests for *Salmonella* on whole chickens at large plants are negative. "Americans eat about 160 million servings of wholesome chicken every day, virtually all of them safely," said the chicken lobby.[17]

The industry also cited a report by the Interagency Food Safety Analytics Collaboration Project (IFSAC) finding that chicken isn't among the top contributors to salmonellosis. Other contributors include seeded vegetables fruits, sprouts, eggs, beef, and pork.[18]

The chicken lobby was unhappy with proposed pathogen performance standards for chicken parts and ground chicken. The USDA's Food Safety and Inspection Service, on January 26, 2015, proposed a maximum acceptable percent positive performance standard for raw chicken parts of 15.4 percent for *Salmonella* and 7.7 percent for *Campylobacter*. Prior to the FSIS announcement, there was no established regulatory standard for *Salmonella* on raw poultry parts, although the most recent 2011–2012 reported industry average was 25 percent.

Ashley Peterson, NCC senior vice president for scientific and regulatory affairs, urged the FSIS to allow two years for poultry plants to evaluate the final performance standards. She said it's "not appropriate to post categories while establishments are still adjusting to the new performance standard. FSIS estimates that a large percentage of establishments initially will not meet the proposed performance standard. Posting the names of these establishments—which are producing lawful, non-adulterated product—before they even have a chance to adjust to the new performance standards is unnecessarily detrimental to the regulated industry and to the agency and will not further food safety."[19]

However, the FSIS in February 2016 finalized its standards to reduce *Salmonella* and *Campylobacter* in ground chicken and turkey products, as well as in raw chicken breasts, legs, and wings. Some 90 days later, the agency began measuring how processors are meeting the new pathogen reduction standards.[20]

On Capitol Hill, Reps. Rosa DeLauro (D-Conn.) and Louise Slaughter (D-N.Y.) welcomed the new standards, but they said the FSIS should also declare *Salmonella* to be an "adulterant" for regulatory purposes.[21]

Salmonella in Peanuts Triggers New FDA Legislation

Michael Taylor, who declared *E. coli* O157:H7 an adulterant in 1994 while serving at the USDA, went on to become FDA deputy commissioner for foods and veterinary medicine. The USDA's FSIS oversees the safety of meat and poultry, while the FDA oversees the safety of all other food products—a curious historic division of labor between the two federal agencies.

Having overhauled the meat and poultry safety program in the USDA in the 1990s, Taylor found himself taking on a similar challenge at the FDA in 2009. President Obama came into office that year amid a widely publicized scandal in which a Peanut Corporation of America (PCA) plant in Georgia knowingly shipped *Salmonella*-contaminated products that caused 9 deaths and sickened more than 700 people in 43 states across the country. Two months into his presidency, Obama called on Congress to improve food safety laws.[22]

Taylor returned to the FDA in July 2009 to serve as senior advisor to the commissioner. Confronted with the PCA scandal, FDA officials acknowledged that seemingly "low-risk" products such as peanut butter, spinach, or cantaloupes could be as dangerous as undercooked hamburgers contaminated with *E. coli* O157:H7. The PCA's peanut customers ranged from small, family-owned businesses to global, multibillion-dollar food companies. Nearly 4,000 human and pet food products made with potentially contaminated PCA peanut products were recalled.

Stewart Parnell, former owner of the PCA, was found guilty of criminal charges, including conspiracy, wire fraud, and obstruction of justice in connection with the major salmonellosis outbreaks in 2008 and 2009. He received a 28-year prison sentence in 2015. An important lesson from the PCA case was buyers' need to verify that their suppliers are using appropriate food safety controls.[23]

The PCA scandal and other foodborne illness outbreaks gave rise to the FDA Food Safety Modernization Act (FSMA), which was signed into law in January 2011. The FSMA is widely considered the most significant food safety legislation since the 1930s. Supported by both consumer advocates and food industry trade associations, this law represented a bipartisan legislative response to foodborne illness outbreaks in the United States and abroad.

In addition to homegrown foodborne illness outbreaks, imported foods also became a concern to consumers. In China, infant formula adulterated with toxic melamine by unscrupulous manufacturers sickened and even killed babies, raising a cloud of suspicion over all products imported from that country.

The concerns about Chinese imports extended to imports from other countries, which are substantial. The FDA estimates that 15 percent of the U.S. food supply is imported, including 50 percent of fresh fruits, 20 percent of fresh vegetables, and 80 percent of seafood. Yet, the FDA has resources to inspect only about 2 percent of imported food.[24]

The consumer advocacy group Food & Water Watch (FW&W) paid close attention to questionable food imports from other countries, including Canada and Australia, which allowed company employees to conduct meat and poultry inspection. The group was also suspicious of seafood imported from countries in Southeast Asia.

In an October 21, 2015, letter, Rep. Rosa DeLauro urged U.S. trade representative Michael Froman to release provisions of the Trans-Pacific Partnership (TPP) free trade agreement that affect seafood safety. She noted that several countries involved in TPP negotiations, particularly Vietnam and Malaysia, have "notoriously lax" food safety standards.[25]

When the full TPP text was released in November 2015, F&WW, the CFS, and other advocacy groups expressed opposition to the free trade agreement. Debbie Barker, CFS international programs director, called the Investor State Dispute Settlement in the agreement "an extrajudicial legal body that allows private corporations to sue national governments over rules that companies believe inhibit their profit-making ability."[26]

The FSMA law directs the FDA, working with a wide range of public and private partners, to build a new system of food safety oversight focused on *preventing* foodborne illness rather than merely investigating illness outbreaks. Processors of all types of food are now required to evaluate the hazards in their operations and have a plan to take corrective actions. The FDA now has new enforcement tools, including mandatory recall, that allow it to remove contaminated food from the market. The agency has been required to design a product tracing system for foods it designates as "high risk."

The FSMA also required the FDA to set science-based standards for the production and harvest of fruits and vegetables and implement risk-based inspection of food-processing facilities. All high-risk domestic facilities were required to be inspected by 2016 and no less frequently than every three years thereafter.

As for food products coming into the United States, the FDA can now require that importers verify the safety of food from their suppliers and reject foods from facilities or countries that refuse its inspection. The agency promised to work more closely with foreign governments and increase inspection of foreign food facilities.[27]

Antibiotic Resistance Finally Gets Widespread Attention

Antibiotic resistance is a critical health issue in the United States and elsewhere. At least 23,000 people die each year because their bacterial infections are resistant to even the most powerful drugs. Overuse of antibiotics by physicians and animal agriculture creates antibiotic resistance. Antibiotics are routinely used to promote the growth of food animals and to prevent, control, and treat disease. Most antibiotics distributed in the United States are used for food animals.

The FDA released data in December 2015 showing that sales and distribution of antimicrobial drugs approved for on-farm use increased 23 percent between 2009 and 2014. "This report demonstrates what I have been saying for years, that FDA's policies have been toothless in the face of the continued, widespread misuse of life-saving antibiotics in factory farms," commented Rep. Louise Slaughter (D-N.Y.), a longtime food safety advocate with degrees in microbiology and public health.[28]

In September 2013, the CDC issued a "threat report" warning that antibiotics, including animal drugs, play a role in drug resistance. Among the 18 drug-resistant organisms the report highlighted as alarming *Campylobacter*, *E. coli*, *Salmonella*, and *Shigella*. These four are foodborne organisms that become drug-resistant as the foods that carry them are produced or grown.[29]

One year later, the White House announced its plan to make the antibiotic resistance issue a national priority. The President's Council of Advisors on Science and Technology (PCAST) said in its report, "The benefits of antibiotic use in animal agriculture, however, must be weighed carefully against the serious potential risks to human health posed by antibiotic resistance."[30]

The report recommended limiting the use of antibiotics in animal agriculture in line with the FDA's new guidance, including rulemaking to update the language of the Veterinary Feed Directive. Then, the USDA, through its Cooperative Extension Service, was urged to lead a national education and stewardship program to assist farmers, ranchers, and animal agriculture producers across the United States in complying with this FDA guidance.

Meanwhile, the FDA was urged to assess progress by monitoring changes in the total sales of antibiotics in animal agriculture and, where possible, in the usage of such antibiotics; and by developing and undertaking studies to assess whether decreases are observed in antibiotic resistance among farm animals.

"If the FDA guidances are not effective in mitigating the risk of antibiotic resistance associated with antibiotic use in animal agriculture, FDA should take additional measures to protect human health," the report added.[31]

However, Allan Coukell, senior director of drugs and medical devices at the Pew Charitable Trusts, commented, "It is essential now to ensure that antibiotic use in animals is really reduced and that these important drugs are administered only in medically appropriate ways under the supervision of a veterinarian."[32]

Keep Antibiotics Working expressed frustration that the report didn't include "more effective" actions. "Instead of recommending that FDA move to address overuse of antibiotics for disease prevention and the farming practices that create the need for them, the report recommends a wait and see attitude on reducing antibiotic use in food animals."[33]

The FDA Sought Detailed Data on Antibiotic Use

The FDA in May 2015 proposed a rule that would require antimicrobial drug companies to break down their annual sales and distribution reports to the FDA into major food species, such as chicken, turkey, cattle, and pork.

William Flynn, science policy director for the FDA's Center for Veterinary Medicine (CVM), told the inaugural meeting of the Presidential Advisory Council on Combating Antibiotic-Resistant Bacteria (CARB) in September 2015 that CVM needs more information on disease resistance. "Why is [an animal drug] product being used and under what system?" he asked, adding, "There's a disconnect with resistance information. It's an important gap that needs to be filled to see what is happening. We're coordinating with CDC and USDA to explore around that issue. We have more than one species to deal with—cattle and pigs on one label. How much are the sales for swine and cattle markets?"[34]

However, the Animal Health Institute (AHI), which represents drug manufacturers, argued there is a poor correlation between sales data and public health risk, citing encouraging data from recently released National Antimicrobial Resistance Monitoring System (NARMS) reports. "These data sets show that antibiotics can be and are being used carefully to protect animal health without adding to the human burden of antibiotic resistance," the AHI said.[35]

On October 10, 2015, California governor Jerry Brown signed a bill (SB 27) that would make his state the first in the nation to require a veterinarian's prescription for therapeutic antibiotic uses in livestock, ban other uses (including low-dosage levels used to prevent diseases), and require collection of data on antibiotic use.[36] Brown had vetoed a similar bill in 2014, explaining that it simply codified the FDA's voluntary standard for removing growth promotion claims from animal antibiotics labels and the agency's rule bringing all antibiotics under veterinary oversight. He said it was "unnecessary, since most major animal producers have already pledged to go beyond the FDA standard."

The new law, which would take effect on January 1, 2018, also requires the California Department of Food and Agriculture to start a monitoring program to gather information on medically important antimicrobial drug sales and usage, antimicrobial-resistant bacteria, and livestock management practice data.

In a lead editorial on October 26, 2015, *The Washington Post* commented, "After decades of inaction, concern about the use of antibiotics in animal agriculture is finally gaining traction, not because of federal regulations or congressional legislation, but because smart people around the nation are listening to consumers and thinking creatively about new ways of doing things. . . . What's impressive about the California example is that the law came about as a result of cooperation among representatives of public health, medicine, government, academia and agriculture."[37]

Food companies in March 2016 joined public health advocacy groups in pushing for more detailed data collection on how antimicrobials important to human health are used on the farm. Tyson Foods, Cargill, Hormel Foods, McDonald's, Costco, and Walmart sent a letter to Congress supporting funding requests to implement the National Action Plan for Combating Antibiotic-Resistant Bacteria.[38]

Animal Drug Industry Seeks Collaboration with Health Advocates

The animal drug industry came around to seeking collaboration with the health advocates. AHI spokesperson Ron Phillips said the industry "abandoned the trenches and sees a need to collaborate rather than point fingers."

He noted that the CDC's 18 "threat points" for antibiotic resistance include 2 linked to agriculture, "which we think are much more science-based. Everybody's got a role to play, and it's changing the landscape."[39]

A coalition of advocacy groups, on September 15, 2015, sent letters to the CEOs of the top 25 U.S. restaurant chains, urging them to choose only meat suppliers that don't use antibiotics to promote growth. They also released a 38-page report and scorecard that rated the companies on their antibiotics use policies. The 109-member coalition gave all but five of the companies *F*s for allowing routine antibiotic use by their meat suppliers. The 109-member coalition includes the Consumers Union, Center for Food Safety, and National Resources Defense Council.[40]

Chains receiving failing grades include Applebee's, Arby's, Burger King, Chili's, Dairy Queen, Denny's, Domino's, IHOP, Jack in the Box, KFC, Little Caesars, Olive Garden, Outback Steakhouse Grill and Bar, Papa John's Pizza, Pizza Hut, Sonic, Starbucks, Subway, Taco Bell, and Wendy's. The five chains earning passing grades include Panera Bread, Chipotle Mexican Grill, Chick-fil-A, McDonald's, and Dunkin' Donuts. The coalition said in its letter that the restaurant industry "can use its significant buying power to help stem this public health crisis by developing strong policies to reduce or eliminate antibiotic use in [its] meat and poultry supply chains."[41]

Subway later announced that its 27,000-plus outlets in the United States would start transitioning in 2016 to serving poultry products made only from turkeys and chickens raised without antibiotics.

On the meat industry side, Mark Graves, a corporate strategist for the meat and poultry industry, noticed that the chicken industry is responding to consumer demands for less antibiotic use in the raising of food animals. Major chicken companies have committed to raising chickens without using antibiotics.[42] Graves noted that chicken companies—such as Perdue and Tyson—had developed consumer-trusted brands that resonate with shoppers. "Chicken consumption took off when the major player decided to brand their wares and communicate their virtues," he reported.

The beef and pork industries have been left in the dust when it comes to the antibiotic resistance issue, said Graves. He recommended that big beef companies "come out with protocols for the reduction of antibiotic use in cattle raising and branding their fresh beef offerings. It's not only the right thing to do, it is the smart thing to do if the beef industry ever wants to reclaim its mantle of the consumer-preferred protein it held until chicken surpassed it in 2005."

Chemical Hazards in Foods and Packaging

For many years, U.S. consumers expressed more concern about chemicals added to foods than pathogens that could make them deathly ill. But the tide turned in the 1990s, when the public became aware of foodborne outbreaks linked to *E. coli* O157:H7, *Salmonella*, *Campylobacter*, *Listeria monocytogenes*, and *Norovirus*.

The industry-supported International Food Information Council's annual Food and Health Survey keeps its finger on the public's pulse. In 2014, it was no surprise that 34 percent of 1,000-plus adult respondents expressed concern about foodborne illness, and only 23 percent worried about food additives and chemicals that can migrate from packaging into food.[43] However, the 2015 survey found 36 percent of respondents listing chemicals as their leading concern, while 34 percent remained steady with concern about foodborne illness. Where did the 13 percentage point jump toward chemicals come from? The questions were somewhat different in the two years, but not enough to change the result.

Also troubling, the percentage of consumers who are confident in the safety of the U.S. food supply dropped from 70 percent in 2013 to only 60 percent in 2015. Where did that drop come from? The IFIC believes individuals who aren't confident in the U.S. food supply are "much more likely to be concerned about chemicals in food."

The Environmental Working Group (EWG), famous for its "Dirty Dozen" list of fruits and vegetables contaminated with pesticides, in November 2014 released a similar guide for food additives. The new Dirty Dozen list includes nitrates and nitrites, potassium bromate, propyl paraben, butylated hydroxyanisole (BHA), butylated hydroxytoluene (BHT), propyl gallate, theobromine, secret flavor ingredients, artificial colors, diacetyl, phosphates, and aluminum additives. The report provided details about concerns surrounding each additive. Some of them are known or possible carcinogens, and some can have reproductive and developmental effects. The EWG is also among consumer advocacy groups that claim some additives with "generally recognized as safe" (GRAS) status don't meet the same safety standard as food additives.[44]

In a 2014 report titled "Generally Recognized as Secret: Chemicals Added to Food in the United States," the Natural Resources Defense Council estimated that about 1,000 of the 10,000 food additives in use today are based on undisclosed GRAS safety determinations. The NRDC was able to identify 275 chemicals from 56 companies that appear to be used in food based on undisclosed GRAS safety determinations. Among the requests for FDA review, about one in five notices is rejected or withdrawn from review.

Such a withdrawal, however, doesn't prevent the company from marketing the product for use in food. The report details four chemicals with withdrawn GRAS notices—epigallocatechin-3-gallate (EGCG); gamma-amino butyric acid (GABA); theobromine; and sweet lupin protein, fiber, and flour. Despite safety concerns, each has been listed as an ingredient in some food products.[45]

In August 2014, the Grocery Manufacturers Association announced a plan to make the GRAS process more transparent for its member companies. The FDA in October 2014 agreed to finalize its rule for determining food substances as GRAS. The decision was part of a settlement with the Center for Food Safety (CFS), which sued the agency to vacate its 1997 GRAS proposal. The settlement agreement required the FDA to finalize the GRAS rule by August 2016. If it didn't meet this deadline, the CFS could ask the court to order the agency to fulfill its commitment and issue the rule.

"This is a major victory for consumers and the public," said Donna Solen, CFS senior attorney. "For more than 17 years, FDA has imposed a lax regulatory system [affecting] consumers without affording them their right to participate in the rulemaking process. This is a violation of federal law that will come to an end as a result of this settlement agreement."[46]

The FDA announced in January 2016 it planned to ban three specific types of perfluoralkyl ethyl chemicals used in many pizza boxes and other food packaging to act as oil and water repellants for paper and paperboard, which come in contact with aqueous and fatty foods. The announcement was a response to a petition by the NRDC and eight other consumer advocacy groups.[47]

The CSPI in March 2016 asked the FDA to require warning labels on foods containing Red 40, Yellow 5, and other synthetic food dyes, notifying parents about possible effects on children's behavior. It estimated that more than a half million children in the United States suffer adverse behavioral reactions after ingesting food dyes, with an estimated cost between $3.5 billion and more than $5 billion.[48]

A 2007 study at Southampton (U.K.) University found behavioral changes in children exposed to a mixture of dyes plus the preservative sodium benzoate. The European Union adopted legislation in 2009 requiring a label warning on foods containing these chemicals.

The FDA ran tests that found all exposure estimates for seven dyes well below the acceptable daily intake (ADI) levels it had previously identified. However, the CSPI said the ADIs are too high to protect children, and the FDA's recent exposure assessments are "seriously flawed." The advocacy group also claimed the FDA's website offers "misleading information about dyes and behavior."[49]

Companies Pledge to Ditch Additives and Preservatives

Panera Bread, a chain of bakery-café fast casual restaurants, in May 2015 published a list of artificial preservatives, sweeteners, colors, and flavors that it either didn't use or planned to remove from its food by the end of 2016. The company's "No No List" included high-fructose corn syrup, hydrolyzed soy or corn protein, added monosodium glutamate (MSG), Classes II–IV caramel color, and all parabens, among many other ingredients that had been linked to health problems, were difficult to pronounce, or both.

Panera's announcement came amid a tide of similar initiatives from other restaurants and food companies in response to growing consumer awareness of additives in food and a heightened demand for healthier alternatives. In August 2015, PepsiCo promised to replace the artificial sweetener aspartame in its Diet Pepsi with sucralose and acesulfame potassium (ace-K). Larger food companies were also switching to more natural ingredients. U.S. Kraft said it would make its macaroni & cheese without artificial preservatives or synthetic colors by January 2016. Nestlé in February 2015 pledged to remove all artificial flavors and FDA-certified colors from more than 250 products by the end of that year.

"We are grateful that the Panera team reached out to our experts and listened to our recommendations to improve their fare, eliminating EWG's 'dirty dozen' food additives from their food and using other information from our Food Scores database," said Ken Cook, president and cofounder of the Environmental Working Group. "We commend Panera for stepping up in support of healthier food made with 'cleaner' ingredients."[50]

A Single Food Safety Agency: A Work in Progress

Early in 2015, Sen. Dick Durbin (D-Ill.) and Rep. Rosa DeLauro (D-Conn.) introduced the Safe Food Act to establish a single, independent food safety agency by consolidating the 15 agencies that currently have a hand in food safety. In the 1990s, the Government Accountability Office (GAO), which investigates issues for Congress, recommended a single food safety agency.

In a lengthy blog on his website, David Acheson, a former high-ranking FDA official turned consultant, asked whether a single agency is good, bad, or impossible. Acknowledging he has long been a vocal advocate for a single agency, he commented, "The goals are great. In general the end result is okay and thankfully it is risk-based. But the means of achieving the goal are undefined and, as one would expect, there is no serious mention of funding."[51]

The whole concept of food safety-wide, risk-based inspections and actions is great, said Acheson. "However, the bill includes little detail on how the transfer and consolidation would work. In fact, that detail is turned over to none other than President Obama" to accomplish within a year's time.

Noting that many of the goals are reflective of the FSMA or are the responsibility of the USDA's Food Safety and Inspection Service, Acheson continued, "From our perspective, it is not that these authorities and protections don't exist today—it is that they are the responsibility of different agencies, which, due to the laws written by Congress, will result in different approaches or different standards, different levels of on-site inspections, and different allocations of resources to risks being applied by the different regulatory bodies."

Acheson noted that the proposed food safety administrator is tasked to issue a performance standard (guidance, action level, or regulation) to prevent or control a foodborne contaminant that presents the risk of serious adverse health consequences or death to consumers, causes food to be adulterated, or could promote the spread of communicable disease. "If the bill is truly recommending that this be enacted for every applicable food, it seems to us that requiring such an unreasonable, virtually impossible, task is simply setting up the administrator for failure," he said.

"I have been an advocate for a single food safety agency, and I really like the fact that it continues to have life," Acheson concluded. "But to build a solid structure on top of this foundation, we'd like to see Congress do a little more than put out idealistic mandates, so we are not once again treading the underfunded/under-resourced, missed-deadline, consumer-group-lawsuit path of FSMA.

"So overall good idea—but bad implementation and likely impossible to pay for."

In short, the United States has a lot of unfinished business where food safety is concerned. The FSIS is still grappling with *Salmonella*, *Campylobacter*, and *Listeria.* The FDA needs to implement the Food Safety Modernization Act and cope with antibiotic resistance.

On the bright side, Robert Tauxe, director of the CDC's division of foodborne, waterborne, and environmental diseases, told the USDA's Agricultural Outlook Forum in February 2016 that a "tipping point" might be near in preventing foodborne illness. "We are finding and stopping more outbreaks and finding them when they are smaller," he reported.[52]

Tauxe said 10 laboratories are pilot-testing whole genome sequencing (WGS) and would begin using it to test for pathogenic *E. coli* and *Salmonella* later in 2016. He added that WGS used to take three months, but it can now be completed in a day and may cost less than some traditional methods.

CHAPTER FOUR

Dietary Guidelines Become Fierce Battleground

Dietary Guidelines for Americans are more than advice to individuals. They influence federal food and nutrition education programs, including school meals and national health promotion initiatives. Health care providers, educational institutions, and other public health agencies use the Dietary Guidelines to choose their menus. Foreign countries also take note of the U.S. guidelines.

Who would have guessed that the 2015–2020 Dietary Guidelines would become a fierce battleground between the food industry and vocal health advocates? In the past, experts fussed over individual nutrients with little publicity.

The 2015 Dietary Guidelines Advisory Committee (DGAC), appointed by HHS and USDA, issued a 571-page scientific report in February that angered the meat industry and the processed food industry. The DGAC downplayed the importance of lean meat in the diet and suggested that Americans shift to a plant-based diet in the interest of health and environmental sustainability. The committee also recommended steps to reduce added sugars in processed foods and beverages.[1]

Since 1977, the phrase "eat less" of any food category has been the Third Rail of food politics. Sen. George McGovern (D-S.D.), chairman of the Senate Select Committee on Nutrition and Human Needs, suggested that Americans eat less meat as part of the panel's Dietary Goals, a precursor to the 1980 Dietary Guidelines. He immediately suffered a backlash from the livestock industry in his home state and elsewhere, and the phrase quickly disappeared from the Dietary Goals.

When the 2010 Dietary Guidelines were unveiled 30 years later, a reporter asked Agriculture Secretary Tom Vilsack why they didn't advise consumers to eat less meat and poultry. "The focus here is on calories in and calories out, and people need to eat nutrient-dense foods from a variety of sources," he replied, adding, "In suggesting to eat more fish and seafood, I think that's a way of saying what you're saying. We're not trying to eliminate all foods in all categories. It's about a balanced approach to diet."[2]

Marion Nestle, author of the landmark book *Food Politics*, explained that Vilsack didn't say, "Eat less meat," because "advice to eat less is very bad for business. It's all politics. Since 1979 no one has said anything about eating less."

Nestle was right again when the USDA and the Health and Human Services Department (HHS) released the 2015–2020 Dietary Guidelines on January 7, 2016. "These Dietary Guidelines, like all previous versions, recommend *foods* when they suggest 'eat more.' But they switch to *nutrients* whenever they suggest 'eat less,' she said in her *Food Politics* blog. "In the 2015 Dietary Guidelines: (1) Saturated fat is a euphemism for meat. (2) Added sugars is a euphemism for sodas and other sugar-sweetened beverages. (3) Sodium is a euphemism for processed foods and junk foods.[3]

"If the guidelines really focused on dietary patterns, they wouldn't pussyfoot," she continued. "They would come right out and say: Eat less meat (OK, they do, but only under the euphemism of 'protein' and only for males). . . . So let's count the 2015 Guidelines as a win for the meat, sugary drink, processed and junk food industries."

Frank Hu, a Harvard nutrition professor who served on the DGAC, agreed with Nestle. "Some simple but important recommendations are watered down, especially reducing consumption of red and processed meats and sugar-sweetened beverages. These recommendations would have been easier for the general public to understand and act upon than specific nutrient cutoff points—such as consuming no more than 10% of calories from saturated fat or added sugars—although it's still important to keep these cutoff points in the [guidelines].

"Environmental sustainability, a major topic in the DGAC report, was unfortunately declared out of the scope of the [guidelines] by the USDA, due to political pressure from Congress and the meat industry."[4]

David Katz, director of the Yale-Griffin Prevention Research Center, launched a *Change.org* petition to the USDA aimed at changing the 2015 Dietary Guidelines for Americans to "Food Policy Guidelines for America." He said the current advice could be called "Guidelines to Balance Public Health and Corporate Profit."

The guidelines are informed by public health science and expertise, but equally focused on the economy and monetary advantage for large food industry sectors, from agriculture to manufacturing, he explained. "That is not necessarily bad, provided it is honest. We can all accept that government has diverse priorities. We are, however, entitled by law, to truth in advertising."[5]

In the final guidelines, the USDA and HHS responded to unhappy industries that persuaded Congress to attach riders to the 2015 congressional omnibus budget bill. The riders required the guidelines to reflect "significant scientific agreement" and avoid issues not strictly related to nutrition, such as sustainability. The bill also set aside $1 million for a National Academy of Medicine review of the process of setting federal nutrition advice.[6]

Savoring victory, the North American Meat Institute praised the 2015 Dietary Guidelines, which included new affirmation that meat and poultry are "rich sources of complete protein, iron, zinc and B vitamins. The Dietary Guidelines confirm that a variety of dietary patterns can be followed to achieve a healthy eating pattern. Consumers who choose to eat meat and poultry, as 95% of Americans do, can continue to enjoy our products as they have in the past."[7]

The Dietary Guidelines also drew praise from the National Cattlemen's Beef Association, National Chicken Council, and four dairy trade groups. However, the Sugar Association said it was "disappointed that, despite a lack of scientific evidence, the 2015 Dietary Guidelines for Americans recommend an intake limit or target for 'added sugars' of no more than 10 percent of daily calories."[8]

The Grocery Manufacturers Association [GMA], an umbrella food trade group, said the DGAC's recommendations on sustainable food and taxation "were outside the committee's expertise, and the GMA commends USDA and HHS for not including these provisions in the final guidelines. We look forward to closely reviewing the details of the guidelines to see how the topics of sugars, sodium, lean/processed meats and caffeine are addressed. GMA had expressed earlier concerns that the advisory committee's recommendations in these areas were not based on the best available science."[9]

On the other side of the battle, the CSPI saw some evidence of victory in the 2015 guidelines. "The advice . . . is sound, sensible and science-based," said Michael Jacobson, CSPI executive director. "If Americans ate according to that advice, it would be a huge win for the public's health."

Noting that basic nutrition advice hasn't changed much for the past 35 years, he continued, "The problem is that the food industry has continued to pressure and tempt us to eat a diet of burgers, pizzas, burritos, cookies, doughnuts, sodas, shakes, and other foods loaded with white flour, red and processed meat, salt, saturated fat, and added sugars, and not enough vegetables, fruit, and whole grains."[10]

The Environmental Working Group said the new guidelines should have "clearly called on consumers to eat less meat—both to protect their health and to reduce the harm that meat production does to the environment. Producing meat is a major source of greenhouse gas emissions, and growing the feed for livestock is a leading cause of farm runoff that pollutes our drinking water."[11]

The United Fresh Produce Association was pleased at how well vegetables and fruit were treated in the guidelines: "For the first time, and to reinforce the significance of eating more vegetables and fruits, this recommendation tops the list of ways to improve eating habits and health. To improve public health, United Fresh urges policymakers to align all federal nutrition programs with the 2015–2020 Dietary Guidelines to significantly increase access to fruits and vegetables, and to consider a broad range of policy changes and educational strategies to make fruits and vegetables the easy choice for all Americans."[12]

A veteran consumer advocate on Capitol Hill, Rep. Rosa DeLauro (D-Conn.), warned, "The United States is in the midst of a dual epidemic of obesity and diabetes, and we need to do something to stop it. Science shows that there is a clear link between sugar-sweetened beverages and these health conditions, and I applaud the USDA and HHS for recommending limiting our sugar intake.

"However, Congress should go further and . . . impose a tax on sugar-sweetened beverage products and fund initiatives that include research, increased access to healthy foods in low-income neighborhoods, subsidizing fresh fruits and vegetables, and nutrition education."[13]

DGAC Takes a Holistic Approach

When the DGAC developed its scientific report, the committee took a holistic approach instead of focusing solely on individual nutrients as earlier committees had done. The 2015 DGAC said its work was guided by two stark realities: about half of all American adults have one or more preventable chronic diseases, and about two-thirds of U.S. adults are overweight or obese.

"These conditions have been highly prevalent for more than two decades," the DGAC said in its report. "Poor dietary patterns, overconsumption of calories, and physical inactivity directly contribute to these disorders. Positive changes in individual diet and physical activity behaviors, and in the environmental contexts and systems that affect them, could substantially improve health outcomes."[14]

The DGAC gave its blessing to three dietary patterns: a healthy U.S.-style pattern; the traditional Mediterranean diet, and a vegetarian diet. It said all three diets are characterized by a high intake of vegetables, fruits, nuts, legumes, and grains (mainly unrefined); a low intake of saturated fats; a moderately high intake of fish; a low intake of dairy products, meat, and poultry; and a regular but moderate intake of alcohol (specifically, wine with meals), as in the Mediterranean diet.

The DGAC identified several low-intake nutrients in the average American diet: vitamin D, calcium, potassium, and fiber, plus iron for females. On the other end of the spectrum is overconsumption of sodium across all age groups and too much saturated fat by consumers more than 50 years old. However, the committee eliminated a long-standing recommended limit on total fat in the diet, drawing praise from medical researchers.

The original Dietary Guidelines, issued in 1980, recommended limiting total fat, saturated fat, and cholesterol intake to reduce cardiovascular disease risk. The total fat recommendation was revised in 2005 to a range of 20–35 percent of total calories.

In a Viewpoint article published in the *Journal of the American Medical Association* (JAMA), authors Dariush Mozaffarian, a cardiologist and epidemiologist at Tufts University, and David Ludwig, a pediatrics professor at Harvard Medical School, agreed with the DGAC: "A restructuring of national food policy is warranted to move away from total fat reduction and toward healthy food choices, including those higher in healthful fats."[15]

The DGAC report "highlights that more than 70 percent of the U.S. population consumes too many refined grain products. Many of these foods enjoy a lingering health halo or at least a benign reputation, based on years of government guidelines and industry promotion," the authors concluded.

The DGAC said "strong and consistent evidence shows that intake of added sugars from food and/or sugar sweetened beverages is associated with excess body weight in children and adults. . . . Strong evidence shows that higher consumption of added sugars, especially sugar-sweetened beverages, increases the risk of type 2 diabetes among adults and this relationship is not fully explained by body weight. [These findings are] compatible with a recommendation to keep added sugars intake below 10 percent of total energy intake."

The DGAC also didn't hesitate to foray into policy recommendations. It suggested exploring higher taxes on sugar-sweetened beverages to reduce consumption. It also suggested policy changes for the Supplemental Nutrition Assistance Program (SNAP), aka food stamps, similar to policies in place for the Women, Infants, and Children (WIC) nutrition program. Recipients should be encouraged to purchase healthier options, including foods and beverages low in added sugars, the DGAC said, adding, "Pilot studies using incentives and restrictions should be tested and evaluated."

In March 2016, a study report in the online journal *BMJ Open* (former *British Medical Journal*) found that more than half of calories (60 percent) in the U.S. diet come from "ultra-processed" foods, defined as products containing manufactured ingredients such as artificial flavors or colors, sweeteners, preservatives, and other additives. Examples include soft drinks, packaged snacks, baked goods, chicken or fish nuggets and other reconstituted meat products, and instant noodles and soups.

The lead investigator, Carlos Augusto Monteiro, a nutrition professor at the University of São Paulo in Brazil, told *CBS News* that the United States should review its Dietary Guidelines and "incorporate clear messages to avoid the replacement of real food (minimally processed foods and freshly prepared drinks, dishes and meals) by ultra-processed food and drink products."[16]

The more the 2015 DGAC broke ranks with earlier Dietary Guidelines committees, the more the panel's makeup rubbed some sectors of the food industry the wrong way. The meat industry viewed the committee as geographically and culturally biased toward ivory tower academics in New England, favoring nutritionists chosen from the Harvard T. H. Chan School of Public Health, Boston University, and Tufts University.

In a letter sent to the DGAC on October 17, 2014, the American Meat Institute and North American Meat Association, which would later merge into the North American Meat Institute, warned that a recommended diet must be "realistic, achievable and easily implemented into the American lifestyle. The United States has a diverse population and a one-size-fits-all approach cannot be taken, because it will not work.

"A diet that may be culturally appropriate in New England may not be recognizable to someone living in southern Texas. A comprehensive approach is necessary to avoid risk for rejection."[17]

In December 2015, the conservative Washington Legal Foundation (WLF) charged that the Obama administration had violated Federal Advisory Committee Act in appointing the DGAC. The WLF's *Legal Pulse* cited Section 5 of the law requiring federal advisory committees be "fairly balanced in terms of the points of view represented and the functions to be performed by the advisory committee."

The *Legal Pulse* described the DGAC as "homogeneously academic," quoting a member's comment that "nobody on the committee was a food scientist or had been trained in food science; nobody had a background in food law."[18]

"Sustainability" Is a Fighting Word

The most controversial word in the DGAC report was "sustainability," because the committee recommended a shift to a plant-based diet for environmental as well as health reasons. The meat industry quickly accused the committee of exceeding its mandate and questioned nutritionists' qualifications to tackle this subject.

In its report, the DGAC said its "major findings regarding sustainable diets were that a diet higher in plant-based foods, such as vegetables, fruits, whole grains, legumes, nuts, and seeds, and lower in calories and animal-based foods is more health promoting and is associated with less environmental impact than is the current U.S. diet.

"Current evidence shows that the average U.S. diet has a larger environmental impact in terms of increased greenhouse gas emissions, land use, water use, and energy use, compared to [recommended] dietary patterns. This is because the current U.S. population intake of animal-based foods is higher and plant-based foods are lower, than proposed in these three dietary patterns. Of note is that no food groups need to be eliminated completely to improve sustainability outcomes."[19]

Opponents wasted no time to weigh in on sustainability. Barry Carpenter, CEO of the North American Meat Institute, immediately said in a February 19 news release that the DGAC's charter "tasked them with reviewing nutrition science, which is the field from which committee members were selected. The committee's foray into the murky waters of sustainability is well beyond its scope and expertise. It's akin to having a dermatologist provide recommendations about cardiac care.

"If our government believes Americans should factor sustainability into their choices, guidance should come from a panel of sustainability experts that understands the complexity of the issue and address all segments: transportation, construction, energy management and all forms of agriculture," he concluded. "Total sustainability analyses were not considered by the [DGAC], whose recommendations appear to be based on personal opinions or social agendas."[20]

Agriculture Secretary Tom Vilsack agreed with the meat industry that the DGAC had exceeded its mandate, declaring, "I am going to color inside the lines."[21]

At an October 7, 2015, House Agriculture Committee hearing on Dietary Guidelines, Vilsack and HHS Secretary Sylvia Burwell assured the lawmakers that the 2015 Dietary Guidelines wouldn't include sustainability or other environmental considerations. However, Vilsack added that sustainability remains an important issue: "I think there is a good debate, and an important debate, to take place in the context of agriculture about sustainability. We didn't think that the statutory direction allowed us to have that conversation in this context, but it's certainly in the Farm Bill, certainly in conservation programs, climate change discussions, all that. We definitely want to have that conversation because we think it's an important one."[22]

Kathleen Merrigan, Vilsack's former deputy secretary who became executive director of the Sustainability Institute at George Washington University, told the National Food Policy Conference in April 2015 that sustainability should be part of the Dietary Guidelines, because the science is "compelling and uncontested. Policy enterprise is needed, but agribusiness tries to block it."

Noting that the DGAC report has drawn "battle lines between industry and consumer groups," Merrigan said there's a need to "bring together constituencies and have a conversation with industry," citing the advantages of grass-fed dairy cows. "We want to work with farmers and ranchers," she added, concluding that sustainability would be part of the 2020 Dietary Guidelines. [23]

Merrigan and other public health and sustainability experts at George Washington and Tufts universities argued in an October 9 *Science* magazine article that sustainability should be included in the Dietary Guidelines for Americans (DGA). "We believe the issue of scope is not the overarching concern, but a political maneuver to excise sustainability from dietary discussions," they said. "The meat industry feels especially under attack. Much discussion of sustainable diets has focused on the increase in livestock production that will result from population growth and adoption of Western-style diets by an expanding middle class in the developing world. Whether from a health perspective (e.g., reducing coronary heart disease) or an environmental perspective (e.g., reducing methane emissions and deforestation) the dietary advice is the same: eat less meat. But reducing discussion to a meat-focused debate ignores larger points around food production.

"In addition to the environmental impacts of food production, its economic sustainability must also be considered," the authors concluded. "The challenge is how to produce the most healthful foods in a way that sustains employment in the agricultural sector and minimizes adverse impacts on the environment. All major constituencies concerned with food security and health must wrestle with sustainability and dietary choices together. It is right and proper for the DGA process to lead the way."[24]

"Nutrition Coalition" Emerges to Criticize the DGAC

Meanwhile, critics of the 2015 Dietary Guidelines scientific report organized a Nutrition Coalition. It urged the USDA and HHS to forward the report for reexamination by a panel appointed by the National Academy of Sciences' Food and Nutrition Board (FNB). Coalition board member Nina Teicholz, author of *The Big Fat Surprise: Why Butter, Meat and Cheese Belong in a Healthy Diet*, published an article in the *BMJ* critical of the DGAC report.[25]

Another Nutrition Coalition board member, Joanne Lupton, a Texas A&M nutrition professor and a member of the 2005 DGAC, quickly resigned, explaining, "Since I am a member of the [Food and Nutrition Board], I would not endorse an organization that would be negative about the Dietary Guidelines . . . unless I were presented with the data and I heard a good debate about this. That hasn't happened yet. Thus, I did not want to be associated with an organization that took stands without showing me the data."[26]

One month later, more than 180 prominent cardiovascular and nutrition scientists from 19 countries urged *BMJ* to retract the Teicholz article. "When the errors are stripped away, there is very little of substance left to justify the claim that the Dietary Guidelines Advisory Committee's process was not rigorous or that its advice was not based on the latest sound science," commented Bonnie Liebman, CSPI nutrition director. "If the *BMJ* is to provide scientists and the public with reliable information and repair the damage to its reputation, it should issue a full retraction of Teicholz's error-filled attack on the DGAC report."[27]

In response, the *BMJ* promised to seek an external expert review of Teicholz's controversial article.

Torrent of Nearly 30,000 Comments

Once the 2015 DGAC scientific report was released in February, it generated a torrent of nearly 30,000 comments before the comment period closed on May 8, 2015. The North American Meat Institute said its 44-page comments "emphasize the variety of nutrition benefits of meat and poultry products as convenient, direct and balanced dietary sources of all essential amino acids and rich sources of many micronutrients." The comments were also critical of lean meat's relegation to mere footnote status in the DGAC report.[28]

In addition, the meat institute criticized the DGAC's recommendation to reduce consumption of "mixed dishes" with foods from a variety of groups, asserting that these foods "often drive consumption of foods and nutrients encouraged by the DGAC, such as vegetables, whole grains, fiber, protein and more."

The meat institute noted that the scientific evidence "did not fit the bias of the DGAC, which instead recommended against including red and processed meat as components of a healthy diet." The group urged the federal department sponsors, the USDA and HHS, to revise the final 2015 Dietary Guidelines with the guidance of food scientists and consumer behaviorists, who it said were missing from the DGAC.[29]

Numerous farmers and ranchers bolstered the meat industry's comments. "It is inappropriate to simply recommend reducing consumption of red meat," said a comment from Myrin Ranch in Altamont, Utah. "It does disservice to consumers who can benefit from this dense source of nutrients. It does disservice to farming and ranching families who produce red meat in an environmentally healthy manner. It does disservice to the environment itself, which benefits from proper use by livestock."[30]

Fueling these comments was a perfect storm facing the red meat industry. Beef consumption in the United States had declined for about two decades because of concern about saturated fat. To make matters worse, the International Agency for Research on Cancer (IARC), a branch of the UN World Health Organization (WHO), reported on October 26, 2015, that excess consumption of processed meat can cause human cancer and red meat probably causes cancer. Advice from the new Dietary Guidelines to cut back on red and processed meat would be yet another huge wave in the storm.

"It's our 12-alarm fire, because if [the IARC] determines that red and processed meat causes cancer—and I think that they will—that moniker will stick around for years," Betsy Booren, meat institute vice president for scientific affairs, warned in late July 2015. "It could take decades and billions of dollars to change that. . . . IARC is going to make the Dietary Guidelines look easy."[31]

Riding out the storm, the Beef Checkoff advertising program, funded by cattle ranchers, launched a new program that didn't mention beef at all in the headline. The 30-day Protein Challenge urged participants to boost their protein consumption as high as 30 grams per meal, with online tools to help achieve the goal. Using daily inspirational emails, protein tracking tools, and beef recipes, the program encouraged protein intake of 75–90 grams daily, which far exceeded the recommended daily allowances (RDAs) of 46 grams for the average adult woman and 56 grams for the average adult male.[32]

The DGAC report also raised the hackles of food and beverage companies that rely on added sugar and other sweeteners in their products. "Looking at the details of the process used to support the recommendations by the Added Sugars Working Group of the Committee could certainly put the scientific integrity of the 2015 Dietary Guidelines process in jeopardy," the Sugar Association said.

"Intake recommendations and conclusions that lead the American public to believe any dietary component is a causal factor in a serious disease outcome should only be made based on significant scientific agreement due to a robust review of the entire body of scientific literature by experts in the field of investigation," the association commented. "Such scientific agreement does not exist for the 2015 DGAC 'added sugars' recommendations."[33]

DGAC Critics Sought Support from Congress

Food industry critics of the DGAC scientific report didn't stop with comments. They sought allies in Congress who could prevent the DGAC's report's recommendations from finding their way into the final 2015–2020 Dietary Guidelines.

Leaders of the House Agriculture Committee asked for the playbook for the Obama administration's review of the nearly 30,000 comments that poured in on the controversial DGAC report. On May 14, Chairman K. Michael Conaway (R-Texas) and Ranking Member Collin Peterson (D-Minn.) sent a letter to Agriculture Secretary Tom Vilsack and HHS Secretary Sylvia Burwell calling for transparency in the administration's review process of the report.

"Members of the Dietary Guidelines Advisory Committee greatly exceeded their scope in developing recommendations," wrote Conaway. "At a time when consumers are already subjected to conflicting and often contradictory nutrition and health information, the Dietary Guidelines must provide the public with realistic, science-based recommendations."[34]

Conaway and Peterson said stakeholders had been forwarding studies to USDA they said weren't included in the DGAC review. In their letter, they asked whether both agencies would review each comment received. The next series of questions asked how many staffers had been assigned to review the comments, how long they would be reassigned to the task, and what program areas would be harmed by the temporary staffing changes.[35]

Later in the spring, appropriations bills for the USDA and HHS working their way through the House suddenly contained riders that restricted major updates to the 2010 Dietary Guidelines. Any new changes "(A) shall be based on scientific evidence that has been rated 'Grade I: Strong' by the grading rubric developed by the Nutrition Evidence Library of the Department of Agriculture; and (B) shall be limited in scope to only matters of diet and nutrient intake."[36]

The Obama administration would also be required to release a preliminary draft of the proposed guidelines, along with all scientific studies supporting revisions, for at least 90 days, followed by a 60-day review period within the departments.

Following the money, the CSPI blamed the restrictive riders on food industry campaign donations to members of Congress. Using data from the Center for Responsive Politics, the CSPI calculated that the 30 Republican senators who signed a letter criticizing the 2015 DGAC had "received more than a million dollars from the food industry between 2013 and 2014, with more than half of that total coming from the red meat industry. The 71 House signers of a similar letter received more than $2 million, according to the analysis.

"All but one Republican on the House Appropriations USDA-FDA Subcommittee signed a letter critical of the Dietary Guidelines Advisory Committee circulated by the meat and food industries," the CSPI reported. "On the whole Appropriations Committee, 84 percent of food and agriculture sector contributions went to Republicans and 16 percent to Democrats. On the full Senate Appropriations Committee, 98 percent of food and agriculture money went to Republicans compared to 2 percent to Democrats."[37]

Health Advocates Defend the DGAC Report

On the morning of a public meeting to discuss the DGAC report in Bethesda, Maryland, health advocates published full-page ads in *The Washington Post*, *The New York Times*, and *Politico* headlined "My Plate, My Planet, Food for a Sustainable Nation." They printed an open letter to Vilsack and Burwell urging them to support sustainability recommendations in the DGAC report "calling for less meat and more plants in our diets for the sake of our health."[38]

More than 100 influential groups and individuals, including the CSPI, Center for Food Safety, UCS, Greenpeace USA, and Friends of the Earth, signed the open letter.

The CSPI in May 2015 took credit for generating more than 14,000 comments from individuals supporting the DGAC report, nearly half of 30,000 total comments. "Much of the obesity, heart disease, diabetes, and cancer in the United States is linked to diets deficient in fruits and vegetables and too high in added sugars, salt, red and processed meat, saturated fat, and refined white flour," said Michael Jacobson, CSPI executive director, in a news release. "But besides providing advice to consumers, the federal government needs to support policies that would actually help Americans take advantage of the advice."[39]

The 2015–2020 Dietary Guidelines once again recommended sound, sensible advice about nutrients, but we may have to wait until 2020 to see more forthright advice about food and better implementation of that advice. Adding "sustainability" would be a major asset to the guidelines, but the meat industry is already girding for the next iteration.

CHAPTER FIVE

Marketing to Children in School and Out

Children are perhaps the most vulnerable to the two faces of malnutrition: hunger and obesity. The food industry can influence children in numerous places: restaurants, convenience stores, and school cafeterias; homes with television sets and other electronic media; movie theaters, sports and music venues; and supermarket checkout counters. Consumer food advocates do their best to counter junk food marketing efforts in all these venues.

In the United States, food and beverage companies spend more than $2 billion annually to market food and beverages to children. Children are targeted for marketing because it creates brand loyalty from an early age and strongly influences long-term consumer behavior.[1]

The food industry has long argued that food advertising to children is best handled through self-regulation. In 1978, the FTC issued a staff report concluding that television advertising to young children is unfair, and any remedy short of a ban is inadequate "to cure this inherent unfairness and deceptiveness."[2]

Broadcasters, ad agencies, and food and toy companies vehemently opposed the FTC's efforts to implement the report's findings. They lobbied Congress to pass the Federal Trade Commission Improvements Act of 1980, which prohibited the agency from issuing industry-wide regulations to stop unfair advertising practices.

In 2007, the industry launched the Children's Food and Beverage Advertising Initiative (CFBAI), which asks its member companies to restrict ads to children under 12. Many major food companies belong to the group, but some others don't.

Consumer advocates say the CFBAI doesn't go far enough in restricting food advertising to children. They would extend the controls to age 14, and they would close loopholes that allow food companies to use cartoon figures, such as Ronald McDonald, and toys to lure kids to their products.[3]

The CFBAI took hits from three research reports in scientific journals in 2015. A study reported in the journal *Preventing Chronic Disease*, published by the CDC, found that more than half of food products allowed for marketing to kids by CFBAI fail to meet health standards recommended in 2011 by the federal Interagency Working Group on Food Marketed to Children.[4]

The IWG included representatives of the USDA, FDA, CDC, and FTC. Of the 407 products given the green light in 2014 by the CFBAI, some 214 (53 percent) don't meet the IWG standards, according to the article authored by Rebecca Schermbeck and Lisa Powell, public health researchers at the University of Illinois at Chicago. The authors assessed the products against the IWG's recommended limits for saturated fat, *trans* fat, sugar, and sodium. The study found that a significant share of products exceeds recommended limits for saturated fat (23 percent), sodium (15 percent), and sugar (32 percent).

"Companies manufacture food and beverage products that meet IWG recommendations; however, these are not the products most heavily marketed to children," the authors reported. "Evidence shows that 96% of food and beverage product advertisements (excluding those for restaurants) seen by children on children's television programs were for products high in" saturated fat, sodium, and sugar.

If companies choose to advertise products from the CFBAI's list of approved food products that meet the IWG recommendations, "children's exposure to food and beverage advertising could improve [diets] substantially," the authors concluded. "We recommend continued monitoring of child-directed marketing by public health researchers and that the public encourage the food and beverage industry to market their healthiest products to young consumers."

Government Seen Needed to Regulate Child Nutrition

The CFBAI took another hit in May 2015 from a research report in a scientific journal. The lead investigator concluded the government would need to step in to regulate child advertising. This study, published in the *American Journal of Preventive Medicine*, claimed the CFBAI has achieved only "baby steps" in the nutritional quality of foods advertised to children. Four of every five foods advertised to children (80.5 percent) are classified in the poorest nutritional category, according to HHS guidelines.[5]

"The long-standing pattern favoring nutritionally deficient food products over more-healthy items clearly persisted despite the advent of industry self-regulation," said lead investigator Dale Kunkel, a researcher in the University of Arizona's communications department. "This outcome occurred largely because participants in self-regulation achieved no significant improvement in the nutritional quality of their advertised foods between 2007 and 2013."

Kunkel and his research colleagues came up with two contradictory findings. First, CFBAI-participating companies completely fulfilled all the commitments they made by advertising only products that meet nutritional guidelines stipulated by their parent corporations. However, the researchers also discovered that the nutritional standards employed by companies participating in the CFBAI were less than ideal.

"Many companies classify a product as healthy if a small portion of the undesirable ingredients is removed from its original formulation. This consideration accounts for the disparity between industry claims that companies promote only healthier foods to children, and the study's finding that the majority of products advertised by CFBAI participants fall in the poorest nutritional category," the researchers reported.

"The good news is that the industry has done exactly what it promised," Kunkel told *The Washington Post*. "The bad news is that the industry's definition of what constitutes healthy food is a joke."[6]

The researchers compared a sample of child-targeted food ads aired in 2007 (before CFBAI) with an equivalent sample of 2013 food advertising (after the CFBAI). Over a period of 10 weeks, one episode of each regularly scheduled children's program that aired between 7 a.m. and 10 p.m. was recorded and analyzed.

In this study, the advertised products were categorized according to a rating system devised by the HHS, which distinguishes among three types of products: Go, Slow, and Whoa. Go foods are rich in nutrients and low in calories, fat, and added sugar—such as vegetables, fruits, whole-grain breads/cereals, low-fat yogurt, nonfat milk, and diet soda. Slow foods are higher in fat, added sugar, and calories. Examples include broiled hamburgers, nuts or peanut butter, waffles, most pasta, 100 percent juice, and 2 percent low-fat milk. Whoa foods are high in calories, fat, and added sugar and are low in nutrients. Examples include fried chicken, hamburgers, cookies, ice cream, whole milk, and regular soda.

When using the Go, Slow, and Whoa categories, the researchers found 79.4 percent of food ads in 2007 were for Whoa products, which increased to 80.5 percent in 2013. There was also little change for Slow products, at 16.5 percent of all food ads in 2007 and 18.4 percent in 2013. "Ads for truly health[ful] Go products were so rare that no statistical comparisons could be made," the researchers found.

Another factor in the lack of improvement in food advertising to children is that approximately 30 percent of the ads were from companies that didn't participate in the CFBAI, notably Chuck E. Cheese (pizza) and Topps Company (candy), which accounted for 14.7 percent and 9.0 percent of all food ads, respectively, the study found.

"In the face of pleas for advertising reform, the food industry has achieved what might be labeled as baby steps," commented Kunkel. "Indeed, this study demonstrates that no significant decline in the proportion of food ads devoted to unhealthy Whoa products occurred as a result of self-regulation, even among CFBAI participants. Given that corporate profit concerns unavoidably mitigate more-stringent industry-based reforms, continued reliance upon self-regulation to resolve this problem seems destined to yield only modest benefits.

"With a persistent national obesity crisis, the failure to act more strongly holds adverse implications for America's children," he continued. "As the IOM [Institute of Medicine] suggested in 2006, government restrictions on advertising practices will likely be required to end the predominance of unhealthy products in child-targeted food marketing. Such steps are increasingly being pursued by countries worldwide."

Children's Exposure to Candy Ads Rose by 74 Percent

In yet another report in the September 2015 issue of the journal *Appetite*, the University of Connecticut's Rudd Center for Food Policy & Obesity researchers found children's exposure to candy ads increased by 74 percent between 2007 and 2011. Not all of those ads were explicitly kid directed, the authors acknowledge, but children were exposed to them nonetheless.[7]

In their report, "Sweet Promises: Candy Advertising to Children and Implications for Industry Self-Regulation," the Rudd Center researchers examined types of candy advertisements, as well as how many ads children below the age of 11 have been watching since 2007, the year the CFBAI was established to curb junk food ads to children. The researchers examined the TV ads for 36 brands of candy marketed by 16 companies.

The Rudd Center research team found that from 2008 to 2011, children's exposure to candy advertisements increased from 279 ads viewed in 2008 to 485 ads in 2011. Ads from companies such as Hershey, Mars, Nestlé, and Kraft increased by 152 percent, the team noted.

Of the 485 candy ads kids viewed by the Rudd researchers, 365 came from CFBAI member companies, while 315 came from companies that explicitly said they wouldn't advertise to children under 11. Of these ads, a third reportedly premiered on television networks such as *Nick at Nite* or

ABC Family, which researchers found to attract a "higher than average" number of viewers under 18.

The researchers conceded that these advertisements don't count as direct marketing targeted toward children, as specified by the CFBAI. The Council for Better Business Bureaus (BBB), which created the CFBAI, upheld this claim, contending that none of these companies failed to keep their promise.

However, Marlene Schwartz, coauthor of the Rudd Center study, commented, "While the companies are following the letter of the law in their pledges, this study highlights substantial loopholes. We would like to see CFBAI adopt a more comprehensive definition of 'child-directed advertising' so that these pledges lead to meaningful changes in children's true exposure to unhealthy food marketing."[8]

CFBAI Says Studies Are Flawed

Elaine Kolish, CFBAI director, responded to each of the journal articles with a rebuttal. She said the first journal article "omits key information: It notes that the 2011 IWG recommendations were not formally adopted but fails to state that the recommendations were never intended as the final word. They were published for comment as 'preliminary proposed' guidelines. . . .

"We worked hard to develop CFBAI's nutrition guidelines based on an extensive review of the 2010 Dietary Guidelines and the recommendations of other authoritative bodies," she concluded. "And we intend to review our criteria after the 2015 Dietary Guidelines are issued. In the meantime the criteria are working as intended and improving the children's food advertising landscape."[9]

In a rebuttal to the second journal article, Kolish countered, "The research tool used in this report is significantly flawed, making the results inaccurate and inherently meaningless.[10]

"The simplistic 'Go, Slow, Whoa' categories are outdated," she explained. "They don't reflect either the government's leading advice on nutrition in the [2010] Dietary Guidelines for Americans or the government's standards for foods served to children in the School Breakfast and School Lunch programs. It's time to can the 'We Can' categories used in this report."

Responding to the third journal article, which showed a 74 percent increase in children's exposure to candy ads, Kolish said, "Looking at techniques such as animation or subjective factors, such as whether the ad includes fun/hip messaging, is not a reliable way to determine that an ad is child directed on such programming.[11]

"Teens and even adults also find such techniques or messaging appealing and they are commonly used in ads for insurance and other prosaic products. CFBAI's focus always has been on improving the children's advertising landscape, and we've succeeded in doing that."

After responding to the series of negative journal articles, the CFBAI released a new study showing that more cereals advertised to children are less sugary and more nutritious than ever before, showing industry self-regulation is working.[12]

"CFBAI's nutrition standards are driving numerous improvements to the nutritional content of cereals, and other foods, advertised to children," said Kolish. "Nearly half of the participants' food advertisements on kids' TV are for cereals, so this progress is significant in the fight against childhood obesity."

A one-ounce serving of all the cereals met the CFBAI's limit of 10 grams of total sugars per serving, a drop from the previous 12-gram standard. Half of the products now contain 9 grams or fewer, the group said. Moreover, most of the participants' cereals (77 percent) contained at least 8 grams of whole grains per serving, an amount the 2010 Dietary Guidelines for Americans consider significant, CFBAI said. One-third contained at least 12 grams per serving, and two-thirds listed whole grains as the first ingredient. The group also pointed to improvements in the amount of vitamin D, calcium, and/or fiber in the cereals advertised to young children.

In an annual report issued in December 2015, Kolish said 2014 "marked the first full year that CFBAI's category-specific uniform nutrition criteria were in effect, resulting in more improvements to foods that are being advertised to children. Those changes, along with the hundreds of changes made earlier and since then, mean that today the foods CFBAI participants advertise to children are markedly better nutritionally than when CFBAI started nine years ago."[13]

Removing Sodas from Fast-Food Kids' Menus

Consumer advocates in 2015 succeeded in persuading the so-called Big Three fast-food chains—McDonald's, Wendy's, and Burger King—to remove soda from kids' menus. Burger King in late March quietly joined McDonald's and Wendy's in dropping soft drinks from its kids' meals. Instead of soft drinks, the Burger King menu for kids would offer fat-free milk, 100 percent apple juice, and low-fat chocolate milk.[14]

McDonald's agreed in 2013 to drop soda from its Happy Meal menus, effective 2015. Subway, Chipotle, Arby's, Panera, and Jack in the Box also removed soda as the default option in their children's meals. Applebee's in

December 2015 became the first sit-down restaurant chain to remove soda from its kids' menu.

"In time, soda on a kids' menu will seem as anachronistic as an ashtray in a high school," commented Jessica Almy, senior nutrition policy counsel at the Center for Science in the Public Interest.[15]

However, restaurants aren't the only places where children buy sodas. Convenience stores are to kids what drug dens are to crack addicts. Corner stores are located where they can attract children before and after school. Sodas and snacks are critical for those stores to make money. Coca-Cola discovered that 20 percent of its customers are "heavy users" who buy 80 percent of sodas.[16]

WHO in January 2016 urged governments to tax sugar-sweetened beverages and restrict marketing of unhealthy food products to fight rampant childhood obesity across the globe. "There is sufficient rationale to warrant the introduction of an effective tax on sugar-sweetened beverages," WHO said in a report by its Commission on Ending Childhood Obesity (ECHO). The report noted that low-income families are most vulnerable to obesity and most influenced by price.[17]

Researchers at the Harvard T. H. Chan School of Public Health and colleagues elsewhere suggested that policymakers consider imposing a penny-an-ounce tax on sugar-sweetened beverages, eliminating the tax deduction for marketing unhealthy foods to kids, and enacting nutrition standards for school food. If this tax policy were enacted, the researchers forecast, childhood obesity would decline between 129,000 and 576,000 cases between 2015 and 2025.[18]

The American Beverage Association quickly shot back. "The soda tax is an old idea that has gotten no traction among the American public because it serves only to raise prices and harm small businesses," said ABA spokesperson Lauren Kane. "Since 2008, approximately 30 states and cities proposed taxes on soft drinks; all have failed save one in Berkeley, Calif., a very pro-tax city. That's why the public policy debate in the U.S. has moved away from taxes and onto real solutions."[19]

The CSPI charged Coca-Cola, PepsiCo, and the American Beverage Association with spending at least $106 million to defeat public health initiatives aimed at reducing soda consumption. "The actual amount spent by the soda industry is assuredly much greater, since campaign finance and lobby expenses are not available in 10 out of the 23 jurisdictions that have considered policies aimed at reducing sugar drink consumption," the CSPI reported, adding, "The soda industry ramped up its federal lobbying spending dramatically in 2009. That year, legislators were exploring new federal excise taxes on soda as one potential funding source for health care reform.

It's impossible to know exactly what Big Soda's lobbyists were working on; disclosure reports indicate menu labeling, school nutrition, and the Supplemental Nutrition Assistance Program [SNAP, aka food stamps] were also among the industry's interests. But compared with the industry's pre-2009 baseline spending, CSPI estimates that the industry spent $52 million at the federal level opposing public health initiatives."[20]

Meanwhile, sales of full-calorie soda in the United States had dropped by more than 25 percent over the past two decades. The decline in soda consumption was the single largest recent change in the American diet and accounted for a substantial reduction in the number of daily calories consumed by the average American child.

Temptation at Checkout in Supermarkets

In a 2015 report on "Temptation at Checkout: The Food Industry's Sneaky Strategy for Selling More," the CSPI said placing junk food at checkout counters is a powerful form of marketing for which food manufacturers pay retailers handsomely. In addition, putting candy at children's eye level creates unhealthy norms for snacks and triggers conflict with parents.[21]

The report said about $5.5 billion of foods, drinks, and other products are sold from checkout aisles at supermarkets alone. The majority of foods and beverages at checkout are candy, gum, energy bars, chips, cookies, soda, and other sugary drinks, according to research by the CSPI and others. Another survey found that shoppers who bought candy and soda at checkout are often the same people who deliberately avoid such products elsewhere in the store.

The CSPI made the following recommendations:

- Supermarkets and other stores that sell food, such as Target, Walmart, and 7-Eleven, should adopt food and nutrition standards for checkout, selling only nonfood and healthier food and beverage options in that location.
- Nonfood stores should remove food and beverages from checkout.
- Because food manufacturers have agreed to policies on food marketing to children, they should voluntarily agree not to use placement fees to induce retailers to place unhealthy foods and beverages at checkout.
- Policymakers should set nutrition standards for retail checkout, addressing impulse marketing of foods that increase the risk of chronic diseases.
- Health departments, other government agencies, hospitals, and other institutions should adopt healthy checkout policies for the properties they own or manage.
- Individuals should urge retailers and policymakers to remove unhealthy foods and beverages at the checkout line.

The Aldi supermarket chain announced in January 2016 it would introduce healthier checkout lanes into its nearly 1,500 stores by the end of the year. "Offering a healthier checkout aisle in each store is a terrific step," commented Jessica Almy, CSPI senior nutrition policy counsel. "But in the UK, all checkout aisles in each Aldi store are candy-free."[22]

School Lunch Standards Become Fierce Battleground

School lunch meal standards were relatively noncontroversial for decades. The 55,000 members of the School Food Service Association (SFSA) were fondly described as the "school lunch ladies" and weren't involved in partisan politics. However, the SFSA historically opposed policy changes that might cause school feeding operations to lose patrons and become economically unsustainable.

The landscape changed in July 2013, when the school food lobby (renamed the School Nutrition Association [SNA]) hired the Washington, D.C.–based law firm Barnes & Thornburg for advocacy and legislative services, replacing well-known lawyer Marshall Matz, who had served the school food lobby for more than three decades.

SNA president Sandra Ford explained: "In light of the historic regulatory challenges facing school nutrition professionals and with Child Nutrition Reauthorization on the horizon [in 2015], SNA's board of directors agreed that it was an ideal time for the organization to reflect on its advocacy strategies." She noted that the USDA in 2012 had issued the first update to school meal pattern regulations in more than 15 years, and, in June 2013, the department released the first-ever regulations for junk foods sold in school vending machines that compete with school meals, and à la carte lines.[23]

The decision to replace Matz took some SNA leaders by surprise and sent ripples of shock across the membership. Jane Wynn, a former SNA president, emailed a letter to members questioning the board's decision and warning that the organization risked becoming a run-of-the-mill trade association rather than an advocate for children.

"I am not concerned about Marshall, who is in high demand," Wynn wrote. "I am very worried about the future of SNA and the millions of children we serve each day. We were out front and a leader when we were expanding our programs, but we are on defense when it comes to obesity and health. When obesity started to gain national attention, SNA rejected Marshall's idea to focus our foundation on obesity and jump to the front of the issue. The White House, USDA and allied organizations now see us as a barrier to improving the quality of [child nutrition] programs. That is just terrible."[24]

Elsewhere, Ed Cooney, executive director of the Congressional Hunger Center on Capitol Hill, sent a two-page letter to SNA president Ford, with copies to other major antihunger organizations, urging her board to reconsider its decision.[25]

"Preparation for the 2015 bill needs to begin *now*, not in 2015," Cooney wrote. "Therefore, it is puzzling that, after years of successful SNA leadership on child nutrition issues, the organization would make this change just as all the other nutrition groups are beginning to work in earnest on the 2015 [Child Nutrition Reauthorization]. With national nutrition standards, the entitlement status of school lunch itself, and the nutrition and health status of over 30 million children hanging in the balance, I urge you to bring your most experienced and trusted team to the fight. In my opinion, the A-team here is [the Olsson Frank Weeda Terman Matz law firm (OFW Law)], led by Marshall Matz."

Twisting a knife in the wound, the SNA in July 2014 filed an ethics complaint with the Office of Bar Counsel in the District of Columbia against OFW Law and attorneys Matz and Roger Szemraj. They were reportedly accused of improper communication with USDA officials and conflict of interest.[26]

The ethics complaint was dismissed on March 9, 2015, but that didn't heal a wound that festered over the previous two years. Former SNA president Wynn sent another letter to her friends. "Of course, it is a relief to see this [Bar Counsel investigation] come to an end, but the hurt will continue for Marshall, Roger and many others," Wynn wrote. "I find myself wondering how could this happen? What could motivate SNA to do something so unfair?"[27]

SNA Fights to Loosen School Meal Standards

As authorization of child nutrition programs neared expiration on September 30, 2015, the SNA urged Republican members of Congress to propose legislation for "flexibility" in school meal standards. It argued that stricter meal rules under the 2010 Healthy Hunger-Free Kids Act had resulted in a decline in school lunch participation, particularly among children who pay full price, thus causing financial problems in school districts.

The rules also said that school districts couldn't use money intended for free and reduced price lunches to keep down prices for children from higher-income families, who are supposed to be paying almost the entire cost of lunch.

The SNA released a position paper in January 2015 protesting mandates to offer a greater quantity and variety of fruits and vegetables that "unnecessarily increased costs and waste for school meal programs and caused many students to swap healthy school meals for junk food fare." The group asked Congress "to provide schools adequate funding and flexibility, allowing school nutrition professionals to plan creative, appealing menus that will entice students to eat healthy school meals," including elimination of the requirement to serve a half-cup of fruits and vegetables.[28]

The SNA cited USDA data showing that after the new rules were implemented, 1.4 million fewer children chose school lunch every day. "Declining student participation reduces meal program revenue for schools already stressed by higher food and labor costs under the new regulations," the association reported. "USDA estimates the new rules add $1.2 billion to the cost of preparing school meals [for] fiscal year 2015 alone. As a result, only half of school meal program operators anticipate their programs will break even at the end of this school year, according to a recent SNA survey."

The SNA also reported that Cornell and Brigham Young University researchers found that the new mandate forcing students to take a fruit or vegetable with every meal, even if they don't intend to eat it, had increased waste by 100 percent, with fruits and vegetables valued at an estimated $684 million thrown in the trash every school year.

However, the Food Research and Action Center (FRAC), an antihunger advocacy group in Washington, D.C., disputed allegations that new nutrition rules are largely responsible for the decline in school lunch participation. The organization reported that lower family incomes and improvements to the eligibility process for school meals led to a continuous increase in participation among low-income children. But rules on pricing of meals for other children contributed to a multiyear decline in participation for those with higher family incomes.[29]

Critics claimed new nutrition rules were driving participation down, but FRAC noted they were introduced in the 2012–2013 school year to bring school meals into line with 2010 Dietary Guidelines. The organization said its analysis "reveals that these participation changes have been percolating for a number of years, with multiple factors at play."

Also expressing disappointment with the SNA position paper, the United Fresh Produce Association said the requirement for children to receive one-half cup of fruits or vegetables in school meals "is being successfully met by tens of thousands of schools across the country. This is a modest step for the health of our children, especially in these critical learning years. When health classes teach students to make Half Their Plate consist of fruits and vegetables, it would be unconscionable for the school cafeteria to undercut that message by not serving at least one-half cup in school meals."[30]

In March 2015, Sen. John Hoeven (R-N.D.) introduced his Healthy School Meals Flexibility Act at the request of the SNA. The bill would provide "permanent flexibility" to school districts in complying with the USDA's new nutrition requirements, specifically sodium and whole-grain requirements for school lunch and breakfast programs. It contained no mention of the controversial requirement to serve a half-cup of fruits or vegetables at school meals.[31]

Opponents viewed the Hoeven bill as a gift to major food companies. But *ProPolitico Morning Agriculture* concluded the food industry had little trouble keeping up with the new meal standards required by the Healthy Hunger-Free Kids Act. "Leading companies, including General Mills, Schwan's and Domino's, are increasing their sales—even though about a million kids have left the school lunch program—and the industry as a whole has dialed down its lobbying in the bitter fight on Capitol Hill," the news service reported.[32]

Elsewhere, some of the largest school districts in the United States formed the nonprofit Urban School Food Alliance and partnered with the Alliance for a Healthier Generation, founded by the American Health Association and the Clinton Foundation, to improve school meals. The food alliance represents school districts in New York City, Los Angeles, Chicago, Miami-Dade, Dallas, and Orange County (Fla.), which have meal-related budgets totaling more than $3 billion.[33] The partnership said it intended to drive "innovative market solutions that are nutritionally wholesome, ecologically sound, economically viable and socially responsible," challenging manufacturers to formulate food that ensures students receive nutritious, delicious meals that meet or exceed USDA guidelines.

Obama Administration Sought to Hold the Line

For its part, the Obama administration sought to hold the line on meal standards for whole grains, sodium, fruits, and vegetables, marshalling arguments from health advocates and organizations, including retired military officers. Nearly 400 retired generals and admirals, calling themselves Mission: Readiness, sent Congress a letter urging members not to lower the school meals standards. "We urge all members of Congress to stand united to maintain the science-based nutrition standards in the child nutrition reauthorization," the retired officers said. "When it comes to children's health and our national security, retreat is not an option."

A 2010 report by Mission: Readiness, titled "Too Fat to Fight," estimated nine million young adults—27 percent of all Americans aged 17–24—are too overweight to join the military. The group said improving nutrition in the nation's schools is a "critical and necessary step to combating obesity among youth and young adults."[34]

Responding to Sen. Hoeven's school meals bill in March 2015, Agriculture Secretary Tom Vilsack enlisted leaders of the American Medical Association (AMA), the American Academy of Pediatrics, and the American Heart Association to defend current school meal standards.[35]

At a teleconference with reporters, Robert Wah, president of the AMA, praised the USDA's meal standards as "based on best available science" and a powerful weapon against obesity, which has tripled over the past 20 years. He noted that the AMA has launched a program with the CDC aimed at halting progression of "pre-diabetes" in individuals to full-blown type 2 diabetes.[36]

Senate Bill Seen as Reasonable Compromise

Authorization of USDA child nutrition programs expired on October 1, 2015, but no reauthorization legislation passed that year. Riders in an omnibus budget bill approved by Congress in December allowed schools to ignore whole-grain requirements, and the bill also blocked sodium restrictions pending further research.

However, senators in January 2016 negotiated a compromise child nutrition bill that drew praise from both sides of the school food fight. Agriculture Secretary Tom Vilsack was pleased that the bill would give schools two more years to reach lower sodium levels in school meals. The SNA also expressed support for the compromise on nutrition standards.

But the SNA later changed its mind and lobbied House Republicans to water down the nutrition standards. To the school food lobby's dismay, the House Education and Workforce Committee's bill, released in April 2016, would also make it harder for schools to qualify for universal free meals.

In February 2016, the SNA sought higher reimbursement for cost of school meals. The lunch ladies asked for a 35-cent increase for school lunches and 10 cents more per breakfast to ensure that they can afford to meet requirements of the Hunger-Free Kids Act of 2010, which has "drastically increased the cost of preparing school meals."[37]

Bettina Elias Siegel, a frequent critic of SNA in her *The Lunch Tray* blog, agreed that the United States is stingy toward school meals. "The federal government provides a little over $3 per student per lunch, and school districts receive a smaller contribution from their state," she wrote in a *New York Times* op-ed column. "But districts generally require their food departments to pay their own overhead, including electricity, accounting and trash collection. Most are left with a dollar and change for food. . . .

"Contrast this with France, where meal prices are tied to family income and wealthy parents can pay around $7 per meal. Give that sum to an American school food services director and you may want to have tissues handy as he's likely to break down in incredulous tears."[38]

Children in the United States will remain vulnerable to obesity until school meals are improved and food marketing to children comes under federal restriction. Neither change is likely to happen soon without strong political pressure.

CHAPTER SIX

Hunger in a Wealthy Society

Shortly after his inauguration in 1969, President Richard Nixon promised to "end hunger for all time in America," asking Congress for $1 billion to reform the nation's feeding programs. Health, Education and Welfare Secretary Robert Finch also viewed hunger as a political and social problem that could be solved rapidly.[1] They were both wrong in their forecasts.

Progress was slow, but a major breakthrough came about in 1977, when food stamp applicants no longer had to pay for their benefits. Congress approved a bill that eliminated the purchase requirement and simplified eligibility standards. As a result, more than five million people, many deeply poor, gained access to food stamps for the first time.[2]

However, the war on hunger is never over. A significant segment of the U.S. population believes that food assistance encourages dependence among poor people and discourages their efforts to find work. That same idea flourished in 1536 in England, when King Henry VIII and his chief minister Thomas Cromwell tried without success to get Parliament to pass a "poor law."

"It is an outrage to the rich and enterprising to suggest that they should pay an income tax, only to put bread in the mouths of the work-shy," Cromwell reflects in Hilary Mantel's historical novel, *Bring Up the Bodies*. "[And if I argue] that famine provokes criminality: well, are there not hangmen enough?"[3]

Some things never change. In 2012, the U.S. House of Representatives proposed cutting more than $169 billion from food stamps, now known as SNAP. The proposal enraged Bread for the World, a church-based antihunger organization in Washington, D.C.

"Some representatives argued that feeding hungry people is really the work of the churches," reported Gary Cook, Bread's director of government relations. "These representatives are essentially saying that every church across America—big, small and tiny—needs to come up with an extra $50,000 dedicated to feeding people—every year for the next 10 years—to make up for these cuts."[4]

Despite the difficulties in defining hunger and the hidden nature of the problem, most Americans acknowledge that the condition exists and believe that we have a duty to share our abundance, America's Second Harvest said in a 2004 report supported by the UPS Foundation (founded by the United Parcel Service) and the Congressional Hunger Center.[5]

The problem of defining and quantifying hunger was largely overcome with the introduction of the concept of "food security," defined as "all people in a society obtaining a culturally acceptable, nutritionally adequate diet, through nonemergency sources at all times."[6] The bipartisan National Commission on Hunger, appointed by congressional leaders of both parties, defined hunger as "very low food security," in a report released in December 2015. The commission reported that nearly 7 million people, or 5.6 percent of American households, had at least one member experience hunger at some time in 2014.[7]

"During the Great Recession, the percent of households that experienced hunger increased from 4.1 percent in 2007 to 5.4 percent in 2010," the commission's report continued. "The rate has remained at that level even as the economic recovery enters its sixth year. In addition, too many people who could work remain out of the labor market—labor force participation by working age adults has been declining since its peak in 2000.

"Hunger has far-reaching consequences, not just on individuals, but also on the U.S. health care system, our educational system, and the economy: hunger contributes to nutritional deficits that can undermine people's health, diminish human capital, and impede children's development. These negative effects can translate into greater health care expenditures, reduced worker productivity, and greater rates of worker absenteeism."[8]

Hunger and Malnutrition Affect Child Development

In the early 1990s, the advocacy group Food Research and Action Center (FRAC) undertook benchmark research into the problem of childhood hunger. The FRAC's Community Childhood Hunger Identification Project fundamentally changed the way policymakers addressed the issue. The study estimated that four million children under the age of 12 went hungry, and nearly 10 million more were at risk of hunger.[9]

Lack of food has powerful effects on infants and children. Maternal undernutrition during pregnancy increases the risk of negative birth outcomes, including premature birth, low birth weight, smaller head size, and lower brain weight, according to the American Psychological Association (APA). Babies born prematurely are vulnerable to health problems and are at increased risk for developing learning problems when they reach school age.[10]

Noting that the first three years of a child's life are a period of rapid brain development, the APA reports that too little energy, protein, and nutrients during this sensitive period can lead to lasting deficits in cognitive, social, and emotional development. Protein-energy malnutrition, iron deficiency anemia, iodine, zinc, and other vitamin deficiencies in early childhood can impair the brain.

Failure to thrive, the failure to grow and reach major developmental milestones as the result of undernutrition, affects 5–10 percent of American children under the age of three, according to APA. Hunger reduces a child's motor skills, activity level, and motivation to explore the environment. Movement and exploration are important to cognitive development, and more active children elicit more stimulation and attention from their caregivers, which promotes social and emotional development.

Families often try to keep their food insecurity hidden, and some parents feel shame or embarrassment that they are not able to feed their children adequately, the APA notes. Children may also feel stigmatized, isolated, ashamed, or embarrassed by their lack of food.

A community sample that classified low-income children aged 6–12 as "hungry," "at-risk for hunger," or "not hungry" found that hungry children were significantly more likely to receive special education services, to have repeated a grade in school, and to have received mental health counseling than at-risk-for-hunger or not-hungry children.

Holes in the Safety Net Reopened

In 1981, amid the worst recession since the Great Depression, President Ronald Reagan resumed direct distribution of food commodities, as was the practice in the 1930s. Reagan issued an executive order allowing the USDA to begin distributing stocks of farm-support commodities that had been held in storage to ameliorate market variations. In 1983, Reagan's executive order was converted into legislation with the Emergency Food Assistance Act and establishment of the Temporary Emergency Food Assistance Program.[11]

In 1996, President Bill Clinton fulfilled his campaign pledge to "end welfare as we know it" by signing legislation that resulted in the largest decrease in the federal food assistance safety net since the New Deal. Congress passed the draconian Personal Responsibility and Work Opportunity Reconciliation Act, better known as welfare reform. The food stamp program was reduced by more than $23 billion through repeals of food stamp expansions made in 1993. The legislation also reduced summer food, school breakfast, and the Child and Adult Care Food Program.

In 1998, the strongest economy in U.S. history helped reduce poverty and food stamp participation. Yet the declines in food stamp rolls—33 percent since the enactment of welfare reform—vastly outpaced the reduction in the number of people living in poverty. The number of officially poor people declined by three million between 1997 and 2001, but the number of food stamp recipients declined by more than eight million, according to America's Second Harvest.[12]

During this period, emergency food providers reported a surge in requests for food assistance. Never before in U.S. history did such significant numbers of employed individuals and children seek assistance from pantries, soup kitchens, and shelters. By 2001, one in four individuals in a soup kitchen was a child.

In 2002, Congress reauthorized the food stamp program as part of the larger Farm Bill. A broad coalition of faith-based organizations, emergency food providers, food policy advocates, and state program administrators helped draft food stamp reforms that restored eligibility to most legal immigrants, generally eased access to the program for working poor families, and increased emergency food commodity distributions.

In 2008, the Farm Bill included about $100 billion in annual spending for USDA programs, about 80 percent of which was allocated for food stamps and other nutrition programs, according to Second Harvest. President George W. Bush vetoed the 2008 bill because of its size and cost, but Congress overrode his veto.[13]

Rural-Urban Farm Bill Alliance Falls Apart

In 2012, the longtime alliance between farm state members of Congress and their urban state counterparts fell apart. Dating back four decades to Sens. Hubert Humphrey (D-Minn.) and Bob Dole (R-Kan.), rural lawmakers reached deals with their urban and suburban colleagues to pass Farm Bills beneficial to both. Farm state lawmakers got the agriculture subsidies they wanted, and urban-suburban members got the nutrition programs they wanted to benefit their constituents.

In July 2013, the House of Representatives approved a new Farm Bill that contained farm programs only, excluding the nutrition title, notably food stamps, for consideration in the future. "The bill passed by the House today is not a real Farm Bill and is an insult to rural America," commented Sen. Debbie Stabenow (D-Mich.), chair of the Senate Agriculture Committee.

"We will go to conference with the bipartisan, comprehensive Farm Bill that was passed in the Senate that not only reforms programs, supports families in need and creates agriculture jobs, but also saves billions more than the extremely flawed House bill."[14]

The idea of splitting the Farm Bill surfaced just before the Fourth of July break. Advocates of the split argued that a farm-only bill would be easier to pass, enabling a conference with the Senate on its version of the Farm Bill. The House would deal with food stamps later.

As expected, the farm-only Farm Bill split drew fierce opposition from Democrats, notably Rep. Rosa DeLauro (Conn.), former chair of the House Appropriations USDA-FDA Subcommittee. "The decision by House Republican leaders to drop nutrition and anti-hunger programs—most notably food stamps—from the Farm Bill puts the final nail in the coffin of the coalition that ensured farmers could make a living and struggling families could put food on their table," she warned.[15]

Meanwhile, House Republicans took their cue from a report issued by the conservative Heritage Foundation, recommending that food stamps and farm programs be considered as separate bills. The Heritage Foundation said "combining the two programs into one massive bill creates an unholy alliance of food stamp and farm policy proponents that lobbies for the bill, making it easier to get enacted. This tactic also serves as a way for Congress to rubberstamp legislation without having to take a serious look at its policy implications. If there is to be real reform of food stamps or farm policy, Congress needs to take the time to address them separately."[16]

Heritage said, "Converting food stamps into a work activation program is a crucial step in promoting self-sufficiency and personal responsibility among food stamp recipients. Able-bodied adults should be required to work, prepare for work or at least look for work as a condition of receiving food stamps."[17]

To the dismay of fiscal conservatives, the Great Recession resulted in record enrollment in SNAP. At the end of 2014, food stamps were helping more than 46 million low-income Americans ward off starvation and afford a nutritionally adequate diet. Yet one in six households experienced "food hardship" in 2014, according to the Gallup-Healthways Well-Being Index. Some 17 percent of households answered yes when asked, "Have there been times in the past 12 months when you did not have enough money to buy food that you or your family needed?"[18]

Nevertheless, fiscal conservatives made cuts to the SNAP program in the 2014 Farm Bill. They argued that generous food stamp benefits create harmful dependence on the federal government.

Opportunity Grant Proposal Prompts Lengthy Debate

On July 24, 2014, House Budget Committee Chairman Paul Ryan (R-Wis.) proposed a new "Opportunity Grant" pilot project in a select number of states where the federal government would consolidate a number of means-tested programs into a new program. The largest contributions would come from the food stamp program (SNAP), Temporary Assistance for Needy Families (TANF), child care and housing assistance programs, and the funding would be deficit-neutral relative to current law.

"It is important to note that this is not a budget-cutting exercise—this is a reform proposal," Ryan said in the committee's discussion paper. "This consolidation does not make judgments about an optimal level of spending. Instead, this proposal is concerned with our ability to use resources effectively and to find out what works.

"It allows the federal government to leverage its strengths—vast resources—while also allowing states, localities, and communities to leverage theirs—deep knowledge of their population and the unique challenges they face," he continued. "Therefore, this proposal seeks to create the space and flexibility necessary for local, state, and federal government to add value without making judgments about the right level of spending."[19]

Like welfare reform, the Opportunity Grant program would begin in a handful of states committed to fixing the status quo. Because the program would be deficit-neutral, the state would receive the same amount of overall funding from the federal government. But by giving states more flexibility, the federal government could test a variety of approaches, Ryan said.

The following day, Robert Greenstein, founder and president of the Center for Budget and Policy Priorities, charged that Ryan's Opportunity Grant proposal would likely increase poverty and shrink resources for antipoverty programs over time.

"While Chairman Ryan describes the proposal as maintaining the same overall funding as the current system for each participating state, that would be a practical impossibility," said Greenstein. "His proposal would convert the nation's basic food assistance safety net [food stamps] from an entitlement that responds automatically to increased need into part of a sweeping block grant that gives each state fixed funding for the year and, thus, cannot respond in the same way. This would be a particularly serious problem when need rises, such as in recessions."[20]

While Ryan said he's driven by evidence and research, "his plan would jeopardize basic nutrition assistance for poor children, which research has shown is highly effective not only in reducing child malnutrition, but also in improving children's long-term prospects," Greenstein continued, warning that the Ryan plan would eliminate poor families' entitlement to SNAP.

Ryan said that the federal block grant funds would have to be used for the poor, "but that wouldn't prevent states and localities from substituting some of these funds for existing state and local funds that they now use for some of the same purpose," said Greenstein. "With broad block grants of this nature, some substitution by state and local governments is almost impossible to prevent.

"History clearly shows that when policymakers combine a number of programs into a block grant, federal funding typically declines over time, often dramatically," Greenstein concluded. "When a broad array of programs are merged into a block grant, policymakers find it virtually impossible to identify a specific level of needed federal funding—or the likely human impact of program cuts. As a result, the broad block grant often becomes easy to squeeze in the competition for federal budget dollars."

Greenstein's critique of Ryan's Opportunity Grants received widespread attention from the media. Scott Winship, a fellow at the conservative Manhattan Institute, felt obliged to write a rebuttal, which was published by *Forbes*. Claiming that welfare reform legislation in the late 1990s helped poor people, Winship said groups such as Greenstein's "ignored the real harm done by the status quo. We also severely underestimated the ability of would-be beneficiaries of means-tested programs to cope with change and adjust their behavior; we did not take seriously the perverse incentives embedded in federal safety net policy. Finally, we failed to recognize the flexibility built into the system of block grants to states that cash welfare became."[21]

Winship said the official measure of poverty doesn't count as income noncash benefits such as food stamps, housing assistance, or Medicaid, and it fails to include refundable tax breaks such as the Earned Income Tax Credit (EITC) and Child Tax Credit. "These are all key elements of our safety net," he continued. "Nor does the measure take taxes into account more generally, which means that when taxes fall, as they have, the official measure of poverty does not acknowledge an increase in take-home pay. A third flaw is that the official measure uses a cost-of-living adjustment that makes the poverty line a higher and higher threshold over time.

"The implication is that moving further in the direction of work promotion, as the Ryan plan does, could reduce the poverty-trap aspects of our programs for the poor, allowing more people to benefit from work, while retaining a robust safety net," said Winship.

Greenstein issued his own lengthy rebuttal, charging that Winship didn't adequately address the concern that Ryan's block grant would likely lead to less antipoverty funding over time. The budget policy center president said Winship "has misplaced confidence that SNAP could work effectively as a counter-cyclical tool if it loses entitlement status and is merged into a sweeping block grant."[22]

Winship "gives short shrift to my concerns about converting SNAP into a block grant and seems not to recognize that SNAP is one of the leading success stories in American social policy over the last half-century, helping largely to eliminate severe child hunger and malnutrition and playing a key role as an 'automatic stabilizer' for a weak economy," said Greenstein.

Nevertheless, the House Budget Committee in March 2015 proposed cutting another $125 billion from the SNAP program by raising eligibility requirements, lowering benefits, and converting the program to "block grants" administered by the 50 states.

Elevated to the post of House Speaker, Ryan in December 2015 reiterated his proposal for block grants to the states. Pointing to a work requirement in welfare changes in the 1990s, he said in a speech he'd "combine a lot of [antipoverty programs] and send that money back to the states for better poverty-fighting solutions. Require everyone who can to work. Let states and communities try different ideas. And then test the results."[23]

The Congressional Budget Office (CBO) examined what would happen to households' income if spending on SNAP in 2016—which CBO projected to be about $77 billion—were cut by 15 percent. Such a decline would save $11.5 billion in 2016, putting inflation-adjusted spending roughly on par with spending in 2009. Specifically, CBO examined three illustrative options, each of which would cut federal spending on SNAP in 2016 by 15 percent.[24]

In a speech at the Consumer Federation of America's National Food Policy Conference, Agriculture Secretary Tom Vilsack said some 11 or 12 million food stamp recipients would need help because House budget conferees want to convert SNAP into a block grant program administered by the states, which would likely save money by raising eligibility standards. He noted that 80 percent of SNAP recipients are senior citizens, persons with disabilities, or part-time workers.

"If you want to reduce SNAP [enrollment], increase the minimum wage," he asserted.[25]

National Hunger Commission Shakes Up SNAP Policy

The 10-member bipartisan National Commission on Hunger, appointed by congressional leaders of both parties, shook up SNAP policy in December 2015 by proposing to limit food stamp recipients' choices. Health advocates have never succeeded in restricting food stamp purchases to healthy foods and beverages.

Among 20 proposals in its 96-page final report, the commission recommended that Congress restrict SNAP purchases of sugar-sweetened beverages, which cost tens of billions annually. "Congress should enact legislation to restrict the purchase of a carefully defined list of sugar-sweetened beverages developed in consultation with major health and nutrition organizations . . . nutritionists, and scientific experts," the commission said. "The USDA should ensure mechanisms that provide broad, understandable, and culturally appropriate communication regarding this new restriction."[26]

To no one's surprise, the American Beverage Association opposed that recommendation. "People using SNAP benefits make the same food-buying decisions as we all do; they don't need government telling them which aisles they are allowed to go down and how best to serve their families," the ABA said, adding, "Allowing government to designate foods as 'good' and 'bad' would create a food code more complicated and arbitrary than the tax code. That would put us on a slippery slope of government intrusion into many decisions that have always been left to the individual to decide."[27]

The Hunger Commission also recommended that Congress and the USDA require states to help SNAP recipients gain more skills to find jobs with wages sufficient to enable them to give up food stamps. The report further proposed that the USDA improve nutrition education for recipients, expand shelf space for healthy foods at SNAP-eligible retailers, and "develop mechanisms for incentivizing purchases of healthier foods."[28]

The USDA in February 2016 proposed a rule that would require stores accepting food stamps to stock a wider array of healthy foods on their shelves, including at least seven varieties of dairy products, breads and cereals, meats, poultry and fish, and fruits and vegetables. The National Association of Convenience and Fuel Retailing said the proposed rule could stop many convenience stores from accepting food stamps.

Half Million Adults Expected to Lose SNAP Benefits

In the wake of the National Commission on Hunger's report, the Center on Budget and Policy Priorities (CBPP) forecast that more than 500,000 adults would lose SNAP benefits in 2016 as waivers expire. Affected unemployed childless individuals are very poor and few qualify for other help, the CBPP added.

"More than 500,000 and as many as one million of the nation's poorest people will be cut off SNAP over the course of 2016, owing to the return in many areas of a three-month limit on SNAP benefits for unemployed adults aged 18–49 who aren't disabled or raising minor children," explained the CBPP. "These individuals will lose their food assistance benefits after three months regardless of how hard they are looking for work. The impact will be felt in the 23 states that must or are choosing to re-impose the time limit in 2016."[29]

Ryan and Republican presidential candidates all favored changing food stamps from a federal program to block grants for states. But some states prefer not to help poor families, leaving them surviving on jobs with low wages. The Republican leaders would tear apart one of America's most successful antipoverty programs in the past half-century.

PART II

Emergence of Consumer Advocates

CHAPTER SEVEN

Landscape Shift in Food Advocacy

The next three chapters describe the emergence of influential individuals and consumer advocacy groups in the 1960s and 1970s. During this period, they awakened the public to the problems of hunger, food safety, and unhealthy diets.

One of the best-kept secrets of post–World War II America was the appalling hunger and malnutrition in the rural South and other parts of the United States. Jim Crow segregation was understood to be a way of life at the time, but the public was unaware that many African Americans were malnourished as well as mistreated.

The political landscape in Washington, D.C., didn't encourage attention to hunger in the South or anywhere else. High-ranking USDA officials were beholden to powerful southern Democrats who chaired the House and Senate Agriculture Committees and the Appropriations Committees responsible for funding farm and food programs. The late Rep. Jamie Whitten (D-Miss.), for whom the USDA headquarters building is named, was dubbed the "permanent secretary of agriculture" because he controlled the department's purse strings for almost a half-century.

Southern Democrats insisted on local control of food assistance, which preserved racial segregation, and they viewed nutrition programs as a way to dispose of agricultural surplus.

The veil of silence surrounding hunger was torn asunder early in 1967, when Sens. Robert Kennedy (D-N.Y.), Joseph Clark (D-Pa.), and their colleagues on the Senate Subcommittee on Employment, Manpower, and Poverty held a hearing in the small town of Cleveland in the Mississippi Delta. A tour of homes in the Delta wasn't part of the official schedule, but the senators added it to their itinerary at the urging of 27-year-old Marian Wright, an African American civil rights lawyer who later married Kennedy aide Peter Edelman.[1]

"Wright had testified that people were starving in the cotton-rich Delta, but it was not until she persuaded the two senators to go into the miserable shacks, meet the people, and discover it for themselves that they determined, with the greatest conviction, to demand help for the hungry poor," reported Pulitzer Prize–winning journalist Nick Kotz in his landmark book, *Let Them Eat Promises: The Politics of Hunger in America*.[2]

As described by Kotz, Bobby Kennedy "felt his way through a dark windowless shack, fighting nausea at the strong smell of aging mildew, sickness and urine. In the early afternoon shadows, he saw a child sitting on the floor of a tiny back room. Barely two years old, wearing only a filthy undershirt, she sat running several grains of rice round and round on the floor. The senator knelt beside her.

"'Hello . . . Hi . . . Hi, baby,' he murmured, touching her cheeks and her hair as he would his own child's. As he sat on the dirty floor, he placed his hand gently on the girl's swollen stomach. But the little girl sat as if in a trance, her sad eyes turned downward, and rubbed the gritty rice.

"For five minutes he tried: talking, caressing, tickling, poking—demanding that the child respond. The baby never looked up."[3]

Kennedy went out to the front yard, where the girl's mother was telling Sen. Clark that she couldn't afford to buy food stamps and was feeding her family with some rice and biscuits made from leftover surplus commodities. Controlling his anger, Kennedy whispered to a companion, "I've seen bad things in West Virginia, but I've never seen anything like this anywhere in the United States."

At an earlier subcommittee hearing in Washington, D.C., Wright described how a perfect storm had transformed the Mississippi Delta into a nightmare for African Americans:

- Mechanized cotton farming
- A new minimum wage for farm workers that pushed sharecroppers off their land,
- A huge cutback in cotton planting, and
- The rising battle for civil rights.

"Several hundred thousand Negroes were out of work, hungry and unwanted, as mechanization of cotton planting and picking had eliminated the meager jobs on which they had subsisted for generations," wrote Kotz, summarizing Wright's testimony. "And, as a final blow, many counties were switching from a food program in which the poor were given free surplus commodities to a new food stamp program in which stamps cost more than they could possibly pay."[4]

The widely publicized Kennedy-Clark visit to Mississippi inspired two private organizations—the Field Foundation and the Citizens' Crusade against Poverty—to step up their own efforts against hunger in America. Leslie Dunbar, a soft-spoken white former college professor who headed the Field Foundation, decided in April 1967 to organize his own fact-finding tour of Mississippi, conducted by Harvard psychiatrist Robert Coles and three other physicians.

Driving around Mississippi on Memorial Day weekend, the team of four doctors was appalled by the condition of African American children as they visited Head Start centers throughout the state. In a report titled *Children in Mississippi*, they said, "We saw children being fed communally—that is, by neighbors who give scraps of food to children whose parents have nothing to give them. Not only are these children receiving no food from the government, they are also getting no medical attention whatsoever. They are out of sight and ignored. They are living under such primitive conditions that we found it hard to believe we were examining American children of the twentieth century!"[5]

The Field Foundation's medical team flew to Washington, D.C., for a meeting with top Johnson administration officials: Agriculture Secretary Orville Freeman; HEW Secretary John Gardner; and Sargent Shriver, director of the Office of Economic Opportunity (OEO). However, the doctors were disappointed by their response. Freeman complained of restrictions placed on him by southern conservatives in Congress, and HEW officials stressed political limitations on the Public Health Service.

Meanwhile, the Citizens Crusade against Poverty, a coalition of liberal church groups, unions, and foundations led by antipoverty crusader Richard W. Boone, embarked on a comprehensive investigation of poverty and hunger. They formed a Citizens Board of Inquiry into Hunger and Malnutrition to examine federal feeding programs across the United States. Cochaired by the Field Foundation's Leslie Dunbar and Benjamin Mays, president of historically black Morehouse College in Atlanta, the citizens' board recruited respected figures from medicine, law, universities, foundations, social action groups, and religious institutions.

Teams from the Citizens Board of Inquiry visited the ghettoes of Boston and New York City, Native American reservations in South Dakota and Arizona, rural white slums of Appalachia, rural black slums in South Carolina, migrant camps in Florida, and Mexican American barrios in San Antonio.

"As the Board moved from state to state, stories of the witnesses followed a familiar pattern. Poor people said they were hungry and were not being helped by government food programs," reported Kotz. "Local doctors said that poor people in their areas suffered from malnutrition. Poverty workers described local institutions that resisted efforts to alleviate the misery of the poor. As the Board members investigated, held hearings and examined children, they confirmed that hunger and malnutrition weren't confined to Mississippi. Hunger was a scar across an affluent nation."[6]

The Citizens Board's report on its findings, *Hunger USA*, issued in 1968, met stiff resistance from southern politicians, who viewed the hunger issue as a political ploy by Bobby Kennedy and other liberal politicians to gain African American votes. "There has been hunger since the time of Jesus Christ and there always will be," commented Sen. Strom Thurmond (R-S.C.).[7]

Rep. Jamie Whitten (D-Miss.), chairman of the House Appropriations USDA Subcommittee, and House Agriculture Committee Chairman Bob Poage (D-Texas) undertook separate investigations to discredit the report. Whitten sent FBI agents across the country to investigate what he conceived as a deliberately "framed picture" in *Hunger USA* and a related CBS television documentary, "Hunger in America." He suggested that some of the photos might have been taken in impoverished developing countries.

Summing up Citizen Board survey results from health officers in the 256 "hunger counties," mostly in the South, Poage declared, "The basic problem is one of ignorance as to what constitutes a balanced diet, coupled with indifference by a great many persons who should and probably do not know. . . . Children suffered because a father spent disproportionally large sums either on liquor or on extramarital relations. . . . Jobs were available in a community but rejected by able-bodied men who apparently preferred to remain on welfare rolls. . . . Families on food relief often had television sets and nice automobiles, and often the head of the household was reported to be spending money on whiskey that was needed for purchase of food for the children."[8]

Senate Agriculture Chairman Allen Ellender (D-La.) chimed in, "I know that in my state we had a number of fishermen who were unable to catch fish. Do you expect the government, because they cannot catch fish, to feed them until the fish are there?"[9]

Even Agriculture Secretary Freeman sought to discredit the "shockingly irresponsible" CBS documentary on hunger, telling President Lyndon Johnson he had received thousands of critical letters and had mounted "an important counterattack" in response. He cited minor factual inaccuracies and the film's failure to acknowledge improvements to food programs.[10]

Let Them Eat Promises

In 1969, journalist Kotz thoroughly exposed the scandal of hunger in America in *Let Them Eat Promises*. Critics put his book in the same league as

Ralph Nader's *Unsafe at Any Speed*, which exposed the corrupt practices of the automobile industry.[11]

Born in Texas, Kotz was the grandson of Ukrainian immigrants who escaped pogroms in the 19th century and established a large farm-supply store and a cattle-breeding ranch in San Antonio. His parents divorced when he was still an infant, and he and his mother went to live with his maternal grandparents.

Kotz's life took a turn for the better at age 14, when his mother married an obstetrician-gynecologist in Washington, D.C., and moved there. He was adopted by his stepfather and enrolled in St. Albans School, an elite prep school in D.C. Kotz then attended Dartmouth College, where he graduated magna cum laude and won a prize for his history thesis. He studied international relations at the London School of Economics before joining the U.S. Marine Corps to fulfill his military service obligation.

Fresh out of the Marine Corps, Kotz pursued his dream of becoming a writer, following the example of Ernest Hemingway and other great novelists who started as newspaper reporters. He landed a job with the *Des Moines Register*, where he began on the police beat and worked up the ladder to become a Washington correspondent. Arriving in 1964 at a news bureau in Washington serving both the *Des Moines Register* and the *Minneapolis Tribune*, Kotz was assigned the agriculture beat, a boring subject area often handed to newcomers. However, he soon turned the agriculture beat into the hunger beat as he wrote stories about inadequacies in USDA food programs.

After writing a newspaper series on poverty in Mississippi, Kotz was urged to write a book about hunger. "I'd never written a book before," he recalls. "Then I got a call from a [publisher] at Prentice-Hall suggesting I write the book."[12]

Early in his book, Kotz says he witnessed the realities of extreme rural poverty through the eyes of his wife, journalist Mary Lynn Kotz, during a 1960 trip to her native state of Mississippi. As a reporter in Iowa, he saw similar suffering and injustice in that breadbasket state.

"Returning to Mississippi and other parts of the rural South in 1967 as a Washington correspondent reporting on government programs supposedly designed to alleviate poverty, it seemed to me that the misery was worse than it had been seven years earlier," he wrote.[13]

Let Them Eat Promises revealed the nation's leaders treating hungry Americans with nothing short of contempt. Food company executives were no better than politicians in acknowledging hunger in America. In late1967, Richard W. Boone, who launched the Citizens Board of Inquiry that published *Hunger in America*, wrote a letter to 75 major companies belonging to the Grocery Manufacturers of America (GMA), the nation's largest food trade association. Boone asked the executives if they should be doing more to help poor people access an adequate diet. He suggested providing fortified food products to low-income people who couldn't afford better food.

"I have difficulty seeing why major food manufacturers should be singled out to comment on hunger and malnutrition," replied W. Gardner Barton, president of Thomas J. Lipton. "The matter of hunger is, of course, related to economic well-being, and I fail to see why you should attribute any special competency to the food manufacturers to comment on economic well-being."[14]

George Koch, president of the GMA trade association, was notorious for his opposition to any social welfare or consumer legislation. According to Kotz, GMA lobbyists maneuvered to kill a bill to provide $50 million for two years for emergency food and medical aid to malnourished Americans who couldn't afford food stamps or access free commodities.

In a 1968 memo to the Citizens Board, the consumer advocate Robert Choate, a wealthy Republican, wrote, "We cannot find one single instance of a major food manufacturer supporting a piece of poverty welfare legislation bringing adequate food to the poor unless that legislation meant increased sales for that food line. In their desire to keep the 'market open' even at the poverty end of the population, and in their desire to avoid 'government intervention,' they have supported . . . denial of government-subsidized food to the hungry residents of the United States."[15]

Kotz says the importance of *Let Them Eat Promises* was its timing. The book came out just as the Nixon administration convened a widely publicized White House Conference on Food, Nutrition, and Health in December 1969. The book became a textbook on the hunger issue for conference attendees and a catalyst for action by the many religious groups primed for a new cause to succeed the civil rights movement.

"My book became the bible to educate all these people about the hunger issue," he reports.[16]

But communities were slow to acknowledge hunger and comply with new food policy initiatives. It didn't help that the OEO, created by the President Johnson's War on Poverty, attempted to take over food programs. OEO's move was deeply resented by Agriculture Secretary Freeman. Neither USDA officials nor their congressional overseers wanted to get into running welfare or social service programs. Freeman argued that welfare programs belonged in HEW. Southern Democrats opposed shifting feeding programs from surplus food disposal to nourishing poor children.

Ignoring deficiencies in antihunger programs, President Johnson resisted food policy reform. He associated the hunger issue with his political rival Bobby Kennedy and viewed food assistance to poor people as "welfare."

"There is little doubt that Congress would have taken major steps forward on the hunger issue in 1968 if Lyndon Johnson had only lent his support," commented Kotz.[17]

At the end of *Let Them Eat Promises*, Kotz lamented, "The politics of hunger in America is a dismal story of human greed and callousness, and immorality sanctioned and aided by the government of the United States. But it is also a story that does provide hope that men can change things; that men do care about fulfilling this country's highest ideals, and do care about their fellow human beings."[18]

But the story doesn't end there. The late Richard Boone, who led the Citizens Board that issued the *Hunger USA* report, said in an interview before his death that Kotz's book gave "added life" to the war on hunger because it was comprehensive, well written, and highly readable. "It cast a bright light on the status quo, especially in the South," he said.[19]

Kotz stressed that the Senate Select Committee on Nutrition and Human Needs, launched in February 1969 and chaired by Sen. George McGovern (D-S.D.), carried forward the reforms he hoped for in his book. Conservative Republicans from the nation's heartland, such as Sens. Bob Dole (R-Kan.) and Marlow Cook (R-Ky.), joined the so-called McGovern Committee and also became lifelong converts to the cause of ending hunger.[20]

During its eight-year lifetime, the McGovern Committee held widely publicized hearings with testimony from academics, consumer advocates, health and nutrition experts, school officials, and physicians. As a select committee, it was authorized for only one year at a time, but the full Senate extended it each year, despite opposition from southern Democrats.

The panel is credited with strengthening the food stamp, school lunch, and breakfast programs and launching WIC, which provides women, infants, and children with nutritious food at a critical moment in their lives. Although the committee had no jurisdiction over legislation, individual members could introduce legislation on their own. It created a bipartisan constituency for antihunger legislation, led by Dole on the Republican side.

Nancy Amidei, a one-time staff member of the McGovern Committee, said the true heroes of the antihunger movement were African American, Hispanic. and Asian welfare mothers and their allies. "When they organized, when they testified, when they spoke to the media, they often were literally putting their lives on the line. They faced abuse and the cutting off of their welfare grants and worse. And yet they were key players in the National Anti-Hunger Coalition," she reported.[21]

Amidei said every state had at least one state-wide group, and it was often church people who made it possible for their members to travel to the state capital to testify or helped line up interviews with local media.

"The antihunger movement would never have gotten as far as it did without the pressure from local people in every state," she said.

Advocates included farm groups, grocery store clerks, local elected officials, school principals and 4-H leaders in farm states, nutritionists, members of the National Welfare Rights Organization, medical students, and legal services attorneys right out of law school and very idealistic, said Amidei. "They were all part of the antihunger movement, and they brought a special kind of passion and influence to the fight. There was only so much the [Washington] types could do. Without pressure from 'back home,' I doubt there would have been any progress."

Incubators of Advocacy

The early 1970s were a time of ferment for food advocacy. The Nixon administration took over the reins of government in 1969, but a handful of individuals—notably Michael Jacobson, Rodney Leonard, and Ron Pollack—stepped forward to create public interest groups that would have profound influence on the politics of food.

The list also includes Ralph Nader, whose Center for the Study of Responsive Law got an early start on food policy issues. Nader's task forces in the late 1960s, dubbed "Nader's Raiders," issued reports on a variety of problems, including *The Chemical Feast*, a 1971 investigation of the FDA's oversight of the food industry by attorney James Turner. That year the center also launched Public Citizen, a watchdog organization that in 2005 gave birth to the advocacy group Food & Water Watch.

Center for Science in the Public Interest

Armed with a PhD in microbiology from the Massachusetts Institute of Technology (MIT), Michael Jacobson in 1970 dreamed of a career in public interest science. As a researcher at Nader's Center for the Study of Responsive Law, he was asked to write a book about the safety of food additives. However, one year later, Jacobson concluded that the additives were less dangerous to health than the foods containing them, including hot dogs and soft drinks, which were linked to problems ranging from tooth decay to heart disease. An unusual scientist with a flair for public relations, he was able to call widespread attention to the foods he saw as dangerous.

While working on his additives book for Nader in 1970, Jacobson met two like-minded young scientists—chemist Albert Fritsch and meteorologist James Sullivan—and the three of them founded the Center for Science in the Public Interest (CSPI). In the initial edition of their newsletter, published in April 1971, the cofounders described their organization as promoting "people-oriented technology and establish[ing] the legitimacy of advocacy science in the public interest."[22]

They added, "Uncontrolled technology has produced a form of progress in our country that erodes the basic quality of our everyday lives. Although scientific research has provided enormous benefits, applications of new technology are all too often directed toward private ends which virtually ignore the public good." They cited "unchecked automobiles contaminating the air, food additives endangering health, and rampant highway development discriminating against the poor and aged."

The CSPI's original agenda included automobile safety, lead pollution, gasoline additives, strip mining, and a host of other issues. By 1978, two of the cofounders had departed the CSPI, leaving Jacobson to focus exclusively on food safety and nutrition.

He didn't have a business model to sustain the group, which declined to accept grants from the government or the food industry. However, his books—and posters derived from the books—proved to be a fountain of cash.

"CSPI survived just through luck," Jacobson recalled. "In the 1970s, I lived off the royalties from *Eater's Digest*. We converted that book into a poster and sold a ton of those. I wrote another book, *Nutrition Scoreboard*, and we sold over 100,000 copies. We had mailbags filled with orders for the book."[23]

The CSPI in 1974 launched its monthly *Nutrition Action Healthletter*, which offered down-to-earth dietary advice and carefully researched exposés, and began charging a subscription fee in 1975. He gives major credit for the newsletter's early success to Patty Hausman, one of its first editors.

"[From her, we] learned about trading mailing lists and other marketing strategies," said Jacobson. "By the early 1980s we were up to speed. Our subscriptions increased, and we could hire more people. During the '80s our poster sales plummeted, but our newsletter subscriptions took off. We were offering information that people wanted and valued."[24]

Nutrition Action, which gained close to a million subscribers, accounts for about 80 or 90 percent of the CSPI's revenue, which totals about $20 million. Some subscribers also make contributions in addition to paying the annual subscription fee, Jacobson noted.

By focusing on unhealthful food products, Jacobson became the scourge of the food industry, causing critics to call the CSPI "the food police." For the next 40 years he encouraged American consumers to think twice about buying hot dogs, bacon, theater popcorn, greasy Chinese food, Olestra fat substitute, potato chips, and numerous other food products.

"We're the consumer watchdog that has stopped countless deceptive ads and labels for products made by some of the nation's biggest food marketers," he wrote in a 40th anniversary report issued in 2011.

"Beyond tooth decay and heart disease, new evidence demonstrated that the typical American diet also was causing obesity, cancer, strokes and diabetes," he said. "In fact, as many as several hundred thousand people a year were dying unnecessarily, just because of what they were eating—and were encouraged to eat by government agencies, dietitians and the food industry."[25]

In the 1997 edition of the *Encyclopedia of the Consumer Movement*, Jacobson reviewed the CSPI's advocacy campaigns since 1980, when the group's scientists, writers, and organizers were bolstered by an in-house legal staff. "When necessary, the organization's legal staff seeks solutions through enforcement of existing laws or adoption of new regulations or legislation," he wrote.[26] The group took the lead in winning passage of the Nutrition Labeling and Education Act of 1990 (NLEA), which mandated the Nutrition Facts label on packaged foods. Jacobson noted that, responding to public demand for healthier food in the early 1980s, "many food manufacturers began promoting the supposed nutritional virtues of their products more aggressively.

"CSPI began to identify numerous product labels and advertisements that were clearly deceptive, if not fraudulent," he continued. "After first seeking a halt to individual deceptions on a case-by-case basis, the organization began to advocate legislation to protect all consumers. That effort culminated almost a decade later with passage of [the NLEA], which mandated clear and useful nutrition information on practically all food labels."

Some companies responded by moving deceptive statements from labels to ads, Jacobson reported, adding, "Yet, again as a result of CSPI's advocacy efforts, in 1994 the [FTC] responded by adopting a policy that called on companies to have their advertisements comply as fully as possible with the nutrition labeling law."

The CSPI was also among the first advocates to call for reduction of sodium levels in foods and curbing consumption of sugary soft drinks.

Community Nutrition Institute

In 1969, Rodney Leonard, USDA deputy assistant secretary in charge of meat inspection and federal feeding programs, was out of a job. Serving as press secretary for Minnesota governor Orville Freeman, Leonard had followed him to Washington when Freeman became agriculture secretary in the Johnson administration. As political appointees, Leonard and Freeman both lost their jobs when Richard Nixon became president.

Leonard was born in 1929, in Eureka, Kansas, to a rural mail carrier and his wife, a devout churchgoer. His father was a World War I veteran who was lured to Kansas from Minnesota by an Army buddy who then cheated him out of an investment in a fledgling electric company. Growing up in Kansas, Leonard heard nostalgic tales of Minnesota's beautiful lakes and forests from his parents. He earned an economics degree from Kansas State University and was promptly drafted into the military to serve in the Korean War. He was assigned to a clerical unit that produced a daily newspaper for the troops.

Bitten by the journalism bug, Leonard decided after his discharge to enroll in a graduate program in the subject at the University of Minnesota. There he met his future wife, Betty Berg, who became the first peacetime female editor-in-chief of the *Minnesota Daily*, the campus newspaper, while Rod served as editorial page editor.

After graduation, both Rod and Betty landed reporting jobs with the *Minneapolis Tribune*, he on the police beat and she on the women's page. However, when Betty became pregnant with twins, Rod couldn't support his family on his cub reporter's salary. He then took a public relations job with 3M (the Minnesota Mining and Manufacturing Company).

Like other former reporters working for 3M, Leonard found time on his hands and wrote political ammunition for the Democratic-Farmer-Labor Party (DFL). He attracted the attention of DFL operatives and was hired as Freeman's press secretary after the governor won reelection in 1956. Leonard followed Freeman to the USDA in 1961.

Although Leonard lost his USDA job in 1969, he saw an opportunity in the 1968 national elections, which changed the food policy landscape. The Nixon administration had no use for the War on Poverty, but it saw political advantage in a War on Hunger. "Hunger is in; poverty is out," was the new guideline. HEW Secretary Robert Finch viewed hunger as a political and social problem that could be dealt with rapidly.[27]

In May 1969, Nixon asked Congress for $1 billion to reform the nation's feeding programs, promising to "end hunger for all time in America."[28] Money for antipoverty programs grew scarce, but money to fight hunger was available. Leonard became a nutrition consultant to the Children's Foundation, a public interest group launched by former Kennedy administration officials.

Leonard launched his own public interest group in 1969, the Community Nutrition Institute (CNI), and applied for an OEO grant to help improve the federal feeding programs he had run while at the USDA. It was something of a miracle that Leonard was able to win approval of the OEO grant application. Moderate Republicans such as Sen. Chuck Percy (Ill.) were able to persuade the Nixon White House to approve the grant.[29]

Leonard viewed the CNI as a vehicle to bring order to the chaos of federal feeding programs, which were funded by the USDA but administered by welfare and education officials at the local level. "Looking back at the '60s, we created a whole new genre—modern food policy," he recalled. "Everyone assumed there would be a mechanism to organize, manage, and expand the programs. We opened the funding faucet, but there was no structure to carry out the programs.

"We agreed to fund child nutrition programs that state education and welfare agencies would be running. The authority and funding came through the USDA, but the programs landed in the states in a different set of program areas. The state agencies weren't interested in nutrition. Food stamps came out of the USDA, but they went to welfare programs in the states. If the policy makers had wanted welfare, they would have done it there."[30]

Leonard reported conversations with state officials and consumer advocates wrestling with implementation of food stamps. "Operational elements of the program never got to either of these groups. We'd issue a rule in D.C., but two months later people in the field weren't aware of it. 'Why should we at the state and local level be concerned with what's going on in D.C.?' they would ask."

A key component of Leonard's OEO grant, in 1971, was a newsletter, *CNI Weekly Report*, which informed program officials in the field what was going on in the federal agencies. It also published reports on what was happening at state and local levels.

"I wanted *CNI Weekly Report* to channel information coming from D.C.," recalled Leonard. "I also wanted to let the D.C. folks be aware of problems at the state and local levels. I wanted to get information to advocacy groups so they'd know about programs operated by departments of education and welfare."

CNI Weekly Report, however, caught the attention of Howard Phillips, a right-wing OEO official who later became director of the agency. In 1971, he succeeded in inserting a condition in the CNI grant requiring agency approval of articles in CNI's "technical assistance bulletin." Leonard swallowed hard at the censorship provision but reluctantly agreed to the condition as a price for the grant.[31]

The OEO's censorship of *CNI Weekly Report* was conducted with a very light hand during the first year and a half of the grant. Newsletter copy was submitted in advance to the OEO's Office of Health Affairs, which occasionally suggested altering a controversial article to avoid trouble with the Nixon administration.

Following President Nixon's reelection in 1972, Howard Philips was appointed OEO director with instructions to dismantle the agency, which he said was based on a "Marxist notion."[32] He hadn't forgotten *CNI Weekly Report* and set about limiting its journalistic freedom to the point of destruction. Newsletter copy was now forwarded to the OEO public affairs office for review, and entire articles were ruled out of bounds.

Meanwhile, Leonard shrewdly set about building a circulation base of some 16,000 readers who received *CNI Weekly Report* for free. As the OEO began censoring entire articles, Leonard calculated that he could return the remainder of his OEO grant to the federal government in dramatic fashion and convert many of the newsletter's readers into paid subscribers.

On April 8, 1973, the CNI held a news conference at which Leonard announced that he was returning OEO grant funds rather than submit to further censorship. *The Washington Post* reporter Nick Kotz wrote a story illustrated with CNI articles crossed out for censorship.

The Nixon administration was furious over this public relations debacle, which foreshadowed the Watergate scandal later that year. Meanwhile, *CNI Weekly Report* quickly built a base of paid subscribers and went on to publish for three more decades. Renamed *Nutrition Week*, the newsletter was the glue that held together the antihunger community, including professionals who ran federal feeding programs at the local level.

The CNI can claim several major accomplishments beyond publication of *Nutrition Week*. In the 1997 edition of the *Encyclopedia of the Consumer Movement*, Leonard noted that he conceived and lobbied for WIC. The organization was also responsible for designing the training program for the Older Americans Nutrition program and writing the training manuals and training the first program managers in hundreds of communities in some 25 states during the 1970s. It sponsored the first graduate intern program for nutritionists to become managers of local school food programs.[33]

Leonard said the first nutrition labeling system implemented by the FDA was developed by the CNI in the 1970s, and the CNI created the format still used by the FDA to select and train individuals who participate as citizen advisers in the agency's activities.

Litigation initiated by the CNI on food safety rules and on citizen participation in rulemaking reached the U.S. Supreme Court and has become part of case law, Leonard noted. The group also helped launch World Food Day, a national educational effort to organize communities' activities.

The CNI suffered severe setbacks when Reagan was elected president in 1980, because key federal contracts weren't renewed and *Nutrition Week* lost subscribers who were forced to reduce their own budgets. Leonard attempted to launch a new magazine, *The Community Nutritionist*, but it failed to attract enough subscribers to make up for the other losses. The CNI's consumer division decamped to form a new organization, Public Voice for Food and Health Policy.

After Leonard returned to Minnesota, the CNI continued operating on a smaller scale until 2005. Meanwhile, he wrote a biography of former governor and U.S. agriculture secretary Orville Freeman that was published in 2015.

Food Research and Action Center

The son of Jewish immigrants who escaped Germany in 1937 before the Holocaust, Ron Pollack became a critical antihunger advocate in the 1960s and 1970s. Like many college students at the time, he got caught up in the civil rights movement. His parents had shown him a clear commitment to social justice, he said, but their experiences were molded by the pre-Holocaust period in Nazi Germany.[34]

Pollack was the student body president at Queens College in New York City in 1964. As a student leader, he recruited Queens College students for Freedom Summer, when students from the North visited Mississippi to encourage voter registration among African Americans. Among Pollack's recruits was Andrew Goodman, one of three civil rights workers slain by members of the Ku Klux Klan near Philadelphia, Mississippi. During a phone call from President Lyndon Johnson before their bodies were found, Sen. James O. Eastland (D-Miss.) dismissed the incident as a "publicity stunt" engineered by African Americans with the help of communists.[35]

After graduating from Queens College, Pollack enrolled in New York University Law School. Undaunted by the perils of Freedom Summer, Pollack risked his life by visiting Mississippi between semesters in the summers of 1965, 1966, and 1967. He worked on school integration and voting rights issues, but he was especially struck by the widespread hunger and malnutrition throughout the state, especially in Bolivar County in the Mississippi Delta.

After graduating from New York University Law School in 1968, Pollack planned to practice civil rights law in the Mississippi Delta. However, the NAACP Legal Defense and Education Fund had run out of funds to help launch his practice.

Pollack's second choice, joining the Center on Social Welfare Policy and Law in New York City, turned out to be providential. During law school, he had been awarded an Arthur Garfield Hays Civil Liberties Fellowship;

and, in that capacity, he worked on the legal brief for the first welfare case that was heard by the U.S. Supreme Court.

"Through that work, I became intimately familiar with the center—where the litigation was initially handled—and so I found it a good alternative as my first professional work after law school graduation," Pollack said. The center provided key legal backup for legal services programs across the United States, and it prepared hunger- and welfare-related class action lawsuits on behalf of the poor.

Pollack and his colleagues discovered that roughly 1,000 of the 3,000 counties in the United States had failed to implement the food stamp program. Texas had 109 delinquent counties, Missouri had 82, and California had 16.

The Social Welfare Policy and Law Center filed 26 lawsuits on the same day against the USDA and state agriculture departments for their neglect of food stamps. In California, 15 of the 16 hold-out counties immediately complied with a judge's court order. The lone remaining county called food stamps "a communist conspiracy" and denied benefits to students and long-haired "hippies."

In 1970, Pollack got a call from the OEO suggesting that he organize a conference on federal food programs for lawyers like himself. Turning down that offer, he instead asked for a $250,000 grant to launch a long-term anti-hunger organization, which became the Washington, D.C.-based Food Research and Action Center (FRAC).

As the FRAC's first executive director, Pollack scored a major victory by dramatically expanding WIC, which provides food to low-income pregnant women and young children. Sen. Hubert Humphrey (D-Minn.) had succeeded in passing legislation for a two-year pilot program costing $20 million in fiscal years 1973 and 1974. However, by June 1973, it was clear that the USDA had made no effort to implement the WIC pilot. It hadn't even proposed regulations.

The FRAC filed a lawsuit asking the USDA to implement the pilot program. When the agency declined to budge, Agriculture Secretary Earl Butz was held in contempt of court. As a remedy, the FRAC asked that the USDA spend the $40 million by the end of fiscal 1974.

Sen. Humphrey seized on the USDA's delays to win passage of a full-fledged WIC program funded at $250 million for fiscal 1975. "So the WIC pilot exploded into a huge program due to Earl Butz's intransigence," recalled Pollack. "WIC grew enormously by accident!"[36]

The FRAC ceased receiving government grants in 1973, when the new OEO director was directed to dismantle the War on Poverty and kill any programs smacking of advocacy. After losing federal funds, however, the organization immediately attracted support from private philanthropies and has survived to this day. Among its many achievements, the FRAC helped pass the landmark Food Stamp Act of 1977, which eliminated a requirement that recipients pay part of the cost for food stamps.

In 1980, Pollack resigned as FRAC's executive director and moved to its board of directors. He became dean of Antioch University Law School, which was dedicated to training public interest lawyers. He went on to found and lead FamiliesUSA, a nonprofit advocacy organization that offers resources on finding, choosing, and using health coverage.

Meanwhile, the FRAC in 1981 successfully defeated a Reagan administration proposal to reduce portion sizes in school lunches and allow ketchup and pickle relish to be counted toward meeting vegetable requirements.

In the 1980s, the group also released the first comprehensive nationwide study of childhood hunger ever conducted—the Community Childhood Hunger Identification Project—which estimated that one in eight children under 12 in this country was hungry. This study later became the basis of the current survey used by the USDA to measure hunger.[37]

Working with hundreds of national, state, and local nonprofit organizations, public agencies, corporations, and unions, the FRAC became the leading national nonprofit organization working to eradicate hunger and undernutrition in the United States. *Congress Daily* described it as "the premier anti-hunger group in Washington."[38]

Along with the CNI and CSPI, the FRAC changed the landscape of food advocacy in the 1970s and 1980s and went on to gain places at the table for food policy in later decades. They and other groups would become critical players for a national food policy.

CHAPTER EIGHT

Transforming the U.S. Agriculture Department

This chapter describes three remarkable individuals who transformed the U.S. Department of Agriculture in the areas of food safety, nutrition programs, and school meals.

Carol Tucker-Foreman

President Jimmy Carter's decision in 1977 to name Carol Tucker-Foreman as a USDA assistant secretary shook the century-old foundations of the department and the agribusiness establishment. In this capacity, she had responsibility for meat and poultry inspection, food assistance, and nutrition programs.

Almost 100 years earlier, Abraham Lincoln called the USDA "the people's department," because the vast majority of Americans were engaged in farming. By the time Carter took office, U.S. agriculture had undergone a transformation, and so had the USDA. Only 4 percent of Americans listed their occupation as farming. They produced more than enough food to feed the U.S. population and support substantial exports.

Congress had expanded the USDA's portfolio far beyond education and assistance for farmers. The department was charged with establishing safety standards for meat and poultry, helping low-income people purchase food through food stamps, and improving child nutrition and health through school lunches and special food packages designed to meet the needs of pregnant women, nursing mothers, and very young children. Food assistance programs grew to over half of the USDA's budget. The department also took on major responsibilities for conducting nutrition research and protecting the environment.

Carter directed that virtually all of the USDA programs designed to serve consumers be combined into a new subcabinet office, and he appointed Tucker-Foreman, executive director of the Consumer Federation of America, to the position. She became the first presidential appointee in the USDA's history devoted to consumers rather than producers. In addition, she was only the second female presidential appointee.

Tucker-Foreman had arrived at Washington, D.C., in 1960, with bright hopes of working on Capitol Hill. A newly minted graduate of Washington University in St. Louis, she was born into a prominent Democratic family in Arkansas. Her father was a state treasurer, and her brother became a member of the U.S. House of Representatives.[1] After graduate study at American University, she landed jobs with Sen. John McClellan (D-Ark.) and Rep. Wilbur Mills (D-Ark.) and worked as a lobbyist for various groups before being hired, in November 1973, as executive director of the Consumer Federation of America (CFA).

Tucker-Foreman's nomination for USDA assistant secretary ignited substantial opposition among members of Congress, old USDA hands, and meat trade associations fearing an end to their cozy relationship with the USDA's top meat inspectors. Former Agriculture Secretary Earl Butz, in speeches around the country, called her appointment "the greatest insult ever" to America's farmers.[2]

The National Cattlemen's Association began rounding up votes to prevent confirmation by the Senate Agriculture Committee. Ranking member Bob Dole (R-Kan.) said the committee needed to examine at length Tucker-Foreman's history and suggested her husband's employment with a trade union might be a conflict of interest with her duties at USDA.

However, Tucker-Foreman brought formidable skills and significant experience to the job. While at the CFA, she had noticed that high retail prices for beef weren't being passed along to farmers, and she reached out to small-scale cattle ranchers in South Dakota and Montana to join CFA in educating the public about the inequity.

The opposition against Tucker-Foreman on the Senate Agriculture Committee didn't last long, because members learned during the hearings that she could answer questions on farm policy issues. President Carter directed the White House lobbying staff to be sure she was confirmed, and consumer and women's organizations organized a letter-writing campaign in her favor.

Once confirmed in the White House Rose Garden, Tucker-Foreman formed a close relationship with Agriculture Secretary Bob Bergland, whom she described as the most straightforward and honorable man with whom she had worked. Neither Bergland nor the White House staff ever told her to stop making reforms, she said. She started making changes to meat and poultry inspection that foreshadowed the later emphasis on Hazard Analysis and Critical Control Point (HACCP) systems, which aim to prevent pathogens from contaminating raw meat. The new inspection program was called "quality control assurance."

"I was looking for more modern ways to do poultry inspection than just looking at birds flying by on the line," she explains. "However, the inspectors didn't want to change anything."[3]

By the late 1970s, scientists reported that nitrosamines, chemical compounds formed in bacon cured with sodium nitrite, caused cancer in laboratory animals and were likely human carcinogens. The meat industry insisted that it was irresponsible to take sodium nitrite out of bacon because it prevented formation of botulinum toxin.

The USDA promulgated a final regulation establishing a zero tolerance for nitrosamines. It's still in place, but once the regulation requiring use of sodium nitrite in bacon stopped forcing all bacon manufacturers to do it the same way, they developed a variety of new ways to make "uncured" but safe bacon. Those consumers who want bacon made the old way can buy it with no nitrosamines. Those who want it "uncured" get it with a high level of safety from botulism.

Later, in an FDA-commissioned study, Harvard scientists concluded that nitrites in food are carcinogenic on their own. But the House Agriculture Committee demanded a second opinion, which found the Harvard study to be flawed.

One issue the Carter administration didn't have on its agenda was put there by the Supreme Court. In the 1977 *Jones v. Rath Packing* decision, the court ruled that the USDA's rules on net weight labeling were too vague to be of value to consumers.

"State governments were upset. They wanted more precise regulations on just how much water companies could add to their meat and poultry during processing," Tucker-Foreman said. "Most of the water leaked out into the package, but consumers were charged for it as though it were chicken meat. I sure thought and still think that companies shouldn't charge consumers for dirty water drained from chickens.

"However, I had my head handed to me," she continues. "We didn't have the data to show how much the loss to consumers amounted to nor whether most shoppers understood they were being charged for the excreted water. The GMA [Grocery Manufacturers of America] launched a major campaign against the rule. The states that had petitioned the USDA to make the change not only withdrew their support, but some joined with the GMA on the other side. There was a lot of money at stake, and it was clear they were going to fight to the end to prevent any change. Absent compelling data to back up the new rule, we gave it up."[4]

The conservative columnist James J. Kilpatrick took up the industry's cause, writing a column defending the current net weight rules and dubbing Tucker-Foreman "the dragon lady." He also used the insult in speeches, including a talk delivered to a poultry convention in Arkansas.[5]

"When Kilpatrick called me 'the dragon lady,' all eyes shifted from him to my brother, [Rep. Jim Guy Tucker, unrecognized by Kilpatrick], who was also sitting at the head table," noted Tucker-Foreman.[6]

Dietary Goals and Guidelines

The 1977 Farm Bill broke ground with regard to nutrition research. Sen. Hubert Humphrey (D-Minn.), then terminally ill with cancer, successfully inserted language designating the USDA as the lead federal agency for nutrition research. After the Senate Select Committee on Nutrition and Human Needs, chaired by Sen. George McGovern (D-S.D.), put out its controversial Dietary Goals in 1977, Tucker-Foreman led efforts to publish the first set of U.S. Dietary Guidelines in 1980.

The Dietary Goals, which sought to combat chronic diseases such as atherosclerosis, stroke, and certain cancers, raised a firestorm of opposition from the food industry, because the goals recommended eating less high-fat meat, eggs, and dairy products. The "eat less" recommendations triggered strong negative reactions from the beef, dairy, egg, and sugar industries, including cattle ranchers from McGovern's home state of South Dakota.

The AMA also took offense, arguing that individuals should seek dietary advice from their physicians. Some scientists called for further expert review, while others said recommendations should be issued by the National Research Council's Food and Nutrition Board (FNB).

Philip Handler, president of the National Academy of Sciences, reportedly remarked that the FNB "would never support such kind of nonsense."[7]

Responding to pressure, the McGovern Committee held further hearings and issued a revised set of guidelines in late 1977 that adjusted some of the advice regarding salt and cholesterol and watered down the wording regarding meat consumption.

Tucker-Foreman said she was the only federal official who wanted to publish U.S. Dietary Guidelines that responded to the Senate committee's Dietary Goals. She ran into resistance from the NIH, the FDA, HEW Secretary Joe Califano, and numerous USDA officials, not to mention the food industry.

"Industry wanted the USDA to say, 'Eat anything you want.' But the USDA spends billions on nutrition. It's up to us to say something," Tucker-Foreman recalled. "I had to spend millions of dollars to feed people through food stamps and WIC. I had to feed my own kids, too. Was I doing the right thing? We should be able to say, 'This is what we know. This is what we're not sure of.' "[8]

Tucker-Foreman was determined that the USDA draft its own Dietary Guidelines. She gained support from Frank Press, President Carter's science advisor and future president of the National Academy of Sciences. She also sought help from officials at the Health and Human Services Department (formerly HEW), arguing, "We all know enough to do that. We'd like to have HHS join us. It's easy for HHS to say something about health, diet, and nutrition."

Tucker-Foreman enlisted Mark Hegsted, then a prominent nutritionist at the Harvard School of Public Health, to draft the Dietary Guidelines. He was assigned to come up with a book of menus as well as general recommendations.

"The Dietary Guidelines became a big issue," Tucker-Foreman recalled. "The cattlemen hated it." Under pressure from cattle ranchers in Missouri, Sen. Thomas Eagleton (D-Mo.) insisted on a Dietary Guidelines Advisory Committee to oversee the USDA's efforts. Critics joked that the panel should be named GAG, for Guidelines Advisory Group, because it would limit what could be said.[9]

"I argued that the government needed some standard to use in deciding how to spend the money to support food assistance programs, particularly child nutrition programs, and it didn't hurt to give Americans some simple advice on eating healthy," she said.

The Reagan administration withdrew the 1980 Dietary Guidelines and destroyed menus published as helpful tips for consumers. Later the administration reversed course after the FNB published a diet and cancer report in 1982 that supported much of the philosophy behind the guidelines. The USDA and HHS published a 1985 version of the Dietary Guidelines on schedule.

When President Carter was defeated for reelection in 1980, Tucker-Foreman left the USDA. She worked as a lobbyist, started a public affairs firm, and worked for Walter Mondale's presidential campaign. In 1986 she organized the Safe Food Coalition, which included the Consumer Federation of America (CFA), the CSPI, Public Citizen, the Government Accountability Project (GAP), and numerous other consumer advocacy groups. Presenting a solid front to Congress, the coalition influenced the actions of three administrations, especially Bill Clinton's and George W. Bush's.

The coalition played a major role in getting the USDA to reshape the HACCP for meat and poultry inspection. The USDA's original concept of the HACCP had little to do with food safety, Tucker-Foreman said. The Safe Food Coalition told the USDA and Clinton that it wanted the HACCP plan to assure that food coming off the end of the line, especially raw meat and poultry, was cleaner, safer, and less likely to cause foodborne illness than food produced under the old system.

In 2000, the coalition persuaded Agriculture Secretary Dan Glickman to set a zero tolerance for pathogenic *E. coli* O157:H7 and *Salmonella* in ground beef purchased for school lunch programs. He announced that ground beef purchased for the coming year's school lunches would have to be tested and show no sign of O157:H7 or *Salmonella*.

However, the National Meat Association was outraged, as were the fairly small number of companies that supply most ground beef to school lunch programs. The price for ground beef went up in the first few months of the new system because the USDA acted so late that the companies couldn't make the adjustment without raising prices.

After George W. Bush was elected president, the NMA campaigned to drop the requirement, and it was removed from the USDA's Agricultural Marketing Service website on March 31, 2001. Tucker-Foreman quickly notified Sen. Dick Durbin (D-Ill.), *The New York Times*, and *The Washington Post* of the change.

Tucker-Foreman and Durbin held a Capitol Hill press conference on the morning of April 1, 2001. By the time she got to her office, she received a phone call from Agriculture Secretary Ann Veneman saying it was all a mistake. Veneman said USDA never intended to ditch the testing and micro standard, had taken down the notice, and would be publishing a statement. The news article made the front page of both the *Post* and *Times*.[10]

Tucker-Foreman founded and led the Consumer Federation of America's Food Policy Institute from 1999 to 2010 and then became a distinguished fellow at the institute.

Robert Greenstein

Robert Greenstein made major changes in the USDA's administration of federal feeding programs and continued his advocacy on behalf of poor people.

In 1972, he was teaching high school half-time in Newton, Mass., so that he would be able to spend the rest of his time writing a book commissioned by a Ralph Nader task force. Then the publisher cancelled the book project, and Greenstein was left with a half-time job.

The son of a lawyer in Philadelphia, Greenstein had graduated in 1967 from Harvard College, where he majored in modern European history. He spent the next year at the London School of Economics and then enrolled in an American history program at the University of California at Berkeley. After one year at UC Berkeley, Greenstein came back East and began teaching high school in Newton. On the advice of an old friend, he enlisted as one of Nader's Raiders in the summer of 1969. His mentor on the Raiders was food safety investigator Harrison Welford, who suggested that Greenstein work full-time for a public interest group in Washington, D.C.

When Greenstein's book project was cancelled, Welford provided him with job leads in Washington, including an interview with Rod Leonard at the Community Nutrition Institute. The two hit it off, and Greenstein began working for *CNI Weekly Report* as a specialist in food additives. Later he was assigned to report on a summer feeding program in New York City.

"During my first year at the CNI, I realized I was more interested in food programs than anything else. Rod was gracious in letting me do other things besides write for the newsletter," he recalled, noting that he provided analysis to the Senate Select Committee on Nutrition and Human Needs chaired by Senator McGovern.[11]

Greenstein's expertise also attracted the attention of John Kramer, a Georgetown University law professor and antihunger advocate, and Arnold Mayer, an antihunger lobbyist for the meat cutters union. Both men enlisted Greenstein as an unpaid research assistant.

Church groups and labor unions soon sought out Greenstein to provide them with talking points on Capitol Hill and elsewhere. When the Ford administration, in 1974, proposed regulations to cut the food stamp program, Greenstein issued a 10-page analysis of the cuts, and the proposed cuts were blocked.

After Greenstein was invited to testify on food stamps before a House Agriculture Committee hearing, he began working with several members, including future House Speaker Tom Foley (D-Wash.). He helped Foley beat back an effort by House Agriculture Chairman Bob Poage (D-Texas) to cut food stamps. "The hodgepodge bill never came to the floor," Greenstein recalled.[12]

Greenstein soon became an unpaid consultant to Rep. Bob Bergland (D-Minn.) and other House Democrats interested in nutrition issues. "You can be the staff for the group," Bergland told him.[13]

When Jimmy Carter was elected president, Bergland became agriculture secretary and quickly hired Greenstein as his special assistant for food programs. Greenstein was handed a draft Farm Bill with a radical new food stamp title written by Georgetown University's John Kramer that eliminated the longtime requirement that food stamp recipients pay part of the cost of food stamps.

Greenstein's boss was Assistant Secretary Carol Tucker-Foreman, who had responsibility for USDA's food assistance programs. She says before Carter was elected, there was substantial agreement among consumer advocates on the key elements of the food stamp bill, including elimination of the purchase requirement.

"The purchase requirement not only denied food stamps to some people who needed but couldn't afford them, but it also encouraged some of the fraud and abuse that existed in the program," said Tucker-Foreman. "The USDA had to find companies that would sell food stamps in parts of town that weren't served well by banks. A fair amount of that money never got back to the U.S. Treasury Department. It gave opponents a great club to beat the program with."[14]

Tucker-Foreman said Carter favored removing the purchase requirement, but he was under pressure from HEW Secretary Joe Califano to abolish food stamps entirely and fold them into a welfare reform package under development by his department. She joined Greenstein and Bergland for a critical meeting at the White House with President Carter, HEW Secretary Califano, and Domestic Policy Adviser Stuart Eisenstadt. The USDA officials won their argument to keep food stamps and eliminate the purchase requirement.

Tucker-Foreman and Greenstein then walked the halls of Congress for weeks, "and his massive knowledge of food stamps disarmed congressional opponents," she said. "The food stamp legislation was an early and important victory for Carter and for the nation's poor."[15]

Greenstein views the 1977 food stamp bill as his signal legislative achievement in the nutrition arena because it eliminated the purchase requirement and simplified eligibility standards for applicants. As a result, more than five million people, many deeply poor, gained access to food stamps for the first time.

Greenstein and Tucker-Foreman also secured the future of WIC, which would likely have been abolished by the Reagan administration in the 1980s. In a study analyzing WIC's economic benefits, he showed that the extra food provided by the program reduced the incidence of low-birth-weight infants, which result in extremely high hospital costs.

Despite his relative youth, Greenstein was appointed administrator of the USDA's Food and Nutrition Service (FNS), which oversees nutrition programs with budgets in the billions. During his two years there, he expanded a small policy-evaluation shop into a major division with three dozen professional employees.

Greenstein's job as FNS administrator ended when President Carter lost the election in 1980. Greenstein was able to use his expertise to create a new organization, the Center on Budget and Policy Priorities (CBPP), which was launched with a grant from the Field Foundation. "The FNS policy-evaluation shop was the predecessor to my organization. We used in-depth analysis to promote or critique proposals," he said.[16]

The late Richard W. Boone, executive director of the Field Foundation at the time, recalled in an interview that the media uncritically reported President Reagan's assurances that poor people were doing fine under his new administration. "The media didn't have its own research to counter what was coming out of the White House," he said.[17]

Boone asked his board of directors to set aside $200,000 for a campaign to counter the Reagan administration's assertions. "The purpose became reporting on what was really happening to poor people, especially with relation to food," he said, but it was unclear who might run the campaign.

Offered the job, Greenstein was initially reluctant to head up the Field Foundation initiative, favoring a job offered by another organization. "I'm offering you an opportunity to run a program, not just be part of one," Boone insisted.

"We stuck with Greenstein, and he decided to take the job, and the rest is history," Boone added. "He's one of the smartest people I've ever met. He's done a fabulous job trying to keep reporting on hunger and other programs honest and current. Most researchers aren't current, but Greenstein keeps current. He's been able to do that and has not been viewed as partisan, as other think tanks are."

Noting that Greenstein has a "great staff" of more than 100 people, Boone commented, "These are hard times for us [antipoverty advocates], but he's one of the few able to command attention in these ongoing battles."

The CBPP came into being in 1981, just in time to resist efforts by President Reagan and Senate Agriculture Chairman Jesse Helms (R-N.C.) to cut food program budgets. During its first couple of years, the center worked closely with Senator Dole to modify Reagan's proposed budget cuts.

After reading White House budget director David Stockman's "black book" on proposed cuts, Greenstein complained to Dole's staff. "Dole called Stockman, and the food stamp cuts were cut in half," Greenstein recalled.[18]

In 1982, when President Reagan proposed even deeper cuts in food stamps and Helms sought cuts still-deeper than Reagan's, Dole called Greenstein for help. Greenstein said there should be no further cuts, but Dole faced stiff opposition from Reagan and Helms. Dole said he'd lead the opposition to Reagan and Helms, but to do so he must have a package of his own of much smaller cuts.

Dole asked Greenstein to design such a plan for him, saying that either Greenstein could design it or Dole could ask someone else to do it, but Greenstein's version would cause the least damage to low-income people. Greenstein reluctantly agreed, and Dole's plan prevailed in the Senate.

Greenstein acknowledged that some antihunger advocates might find disturbing his willingness to aid Dole in these circumstances. "What's more important—to be 'pure' or to chart a course in real practical terms to do the least damage?" he asked. Things could have turned out much worse.[19]

"Bob Greenstein and I were good friends even though we were with different parties," recalled Dole, who has served "of counsel" to a Washington law firm. "He helped me a lot with food stamp legislation and the school lunch program, too. He would help on anything I needed. He was a strong advocate for helping low-income people. Greenstein did help get the compromise legislation that had some food stamp cuts but wasn't a disaster. He avoided the worst of the cuts proposed by the Reagan administration."[20]

Over the past three decades, Greenstein's CBBP has become one of the most influential think tanks in Washington. The center seeks to affect public debates over proposed budget and tax policies and ensure that policymakers consider the needs of low-income families and individuals. It also develops policy options to alleviate poverty.

In addition, the CBPP examines the impacts of proposed policies on the health of the economy and the soundness of federal and state budgets. The center explores whether federal and state governments are fiscally sound and have sufficient revenue to address critical priorities, both for low-income populations and for the nation at large.

Among other issues, the CBPP has focused on food stamps, WIC, and child nutrition programs.

In 1996, Greenstein was granted a MacArthur Fellowship (commonly known as a "genius award") for making the CBBP "a model for non-partisan research and policy organizations." He has since received numerous other awards for his work on behalf of America's low-income citizens.

Ellen Haas

Ellen Haas will be remembered for seeking to overhaul the USDA's National School Lunch Program so that school meals could meet the U.S. Dietary Guidelines for the first time in 50 years.

She began her career as a consumer advocate as a homemaker who launched the Maryland Citizens Consumer Council in her basement. She focused on food and nutrition issues, including a boycott in 1973 to protest record high beef prices. Haas became acquainted with Rod Leonard, CNI executive director, through local politics, and in 1976 she agreed to work part-time for him. Asked to form a consumer advocacy division within the CNI, she reached out to the food industry but was given the cold shoulder by George Koch, president of the Grocery Manufacturers of America.

Haas had more luck with the Food Marketing Institute (FMI), which represents the nation's supermarket chains. Working with Tim Hammonds and Karen Brown at the FMI, she conceived the idea of an annual food policy conference bringing together representatives of government, industry, and consumer advocacy groups. Launched by the CNI in 1977, the annual food policy conference continued for nearly four decades and is now organized by the Consumer Federation of America's Food Policy Institute. The early conferences focused on legislative goals, such as a landmark nutrition labeling bill in 1990, which enables consumers to know the key nutrients in their food.

Throughout her career, Haas built long-lasting relationships with all sectors of the food system, including growers, manufacturers, and retailers. But that involved a continuous uphill battle. She remembers Earl Butz, agriculture secretary in the Nixon and Ford administrations, treating consumer advocates as *persona non grata*. "We took to protesting and picketing Butz," she recalled. "He cared more about cows and pigs than people.

"There was no framework for including consumers in policy deliberations, even during the Carter administration," she said. "There were no sustainable processes. Attempts at including consumers were very shallow. Now consumers have lots of access."[21]

Haas said that at the CNI, she was the first consumer advocate to break into the agricultural establishment. "I was given a platform," she said. "My accomplishment was to break down barriers. We petitioned the USDA on beef grades, and Assistant Secretary Dick Lyng granted our petition. How do you give information about meat that will change behavior? Low-fat USDA 'good' beef became USDA 'select,'" making it more attractive to consumers.

"Grudgingly, agriculture and the food industry had to accept us into the policy process. We had no voice in 1970 and slowly but surely gained a voice," said Haas. "How far we have come!"

Haas left the CNI in 1982 to found the Public Voice for Food and Health Policy, an advocacy group focused on improving seafood safety, nutrition labeling, and beef grading, among other issues. The Public Voice was later incorporated into the Consumer Federation of America as its Food Policy Institute.

In 1993, President Clinton appointed Haas as USDA undersecretary for food, nutrition, and consumer services. She sought to overhaul the National School Lunch Program, so that school meals could meet the U.S. Dietary Guidelines for the first time.

In the early years, the focus of most school nutrition campaigns was to encourage children to gain weight, reported Susan Levine in her book, *School Lunch Politics: The Surprising History of America's Favorite Welfare Program*. "In one program, children who gained properly were placed at one end of the class[room] and those who did not gain at the other," she wrote.[22]

At the USDA, female home economists took a back seat to agricultural economists in developing policy and forming relationships with legislators, Levine said. "In the end, nutrition science provided a convenient and appealing justification for a school lunch program designed primarily as an outlet for surplus food. . . . In the arena of congressional politics, nutrition reformers were forced to compromise on the content of school lunches and to entirely give up any sustained support for nutrition education in the schools."

In 1969, Agriculture Secretary Orville Freeman announced a new set of regulations that would allow school districts to contract with private companies to run, operate, and manage their lunchrooms. Three years later, the USDA opened the door to soft drink vending machines in schools, Levine reported.

By the early 1970s, school food service increasingly adopted the fast-food model in school cafeterias. Both the USDA and the School Food Service Association encouraged a business model that would attract paying children into the lunchroom with tacos, pizza, and French fries.

In 1980, the USDA made final a proposed rule restricting the sale of "foods of limited nutritional value" in schools if they competed with the federally supported feeding programs. The so-called junk food rule was based on language in the 1978 School Lunch Act. The rule prohibited the sale of a few items on school premises until the end of the last lunch period each day. Banned as "junk food" were sugary sodas and other drinks, hard candy, and chewing gum. Diet sodas weren't banned. Federal courts upheld the substantive portion of the law but ruled it was an unreasonable extension of the statute for the school administration to control school cafeterias or vending machines.

The Healthy Meals for Healthy Americans Act of 1994, which required federally subsidized school meals to conform to the U.S. Dietary Guidelines, was later overturned by the Healthy Meals for Healthy Children Act of 1996, in which Congress gave school districts wide leeway in conforming to the guidelines.

"When Congress passed and the President signed the 1994 amendments, we all believed that schools would be allowed to use a food-based system to meet the dietary guidelines for the school meals program," explained Rep. Pat Roberts (R-Kan.) during debate on the 1996 bill. "Unfortunately, the regulations implementing the 1994 amendments did not provide this flexibility to schools.

"Local school employees involved in the planning and preparation of school meals work very hard to make sure that the meals are nutritious and good tasting," Roberts continued. "A meal not eaten provides no benefit to anyone. Their challenge is to balance good nutrition with what children will eat."[23]

Haas's goal of strict nutrition standards for school lunches wasn't realized until Congress passed the Healthy, Hunger-Free Kids Act of 2010, which gave the USDA the authority to set new standards for food sold during the school day, including food and beverages from vending machines.

When Haas took over leadership of the USDA's child nutrition programs in 1993, she organized the Team Nutrition campaign, which engaged 200 food and health companies and organizations to educate children about healthy food choices. Team Nutrition involved schools, parents, and the community in efforts to continuously improve school meals and to promote the health and education of 50 million school children in more than 96,000 schools nationwide. Schools were invited to enroll as "Team Nutrition Schools," affirming their commitment to take the lead in making nutritional changes, conducting nutrition education activities and events, and using innovative materials from the USDA's Food and Nutrition Service (FNS). State agencies were encouraged to recruit Team Nutrition Schools as well as develop training support systems necessary for local implementation.

However, Team Nutrition was not without controversy. In 1996, Haas was twice summoned before the House Agriculture Committee to justify her policy management. Chairman Pat Roberts demanded her resignation. Haas was accused of giving lucrative government contracts to friends, traveling in luxurious style as a government official, and engaging in careless management practices. Republican critics charged that Haas promoted Team Nutrition with high-priced public relations consultants and famous chefs and conducted focus groups on food stamps by a Democratic polling firm.

"From the beginning, Team Nutrition has been agenda-driven," said Chairman Roberts, "and that agenda has been personal, self-aggrandizing, political, and not in keeping with accepted government procurement and ethical conduct."[24]

Haas said Roberts and his Republican allies were simply "grandstanding" for political gain as Roberts ran for the Senate. No formal action was taken against her alleged mishandling of Team Nutrition. She noted that Team Nutrition had continued much longer and laid a foundation for the Healthy, Hunger-Free Kids Act of 2010, which increased consumption of vegetables and made changes to school vending machines.[25]

"Ellen Haas was certainly a visionary on what should be the path forward for nutritionally superior lunches served in schools," commented Ed Cooney, executive director of the Congressional Hunger Center. "She sometimes faced challenges from critics who reacted to her 'tone.'"[26]

After leaving the USDA in 1997, Haas formed and eventually sold a healthy lifestyle company, FoodFit.com. She then became a strategic consultant and "of counsel" to the Podesta Group, a Washington-based public relations and lobbying firm.

CHAPTER NINE

Churches, Newspapers, and Universities Get Involved

Churches, newspapers, and universities joined other institutions in making major changes in the food policy landscape.

Bread for the World

Arthur Simon and his famous older brother, the late senator Paul Simon (D-Ill.), were sons of a Lutheran minister in Eugene, Oregon. Arthur, the shy son, was overshadowed by his ambitious brother. However, he eventually found his way to a Lutheran parish ministry in New York's Lower East Side. His encounter with hunger there led him to coauthor a book in 1973 with his brother, *The Politics of World Hunger*.[1] The book acknowledged the importance of private enterprise, voluntary assistance, and government policy. But the coauthors were struck by the neglect of government policy in addressing the hunger issue.

In his own memoir, *The Rising of Bread for the World: An Outcry of Citizens against Hunger*, Art Simon recalled asking, "What could the churches do that they are not doing? Like many congregations, ours gave direct assistance locally and participated in supporting relief and development abroad.

"But it struck me that Christians were not being challenged to weigh in as citizens to help shape decisions by the government that have a huge bearing on hungry people. The nation was paying scant attention to hunger, and many of its policies were woefully inadequate. By doing little or nothing about this, Christians were silently approving those policies and reinforcing hunger."[2]

Taking his cue from the civil rights movement, Simon decided to start a citizens' movement to combat hunger in the public policy arena. He pulled together a citizens' committee of seven Protestants and seven Catholics. Bread for the World, as they eventually called themselves, began as a pilot project in New York City before moving to Washington, D.C.

From time to time, Bread has debated whether to describe itself as an interfaith organization rather than a Christian organization. While it remains open to non-Christian members and participating congregations, it retains its Christian identity as a strong selling point to church members.

In 1973, Bread promoted its first campaign urging its several hundred members and local churches to send letters to members of Congress. The letters supported U.S. funding for the "soft loan" window of the World Bank, which lends money at almost no interest to the poorest countries. When the House soundly defeated the bill, Bread testified before the Senate Foreign Relations Committee in March 1974.[3]

Bread began growing at a healthy pace. It had nearly 6,000 paid members by the end of 1974 and close to 10,000 by May 1975. The Simon brothers revised their earlier book on world hunger, and it won a National Religious Book Award the following year. As Bread's membership grew, it set a goal to recruit and train 500 leaders to spearhead its work in congressional districts across the nation.

In 1975, Bread published a manifesto titled "The Right to Food," with nine objectives, which included "an end to hunger in the United States" and "control of multinational corporations, with particular attention to agribusiness."[4]

Congress paid no attention when the nonbinding Right to Food resolution was introduced in the fall of 1975. Then, letters Bread had encouraged began arriving in congressional offices—"first a trickle, then a flow, and soon a small avalanche," Simon recalled.[5]

"How did Bread for the World, with a membership of about 12,000 when the resolution was introduced, manage to drum up 10 or 15 times that many letters to Congress within a year?" he asked. "The answer lies in our connection to the churches and our instrument of an annual 'Offering of Letters.' The Offering of Letters is a way of inviting parishioners to 'contribute' by writing to their member of Congress about a specific hunger issue, and then offering the letters in church, usually during worship. In this way, we visibly offer to God the power we have to help shape government policies that can enable hungry people to feed themselves."

Bread in 2016 had some 74,000 members, including 3,000 participating congregations.

When Bread's letters reach members of Congress each year, those views are taken seriously. One of Bread's many fans in Congress was Sen. Olympia Snowe (R-Me.), who said Bread for the World "is a strong and respected voice on Capitol Hill for those who suffer from hunger at home and around the world."[6]

In 1991, the Rev. David Beckmann, a Lutheran minister and former World Bank economist, succeeded Art Simon as president of Bread for the World. In 2010, Beckmann and the president of Heifer International shared the World Food Prize, which is considered the Nobel Prize for agriculture. They were lauded for their "landmark achievements in building two of the world's foremost grassroots organizations leading the charge to end hunger and poverty for millions of people around the world."[7]

Rep. Frank Wolf (R-Va.), who retired from the House at the end of his term in 2014, was a strong Bread supporter throughout his career. He successfully pushed for creation of a National Commission on Hunger, which was included in the 2014 omnibus appropriations bill. The commission was instructed to encourage public-private partnerships and greater involvement by community and faith-based groups to reduce the need for government nutrition programs.

The commission, which was endorsed by Bread and other antihunger groups, consists of 10 individuals: five Republicans and five Democrats. In December 2015, it issued an influential report, "Freedom from Hunger: An Achievable Goal for the United States of America."[8]

The Rise and Fall of Interfaith Action

In April 1975, the Rev. George A. Chauncey, a seasoned civil rights advocate who became director of the Washington office of the Presbyterian Church, assembled colleagues from other denominational offices to form the Interreligious Task Force on U.S. Food Policy.

It was relatively easy for Chauncey to call such a meeting, as many of the denominational offices were located in the United Methodist Building, which was built in 1923 to further the temperance movement. Situated across the street from the U.S. Supreme Court, the Methodist Building is one of the few nongovernmental buildings on Capitol Hill.

The task force would change its name and membership roster over the years, but in 1983, the newly renamed Interfaith Action for Economic Justice comprised 26 members, including mainline Protestant denominations and a variety of religious groups: the American Jewish Committee, Bread for the World, the Center of Concern, the Friends Committee on National Legislation, Jesuit Social Ministries, Maryknoll Fathers and Brothers, the Network (Catholic religious women), and the World Hunger Information Service. The Presbyterian Church provided the lion's share of funding, but the other member organizations chipped in.[9]

"They thought of themselves as a new model of religious cooperation, neither a governing board nor an advocacy group but a working team, which depended not on other staff but on each other to do the work of the task force," Martin McLaughlin, a longtime contributor to the task force, told Steven Tipton, author of *Public Pulpits: Methodists and Mainline Churches in the Moral Argument of Public Life.*[10]

As described by Tipton in a chapter devoted to a history of Interfaith Action, the task force wasn't simply a coalition of denominations and related religious groups. Nor would it become a membership organization such as Bread for the World, although Bread was a member of the coalition.

Conceived as "a community of religious communities," the task force depended on its denominational members for funding and their paid staff members for its own workforce of volunteers. With the approval of their denominational office directors, the volunteers pledged to work together and in their own organizations for a responsible U.S. food policy by monitoring, reporting, and writing on assigned areas of the task force agenda. Each volunteer also promised, "when or if he or she deems wise, [to] call upon his or her constituency to support the policies advocated by the Taskforce" and help secure funding, according to Tipton.[11]

The task force grew quickly, because hunger was a hot issue in the mid-1970s and the churches were looking for a front-burner issue to replace civil rights, which had largely become law. Also, money was available to fund the hunger issue, because the churches didn't have competing agencies and offices on the ground to respond to economic injustice. The churches were focused on charitable giving rather than political advocacy.

"The task force appealed to denominational leaders in order to do the homework and provide the expertise needed to work out policy positions, testify before Congress and help educate church members about the forces creating hunger," Tipton reported. "However, it was an unprecedented step to form an interdenominational organization to engage in direct advocacy on such specific issues and authorize it to speak in its own name rather than the names of member denominations."[12]

From the beginning, the task force experiment in direct advocacy was a "convulsive experience for the interfaith community," according to Martin McLaughlin. Task force founders were concerned about its effects on the denominations and on the collegial relationships among church bureaucrats in Washington.[13]

As food stamp and child nutrition programs came under budget pressure from the Reagan administration in the early 1980s, the task force looked to Robert Greenstein's Center on Budget and Policy Priorities for outside expertise. In the Reagan years, however, the task force's "Food Policy

Agenda for 1980" and beyond became a "litany of non-achievement," according to a task force member quoted by Tipton.[14]

Nevertheless, by 1985, Interfaith Action could look back on a decade of growth with satisfaction. The number of organizations in the coalition, originally 20, had nearly doubled, and its budget had multiplied six-fold to $320,000. The coalition had hired more than a dozen low-paid staff members, and its executive director's role had expanded from office manager to institutional leader.

The new executive director, the Rev. Arthur Keys Jr., a United Church of Christ minister with a background in community organizing, questioned Interfaith Action's relationship with IMPACT, a long-standing organization that produced background papers on major political issues, published a newsletter, and issued alerts urging its members to take action on issues before Congress. However, IMPACT was unauthorized to speak to Congress or the public in its own name or devise legislative strategies.

Keys advocated a merger of the two organizations, "not primarily to build a stronger organization that served the national religious organizations [but rather to] preach God's News to the Poor" and work to improve the common good. Through the merger, Keys said, Interfaith Action could "broaden its funding base with individual congregational members and donors." Meanwhile, IMPACT could extend its reach into lobbying on Capitol Hill and gain stronger financial support from national religious agencies, especially the national mission boards of the mainline Protestant denominations.[15]

After the two organizations merged in 1990 under the name Interfaith Impact for Justice and Peace, it was the primary advocacy organization for 36 religious denominations in the United States, including all the mainline Protestant churches. The merged organization could claim local and regional affiliates in 23 states and some 10,000 individual and congregation members on its rolls.

However, five years later, Interfaith Impact existed in name only. Its offices were closed and its staff dispersed. Its board of directors and their denominations were raising funds to pay off more than $100,000 in debts. Keys blamed the group's failure on unresolved institutional strains evident in the merger. "We had two different models of advocacy we tried to put together," he told Tipton. "If Interfaith Action had been able to 'buy out' IMPACT, we might have been able to make it work. Different institutional actors saw the world differently through different lenses."[16]

Tipton agrees there was conflict between two models of political advocacy: focused policy research and action by established offices of the mainline denominations; and mass mobilization and political organization forged by moral inspiration.

A veteran staff member, Elmira Nazombe, in 1993 reflected on the downfall of Interfaith Impact: "We have lost so much staff and resources that we can't stay in touch with the issues by working on them ourselves in any detail or depth over time," she told Tipton. "The result is we have lost touch with people on the Hill and around town who are working on them. That's the only way you earn respect and trust in this town. That's the only way you earn influence if you don't have money to buy it. Otherwise, you don't know who is doing what on an issue. . . . We are out of touch. We don't know who to call; we're reduced to looking up phone numbers in the *Congressional Directory*. When we do call, they don't know us. They don't owe us or have any real reason to do us a favor."[17]

Interfaith Action staff and associates landed on their feet in Washington, D.C., after the organization collapsed. Past executive director Arthur Keys founded International Relief and Development, a nonprofit organization responsible for implementing development assistance programs worldwide.

Jaydee Hanson, an advocate employed by the United Methodist Church, joined the Center for Food Safety as a policy analyst of genetic engineering. Among Interfaith Action staff, Ferd Hoefner became policy director at the National Sustainable Agriculture Coalition, and Lorette Picciano became executive director of the Rural Coalition.

Transformation of Food Journalism

Marian Burros, a doctor's daughter from Connecticut educated at Wellesley, became a serious food journalist by degrees. After she and her husband moved to Washington, D.C., she began teaching cooking classes in her kitchen. She then started writing columns for various weekly newspapers.

Burros's columns caught the attention of the food editor of *The Washington Daily News*, who asked her to work for the newspaper on a part-time basis. Yet Burros said she didn't do anything daring until she moved to *The Washington Evening Star*, a now-defunct afternoon paper that competed with *The Washington Post*.

"At a food editors' conference, I heard what was going on in the food world," Burros recalled. "Consumers were being cheated. I always hated the idea of being had." Newspaper food sections at the time were known for printing recipes, publishing news releases verbatim, and avoiding controversial issues.

"Nobody ever stopped me at the *Star*," said Burros. "I got braver and braver. I was aware of what was happening at [the CSPI] and other public interest groups. They reported on misinformation, deceptive advertising, and ingredients that shouldn't be in food. Little by little, I wrote about political stuff. I wrote about the 'politics of food' at a time when nobody knew the term. 'What's that?' they would ask."[18]

In addition to writing for the *Star*, Burros worked as a consumer reporter for WRC-TV, owned and operated by NBC. In 1974, because of the work she had been doing, she was hired by *The Washington Post*.

"I used to be able to speak to anyone I went to because they weren't very guarded," she recalled. "I had lots of sources, like an investigative reporter. I had meetings with some of my sources in strange places, like Deep Throat in the parking garage. They had muzzled one of my sources, and she wouldn't talk to me on the phone.

"I met people in Lafayette Park, across from the White House, and in out-of-the-way coffee shops. I talked to lots of people at home instead of at work.

"*The Washington Post* was very careful about facts. I had the backing of editors except for a story on rBST [recombinant bovine somatotropin, which boosts milk production]. I couldn't write about it. My editors quashed the story. Someone else broke the story about what rBST did to cows [causing mastitis and early milk shutdown] and might do to you.

"There have been pressures from time to time, such as stories about use of artificial colors in farmed salmon and passing them off as wild salmon, and methylmercury in tuna. There are all kinds of pitfalls, and you're not always beloved by your newspaper."

Burros in 1981 moved from *The Washington Post* to *The New York Times*, where she now writes occasionally. During her long career, she won numerous awards, including an Emmy in 1973 for her consumer reporting on WRC-TV, the American Association of University Women's Mass Media Award for consumer reporting and nutrition education, and a 1988 citation from the National Press Club for her coverage of food safety issues in the *Times*.

"Marian was the essence of broadcasting [food policy] news," said veteran consumer advocate Carol Tucker-Foreman. "There were some other reporters doing the same, but they dropped by the wayside."[19]

Burros lamented that both the *Post* and the *Times*, and newspapers in general, were doing less consumer reporting in their food sections, "which is sad. It never ceases to amaze me how the problems I wrote about back then are still resurfacing."[20]

The Rise of Food Studies

The daughter of an engineer, Joan Dye Gussow, born in 1928 in Los Angeles, was born too soon. Her insights into industrialized food and agriculture came at a time when the public wasn't ready to buy organic food or fresh food from local farmers and didn't understand other features of today's food movement.

"I used to be considered totally insane," Gussow told an interviewer for *Organic Gardening* magazine. "I was one of those people who'd ruin dinner parties by talking about the planet's future. There's so much more out there now about food, so much talk and action, more farmers' markets, more CSA [community-supported agriculture]. Now 'local' is a tag word people love."[21]

Best-selling food author Michael Pollan acknowledged a major debt to Gussow. "The first time I heard the advice to 'just eat food,' it was in a speech by Joan Gussow, and it completely baffled me," he wrote in his book *In Defense of Food*. "Of course you should eat food—what else is there to eat? But Gussow . . . refuses to dignify most of the products for sale in the supermarket with that title. 'In the 34 years since I've been in the field of nutrition,' she said in the same speech, 'I have watched real food disappear from large areas of the supermarket and from much of the rest of the eating world.' "[22]

After earning a pre-med bachelor's degree in 1950 from Pomona College in Claremont, California, Gussow saw limited opportunities for female physicians who might also want to have a family. Turning her hopes to journalism, she moved to New York City and worked as a *Time* researcher for seven years when the magazine didn't hire women as reporters.

Gussow took five years off to get married and raise two sons. When she decided to return to the workforce, she pursued an Ed.D. in nutrition education from Columbia Teachers College, a part of the university that specializes in training educators. Why nutrition education? She had helped author the book *Disadvantaged Children: Health, Nutrition and School Failure*. She knew she was an accomplished researcher but felt she didn't know enough to be a nutrition expert.

"I didn't want to write any more books with great men," she recalled. "I decided I should go back to school and become a nutritionist. However, I discovered that the field wasn't concerned about things I cared about, like world hunger and the flooding of supermarkets with questionable products. Critiques of the food supply were coming from outside the field. Nutrition professionals had nothing to do with these issues."[23]

In the midst of global concern about hunger, for example, the *American Journal of Clinical Nutrition* ignored the issue "because that is really not our field," she quoted the journal as saying. "It was clear we nutritionists were going to stay in our silos as the world fell apart."

Instead of focusing on vitamins and minerals, Gussow took a holistic view of nutrition education, taking into account farming, food processing, food safety, marketing, and other aspects of the food system. She sympathized with nutrition educators who, as employees, necessarily displayed total obedience to food companies and the industry in general. She felt privileged to be able to speak out.

Gussow first attracted attention in 1972 with articles such as "Whatever Happened to Food?" which criticized the explosion of food processing in the decades since the 1950s, and "Counter Nutritional Messages of Advertising to Children," published in the *Journal of Nutrition Education.*[24]

She feared she would scandalize her professional colleagues when she testified to a congressional committee on the poor quality of foods advertised to children on television. "But, instead, I got letters from more than 50 dietitians saying, 'Thank God somebody said it.' I was a first-year graduate student, but I was invited to speak at dietitians' meetings. I didn't say things that weren't true. I talked to a whole lot of people and became well-known and well received."[25]

In a widely publicized debate at the American Home Economics Association conference in Atlantic City in July 1973, Gussow argued with Paul LaChance, a Rutgers University food scientist, over the wisdom of fortifying dessert foods favored by children. Defending fortified cakes served in school breakfast programs, LaChance said, "I think we have to face up to the fact that a lot of children are eating cake, and in some cases they aren't eating anything.

"I still don't believe that a breakfast cake is a good idea," LaChance acknowledged. "I think it should be served as a dessert component at lunch or something like that." He said he preferred fortified donuts or pastries for breakfast "because they're part of the American tradition."[26]

Opposing the fortification strategy, Gussow warned that "we have a diet increasingly composed of synthetic or highly processed foods from which a lot of 'minor' nutrients were either absent to begin with or have been deliberately removed or have been rendered unavailable by processing."

Gussow said food manufacturers and their advertisers "have changed our eating patterns. Until we in nutrition education understand how they have been able to do this and are willing to act on this understanding, we can preach the four food groups until we are blue in the face."

Sometime in the early 1970s, Gussow remarked, "As for butter versus margarine, I use butter because I trust the cows more than the chemists." She doesn't remember when and to whom she first made that now famous comment.[27]

Almost immediately after receiving her Ed.D., Gussow was appointed chair of the nutrition education program at Columbia Teachers College, where she taught a course once a week. Many of her students told her she had changed their lives.

In 1978, Gussow published her landmark book, *The Feeding Web: Issues in Nutritional Ecology*, which warned of environmental hazards in the increasingly globalized food supply. She has also published *The Nutrition Debate* (1986); *Chicken Little, Tomato Sauce and Agriculture* (1991); *This Organic Life: Confessions of a Suburban Homesteader* (2001); and *Growing, Older: A Chronicle of Death, Life and Vegetables* (2010).

In addition to teaching, Gussow served on the FDA's Food Advisory Committee, the Institute of Medicine's Food and Nutrition Board, the National Organic Standards Board, and the board of the Society for Nutrition Education. "There was a hell of a lot on sexism on some of these panels," she reported. "The guys were researchers and didn't have to deal with practical issues. The women didn't dare to speak up. It was a very threatening environment. As long as you didn't challenge the conventional wisdom, you were safe."[28]

At an advanced age, Gussow still gave talks and remained outspoken. In May 2013, she delivered a speech, "Realism Is Not a Realistic Option," to an audience in Marion, Massachusetts. "Small farmers are nice enough . . . but let's be realistic: we're told, they'll never feed the world or even their own nations," she said.[29]

She then quoted a United Nations report calling for a major paradigm shift in agricultural development in both developed and developing countries. "We need to move," the report urged, "from a 'green revolution' to an 'ecological intensification' approach, which 'implies a rapid and significant shift from conventional monoculture-based and high external-input-dependent industrial production towards mosaics of sustainable, regenerative production systems that also considerably improve the productivity of small-scale farmers.'

"In other words, smaller-scale agriculture is what's going to feed the world," declared Gussow, who didn't back down an inch in her long career.

Marion Nestle

Marion Nestle did all the right things to pursue a career as a nutrition scientist. She graduated Phi Beta Kappa from the University of California–Berkeley; earned a PhD in molecular biology and a master's in public health nutrition, also from Berkeley; and became a nutrition professor at New York University.

Nestle was asked to bring NYU's home economics and nutrition department into the 21st century. She had come to know many food writers and reform-minded advocates, such as Dun Gifford at Oldways Preservation Trust, and she realized there was potential for a food studies program to replace a hotel management program that was being transferred to another school at NYU.

The *New York Times* food writer Burros wrote a story about the NYU food studies program when it was approved in 1996 by the New York State Board of Education.[30] After NYU established food studies as academically respectable, other universities began to pick up the idea.

Nestle broke ranks with her colleagues in 2002, when she published her landmark book *Food Politics: How the Food Industry Influences Nutrition and Health.* Until that moment, Americans rarely uttered the words "food" and "politics" in the same breath. "What's political about food?" people asked.

As a nutrition professional, Nestle tired of attending conferences where speakers blamed childhood obesity on parents' lack of education and neglect of their children's best interests. The conventional wisdom in 2002 was that food choice was a personal responsibility and wasn't influenced by advertising. Anyone who thought otherwise was a "nagging nanny."

Nestle first became aware of the enormous influence industry had on government food policy when she was appointed in 1986 as editor of the first *Surgeon General's Report on Nutrition and Health.* "My first day on the job, I was given the rules. No matter what the research indicated, the report could not recommend 'eat less meat' as a way to reduce intake of saturated fat, nor could it suggest restrictions on intake of saturated fat," she reported.[31]

Nestle realized that she and her professional colleagues had overlooked the food industry's relentless focus on marketing. Adopting the skills of an investigative reporter, she "followed the money" to discover food companies' business model. Their principal goal wasn't improving the health of consumers but earning profits by any means possible. "Food companies lobby government agencies, forge alliances with health professionals, sell junk food as health food and get laws passed that favor corporate health over human health," she wrote.

"I hoped that *Food Politics* would encourage people to stop thinking about food companies as social service agencies," said Nestle in a preface to the 2013 edition of the book. "They are not. The primary goals of food companies are to sell products, increase returns to investors and report quarterly growth to Wall Street. Eating less is very bad for business.

"Many of the nutritional problems of Americans—not least of them obesity—can be traced to the food industry's imperative to encourage people to eat more in order to generate sales and increase income," she wrote.[32]

Nestle said she wrote *Food Politics* to refocus attention on environmental factors—social, commercial, and institutional—rather than personal influences on food choices. "Public health must focus on political strategies to change society so that healthier choices are the easier—the default choices," she added.[33]

Nestle cited initiatives, such as the removal of junk food from schools and the introduction of fresh fruits and vegetables into inner-city areas lacking produce. Other initiatives include attempts to tax and restrict the sale of sodas, remove toys from fast-food meals. and permit foods marketed to children that only meet defined nutrition standards.[34]

Nestle's attack on the food industry wasn't ignored. Before the book came out in March 2002, four anonymous pre-publication reviews were published on Amazon's website, triggered by a February 22 review on *FoxNews.com* by Steven Milloy, host of the industry-friendly *JunkScience.com* website.[35]

"New Nutrition Book Choking on Bad Science" was the headline on Milloy's review, which said Nestle "parrots government claims that rates of overweight and obese children and adults are skyrocketing. But these claims are based on dubious research (telephone surveys without any data verification) and an arbitrary definition of 'overweight' based on 'body mass index.' The BMI, a ratio of weight to height, is problematic because it does not consider body type or state of health."

Milloy denied not only industry's role in influencing food choices but also the existence of an obesity crisis. It's worth noting that he was a paid consultant to the tobacco industry.

Mary Grabar, a researcher at the John William Pope Center, a think tank in Raleigh, North Carolina, that specializes in higher education policy, attacked food studies in general. In "Food Fetish on Campus," Graber said food studies have "become an academic growth area, adding to the deterioration of the humanities and to the advancement of leftist ideologies. No doubt our universities will be producing many more 'scholars' investigating all aspects of food: food and race, food and capitalism, food and gender, etc. But we will have fewer graduates familiar with literary and philosophical masterpieces. Fewer will be able to produce good writing—or real food."

Grabar added that food studies have "little to do with legitimate intellectual endeavors like agriculture or nutrition science. Instead, food becomes another lens through which to examine oppression, sustainability and multiculturalism."[36]

In a rebuttal posted on her *Food Politics* blog, Nestle acknowledged that food studies, which tend "to promote local, organic, seasonal, sustainable and healthful food, inherently question the industrial food system." They also promote food equity, food justice and food sovereignty. No wonder they worry conservatives, she wrote.[37]

Noting that she teaches courses in food policy, politics, and advocacy, Nestle said she instructs students "how to analyze food systems and advocate those that promote the health of people and the planet. When my academic department at NYU inaugurated our undergraduate, master's and doctoral programs in 1996 . . . we could hardly have predicted how quickly the field would spread to other universities or how brilliant and exciting so much of its scholarship would turn out to be."

PART III

Problems Can Be Solved

CHAPTER TEN

The End of Food as We Know It

The final chapters in this book offer solutions to the problems described by the four food advocates in their 2014 proposal for a national food policy.

Climate change will affect all Americans, including farmers and ranchers, in the upcoming decades. Because action has been delayed for so long, humanity can't avoid very serious climate effects, which raise pressure for steps toward sustainable agriculture.

Agricultural practices have harmed the planet, animals, and laborers throughout the supply chain. The current systems are not sustainable. This chapter extrapolates from current trends to describe what could happen if things continue with or without change.

The USDA's annual Agricultural Outlook Forum in February 2016 introduced a novel theme, "Transforming Agriculture: Blending Technology and Tradition." But the opening session focused more on behavior than technology.

Agriculture Secretary Tom Vilsack quizzed Howard Buffett, a farmer and conservationist who is a son of billionaire investor Warren Buffett. Buffett made a strong case for no-till farming and cover crops, which enable him to make more money than his neighbors.[1]

"This is not a choice. It's what we have to show the world how to do," said Buffett. "We still have time left. We need a lot of urging to beat the regulators [who would require changes]."

Buffett congratulated Vilsack for "putting conservation on the map," but he acknowledged that "changing behavior is a great chore . . . Nothing is easy. It requires right knowledge, right equipment, and right information. It takes six months to learn biodiversity. It's underrated and presented in a negative way. U.S. farmers are the biggest conservationists in the world. If 95 percent of U.S. farmers grabbed on to biodiversity, we'd be heroes. We'd be leading globally. We could do it!"

Buffett said organic farming conflicts with sustainable agriculture because it postpones no-till for three years during the transition from conventional farming. "I have yet to find an organic farm that's on a conservation base," he said. The U.S. organic industry has enjoyed steadily increased sales to consumers, but the number of farms hasn't grown to meet the demand.

Laura Batcha, executive director of the Organic Trade Association, responded later that Buffett has "just a narrow vision of no-till corn."[2]

Chris Clayton, author of *The Elephant in the Cornfield: The Politics of Agriculture and Climate Change*, reported that American farmers and agribusiness leaders are "quick to tell you that they need to ramp up production to meet the food demands of 9.6 billion by 2050. Others in the food conversation are questioning what the conditions are going to be like to grow food for that many people every year. As we move deeper into this century, our growing zones for crops move as well. Springfield, Illinois, will look more like Dallas."[3]

Clayton quoted Don Wuebbles, an atmospheric scientist at the University of Illinois: "If you've ever been in Dallas, the climate there is very different than what we're used to in Illinois. We're not used to a month of 100-degree days and a summer that's above 90 degrees every day—but that's what you get."[4]

Climate scientists in Nebraska concluded that most of the Cornhusker state would experience drought increases from 45 percent to 85 percent between now and 2050. "Drought is a big fear," commented Clayton. "Nobody on the planet is stockpiling the way Joseph did for the Egyptians in Genesis."

Climate change is likely to increase malnutrition around the world in the decades ahead, warned a scientific assessment released by Vilsack in conjunction with the Paris Climate Conference in early December 2015. Disruptions of food production and transport could constrain local availability, diminish food safety, and increase food prices, with poor people in tropical regions at greatest risk, according to the report, "Climate Change, Global Food Security and the U.S. Food System," led by the USDA and 12 other federal agencies.[5]

"The past six years have been a success story in terms of global food security. Two hundred million fewer people are food insecure today than six years ago. The challenge we now face is whether we can maintain and even accelerate this progress despite the threats from climate change," Vilsack said.

The report recommends practices and technologies across the food system to improve food security in a changing climate. In addition to advanced methods of crop production in low-yielding agricultural regions, recommendations include reducing food waste through innovative packaging, expanding cold storage to lengthen shelf life, and improving transportation infrastructure to move food more rapidly to markets.

Some major food companies aren't among climate change deniers. In an October 1, 2015, letter sent to global leaders in advance of the Paris Climate conference, 14 U.S.-based companies asked for a strong agreement from the talks. "Climate change is bad for farmers and for agriculture," they wrote. "Drought, flooding and hotter growing conditions threaten the world's food supply and contribute to food insecurity. . . . For companies like ours, that means producing more food on less land and using fewer natural resources. If we don't take action now, we risk not only today's livelihood, but also those of future generations."[6]

Sponsored by Ceres, a nonprofit organization advocating for sustainability leadership, the letter was signed by The Hain Celestial Group Inc., Hershey's, Mars Inc., General Mills, Unilever, Kellogg Company, Nestlé USA, New Belgium Brewing, Ben & Jerry's, Clif Bar, Stonyfield Farm, and Dannon USA. The statement was also later signed by Coca-Cola, PepsiCo, and The Hershey Company.

Climate change isn't the only problem affecting sustainability. Joel K. Bourne, a would-be farmer turned journalist, described in a book a future dystopia where the growing global population outstrips food. The dire predictions of 18th century economist Thomas Robert Malthus finally come true by 2050 if we can't feed nine billion people, he wrote.

"Most agricultural researchers are down-to-earth pragmatists by nature, and the least likely scientists to be alarmists," Bourne wrote in his book, *The End of Plenty: The Race to Feed a Crowded World*. "Yet when I've asked them how we can accomplish that seemingly impossible task, they strain to come up with answers, and I hear grave concern in their voices. . . . No one wants to be lampooned as the next nay-saying Malthus. Yet even these typically staid [researchers] are ringing alarm bells as loud as they can muster.

"The hard reality is that unless we radically alter the way we live, eat and farm—or are blessed with a technological miracle . . . it's hard to see how we will be able to feed more than nine billion people by 2050 without adding hundreds of millions to the burgeoning ranks of the hungry or plowing up every acre of potentially arable rain forest, savannah and prairie in a desperate attempt to make our agricultural ends meet."[7]

Bourne, who grew up in a farm family and earned an agronomy degree from North Carolina State University, took a hard look at three factors in meeting global food needs: the total area harvested, the total annual yield per hectare, and the total human population.

"Unless we start growing substantial amounts of our food in skyscraper greenhouses—a heady but unlikely scenario, given the costs of pumping all that water and burning all those grow lights—humanity will continue to depend on the thin layer of soil that is warm enough, fertile enough and wet enough to grow the crops and pasturelands we need," he wrote.[8]

Bourne forecast that 90 percent of the increase in food over the next four decades must come from land already in cultivation. "To make matters worse, some countries with the highest yields, such as China and the United States, are losing farmland at a rate of about a million hectares a year to roads, housing tracts, office towers and strip malls," he added.

He also noted that some 8 percent of the world's available farmland will be tied up growing crops for biofuels, "the production of which experts from the FAO [UN Food and Agriculture Organization] and the OECD (Organisation for Economic Cooperation and Development) expect will double between 2009 and 2019."

High Food Prices Cause Political Unrest

Warning of political unrest in the future, Bourne cites research comparing the dramatic rise of the FAO's Food Price Index to increasing violence and social unrest in the developing world from 2004 to 2011: "The first big spike, in 2008, coincided with the food riots that occurred in more than 20 nations; the second big spike, in 2011, coincided perfectly with the Arab Spring uprisings that led to violent protests in more than a dozen countries, toppled long-standing regimes in Tunisia, Egypt and Libya, and plunged Syria into civil war."[9]

Bourne's book was published too early in 2015 to take account of the massive exodus of civil war victims in Syria attempting emigration, overwhelming countries in the European Union and creating ugly confrontations at national borders. The Syrian exodus could portend worse problems in the future.

"Here in Europe, you're in the middle of one of the worst refugee crises in decades," Secretary of State John Kerry told world leaders in a speech at the Milan Food Expo. "And I would underscore, unless the world meets the urgency of this moment, the horrific refugee situation that we're facing today will pale in comparison to the mass migrations that intense droughts, sea-level rise and other impacts of climate change are likely to bring about.

"For all of these reasons, it is essential that we address the challenges of food security and climate change in a way that is coordinated," Kerry continued. "In government, we talk a lot about what we call 'climate-smart agriculture.' Basically, that means ensuring that solutions we pursue are aimed at achieving three specific goals, all at the same time:

"First, that we increase agricultural productivity in a way that is sustainable over time. Two, that we make sure our food systems are able to adapt to the climate impacts that we're already experiencing. And three, that we find ways to reduce greenhouse gas emissions from agricultural sources. Most people don't realize that agriculture as a sector itself is actually one of the leading drivers of climate change. Agriculture emits as much greenhouse gases as all of our cars, ships, trains, and airplanes combined."[10]

Author Joel Bourne sees two different paths ahead of us: on the one hand, rising food prices resulting from each climate change shock, soaring meat prices, plummeting fish and shellfish stocks, and immigration pressure rising as poor people clamor to escape countries in Africa and Southeast Asia that can no longer clothe or feed them; or, on the other hand, making secondary education a global civil right, ensuring education equality for women, and investing in basic agricultural research to help farmers become better agronomists.[11]

He sees encouraging signs that a greener revolution is under way, citing thriving organic agriculture and sustainable agriculture that "now seems within our grasp." He notes that his alma mater, North Carolina State, once a bastion of pesticide-friendly agriculture, has established a Center for Environmental Farming Systems that is striving to create "just and equitable food and farming systems that conserve natural resources, strengthen communities, improve health outcomes, and provide economic opportunities in North Carolina and beyond."[12]

At the government level, the CIA agrees that the United States and its allies need to help create skilled farm and food industry workers to combat rising food insecurity in Africa, the Middle East, and South Asia. In a report, "Global Food Security," published in October 2015 by the Office of the Director of National Intelligence, the CIA warned that overall risk of food insecurity in many countries of strategic importance to the United States will increase during the next 10 years because of production, transport, and market disruptions to local food availability, declining purchasing power, and counterproductive government policies. "In some countries, declining food security will almost certainly contribute to social disruptions or large-scale political instability or conflict, amplifying global concerns about the availability of food," the CIA warned.[13]

Food Tank Stresses Small-Scale Women Producers

The Food Tank, a Washington, D.C.–based think tank headed by returned Peace Corps volunteer Danielle Nierenberg, thinks along similar lines. In a 30-page report coauthored by CARE and titled "Cultivating Equality:

Delivering Just and Sustainable Food Systems in a Changing Climate," the authors stressed the importance of small-scale food producers, especially women.[14]

The Food Tank noted that up to 79 percent of economically active women spend their working hours producing food through agriculture, and women comprise an average of 43 percent of the agricultural labor force worldwide. Women make up nearly 50 percent of farmers in Eastern and Southeast Asia and sub-Saharan Africa, and they are responsible for the majority—almost 90 percent—of food preparation in the household.

"Despite their pivotal roles in food systems and agriculture, women are drastically [ignored] and, as a result, unable to reach their full productive potential," the report continued. "Globally, only between 10 to 20 percent of all landholders are women, and women only receive 5 percent of agricultural extension services worldwide. When food is scarce, often because of extreme weather or disasters, women and girls are also less likely or the last of the family to eat."

Empowering women is a powerful tool for bringing sustainable institutional change to agricultural systems in the face of climate change, the Food Tank wrote. "To tackle the issues of hunger, malnutrition, poverty and climate change, women must be given greater access to education, inputs and other resources in order to have greater control and influence over their households.

"Women must also be valued for their roles and their knowledge rather than seen solely as victims of climate change and hunger. Their role as providers of family health and nutrition means they bring a different—and needed perspective—on vulnerability and household needs and priorities."

American Agriculture Seen as Uncharted Territory

Kathleen Merrigan, former deputy to Agriculture Secretary Tom Vilsack and now head of George Washington University's Sustainability Institute, predicted the United States has seen its last Farm Bill, leaving American agriculture in uncharted territory with unlimited potential. "The exciting thing about agriculture now is that the future is unwritten," she told a seminar at the University of Maryland. "We know there are challenges to face, but anything can happen."[15]

Citing an FAO study, Merrigan concluded, "If women had more education resources and more opportunity for leadership positions in the same way men do, food production would increase by 30 percent."

The FAO says 80 percent of the world's food is produced by family farmers and about 72 percent of farms worldwide are less than one hectare, while only 6 percent are larger than five hectares.

To address the challenges faced by small family farmers, the FAO launched a new digital Family Farming Knowledge Platform (FFKP) to support better policies for family farmers and provide data for governments and organizations.[16]

"There was a need to share knowledge on family farming—on the different kinds of policies that governments have implemented and the numerous activities of family farmers and their organizations in the field," said Francesco Pierri, chief of the advocacy unit in the FAO Office for Partnerships, Advocacy, and Capacity Development.

The new digital platform provides information and legislation to build stronger public policies in support of family farming worldwide. "There is a lot of information available on the web, but it's scattered—we wanted one single access point for all the information out there, for anybody working in this field to use," said Pierri. Statistics, academic reports, and case studies will be added to the platform as further research becomes available.

"FAO is democratizing innovation by disseminating to family farmers' creative solutions to the challenges of climate change, resource scarcity, and farm business management," commented Food Tank. "Publicly available information not only improves the visibility of farmer-led solutions but also provides grassroots support for effective public policies that support food producers.

"The data and research gathered by the FFKP have the potential to unlock farmers' solutions to everyday challenges. By engaging farmer networks and organizations via the platform, the FAO expects that the conversations . . . will continue to push for effective policies and raise global awareness of the daily realities of working in agriculture."[17]

Smallholder farmers are seen by the FAO as crucial to achieving sustainable use of natural resources, providing food security and balanced diets to local communities, and breaking cycles of rural poverty. These farmers face immense obstacles such as limited access to land, credit, and technology; poor basic services and infrastructure; and imminent climate threats.

However, policies often fail to recognize the contributions of smallholder family farmers and are not geared to supporting them. The FAO recommends that policies focus on access to credit and finance, improvement of trade and markets, and sustainable use of natural resources. Farmer-led research and extension—amplified by farmers' traditional knowledge—will also be vital to the cultivation of a new generation of family farmers.

Now is the time to recognize and support family farmers' traditional knowledge in the international arena and major multinational institutions. Governments should prioritize implementing the voluntary guidelines on responsible governance of land, fisheries, and forests, which were passed within the FAO Committee on World Food Security.

Much like the four food advocates' call for a national food policy in *The Washington Post* (see Chapter 1), the Chicago Council on Global Affairs issued a 2015 report, "Healthy Food for a Healthy World," urging the United States to use the power of its agriculture/food sector to "reduce the reality and risks of malnutrition globally. Malnutrition—from undernourishment to obesity—is a global challenge affecting every country on earth and placing more than one quarter of the world's population at serious health risk."[18]

The Chicago Council warned that malnutrition rates are on the rise, "increasingly saddling economies with lower productivity and higher healthcare costs. Adults who were undernourished as children earn at least 20 percent less than those that were not, and a staggering 4 percent to 9 percent of most countries' gross domestic product must cover the cost of treating those who are overweight or obese. By 2030 the global decline in productivity resulting from chronic disease could cost $35 trillion. Sadly, more than half of those who are chronically hungry are small-scale farmers."

An article published in *The Lancet* forecast that more than a half million adults worldwide would die in 2050 from changes in diets and body weight due to reduced crop productivity caused by climate change.[19]

Federal agencies are doing what they can politically to improve sustainability. In September 2015, Agriculture Secretary Tom Vilsack and EPA Deputy Administrator Stan Meiburg announced the first-ever national food waste reduction goal—a 50 percent reduction in food waste throughout the United States by 2030. To achieve the goal, the federal government would partner with charitable organizations, faith-based groups, the private sector, and local, state, and tribal governments.[20]

Experts calculate that reducing food loss by just 15 percent would provide enough food for more than 25 million Americans every year. The EPA says wasted food is the "single largest component" of disposed U.S. municipal solid waste and contributes to U.S. methane emissions. Landfills are the third-largest source of methane, a major greenhouse gas, in the United States.

The USDA also launched a new consumer education campaign with information on food loss and unveiled a new section on *ChooseMyPlate.gov* to educate consumers about reducing food waste to help stretch household budgets.

In addition, the food industry also supported the government's efforts to reduce food loss. In 2011, the GMA—along with retailers, restaurants, and food service companies—formed a Food Waste Reduction Alliance to identify sources of food waste, increase contributions to food banks, and decrease food sent to landfills. "Last year, GMA member companies recycled 93 percent of food waste generated from manufacturing and donated 106 million pounds of food to food banks," said Pamela Bailey, GMA president and CEO.[21]

"Sustainability" in Fashion but Vaguely Defined

Against the background of sobering forecasts of future food scarcity, U.S. government agencies, food companies, and consumers have embraced the concept of "sustainability," but there is wide disagreement about what it means.

Writing in GMA *SmartBriefs*, Laurie Demeritt, CEO of the Hartman Group consulting firm, reported that most consumers understand sustainability if it is expressed in terms of "transparency" and "responsibility."

The Hartman group's "Transparency 2015" report found that "awareness of, and familiarity with, sustainability continues to grow, reaching an all-time high of 79 percent in 2015 (up from 74 percent in 2013). There is clear evidence . . . that sustainability is becoming more prevalent in consumers' attitudes and actions:

- "An increasing percentage of consumers define sustainability in terms of natural resource conservation, land stewardship and responsible farming methods;
- More consumers claim that their purchasing decisions are influenced by environmental and social well-being; and
- Almost a fifth claim to be buying sustainable products more frequently."

However, Demeritt said consumers "continue to struggle to identify sustainable products and companies, hindering them in their desire to support sustainable initiatives and contribute to the welfare of society and the environment."[22]

The Washington, D.C.–based Brookings Institution think tank reported in October 2015 that wealthy countries spend about $250 billion each year subsidizing agricultural sectors, which artificially lowers prices for certain crops and blocks market access for poor countries. The report, "Mapping Needs for Food and Nutrition Security," said wealthy nations spend about 20 times annually more on agricultural subsidies than they do on aiding poor farmers. The authors claim the European Union reportedly spends 42 times as much on supporting its farmers as on nutrition and food aid; it supports small-scale farmers' roles in preserving wildlife habitats and beautiful scenery. Japan spends 59 times more on agricultural subsidies than on nutrition and food aid, while the United States spends 16 times as much.[23]

Brookings claimed that "ending world hunger forms a realistic objective, attainable within 15 years, but a new approach is needed. The international community must shift from a pattern of erratic political attention and inadequate measurement of the underlying issues to a sustained, strategic, and evidence-based commitment to food and nutrition security."

The report said that of the 795 million undernourished people in the world, three-quarters live in developing countries' rural areas, meaning that ending hunger is "primarily about promoting transformational change in local food and agricultural systems."

Ricardo Salvador, director of the food and environment program at the Union of Concerned Scientists, criticizes the flow of federal subsidies to large-scale agribusiness. "It is the single most distorted system in market economics," he said in a lecture at Dartmouth College. "These are large corporate farmers. They're the business most capable of sustaining themselves in a natural market, and we're subsidizing them."

As an alternative, Salvador proposed increasing federal support for growing fruits and vegetables, which he said would only cost $90 million.[24]

Could U.S. Farmers Be Heroes?

Chris Clayton, an award-winning agriculture journalist, suggested in his book that U.S. farmers would be the heroes in the struggle for sustainability. He quoted Jerry Hatfield, a USDA soil scientist who has worked on ways for farmers to increase production despite climate change. "Climate determines where we grow crops," Hatfield told a conference in Norman, Oklahoma. "Weather determines how much we grow in a season. What we need is to build agricultural systems that reduce that variation from year to year."[25]

Hatfield said that when farmers talk about yield, they need to consider a new metric on their farms and return on investment. "How much did you produce per unit of nitrogen applied on the crop?" he asked rhetorically. "When producers start asking different questions about their system, then we have those light-bulb moments."

Hatfield pointed out that roughly $12 billion was paid out in the Midwest on crop insurance claims since 1989. If that $12 billion had been invested in soil improvements, the Midwest would look different today.

"We think about crop insurance as a risk management tool, but it doesn't promote good stewardship in terms of how we improve capacity back into the soil," he said. "The conversation with producers is not how are you going to deal with climate change, but how are you going to cope with climate variation.

"The way to have a conversation with the farm community is to not have a conversation about climate change. Those are very polarizing words. You lead with conversations about their experiences and what they are seeing on the land. . . .

"What we're looking for is a way to monetize that and reward producers for the full range of services they offer," Hatfield continued. "We're not there yet. We're still in the Old World mindset of thinking about government payments to effect change."

Clayton concluded that the United States and its agricultural production "are part of the solution to climate change, but for two decades we've largely treated it as a potential emissions problem and regulatory nightmare. There are ways to find a balance between productivity and sustainability.

"You can attempt to get there from a regulatory approach, but that only goes so far," Clayton continued. "A better way is to show society the value farmers, ranchers and agriculture as a whole play in dealing with a hotter, more crowded planet.

"Farmers could be the heroes."[26]

CHAPTER ELEVEN

Some of the Worst Jobs in America

As the land of opportunity became the land of low wages, half of the eight worst-paying jobs in the United States can now be found in the food system: food preparation and service workers, cashiers in fast-food outlets, restaurant hosts. and farmworkers. Meat- and poultry-processing workers are paid somewhat more, but their jobs certainly qualify among the worst. In his novel *The Jungle* a century ago, Upton Sinclair described the work as "stupefying and brutalizing," and more recent observers continue to find it repetitive, filthy, and terribly dangerous.[1]

Much of our food is cheap in restaurants and supermarkets, but we pay for those low prices through our taxes. Many farmworkers and fast-food workers live in or near poverty. Because they receive low wages from their employers, they account for a large fraction of the employed individuals receiving public assistance, according to the University of California at Berkeley's Center for Labor Research and Education.[2]

The center's report, "The High Public Cost of Low Wages," said persistent low wages are costing taxpayers about $153 billion every year in public support to working families. On average, 52 percent of state public assistance spending supports working families, with costs as high as $3.7 billion in California, $3.3 billion in New York, and $2 billion in Texas. Some 52 percent of fast-food workers receive public assistance, compared with 25 percent of families in the entire workforce.

Migrant farmworkers and fast-food workers are at the very low end of the pay scale in America, worsening the inequality of the U.S. economy. Undocumented workers face human rights violations on an alarming scale. Farmworkers have long been out of sight and out of mind in America, despite periodic documentaries such as Edward R. Murrow's 1960 *Harvest of Shame* and the recent film *Food Chain$* about farmworkers in Immokalee, Florida, pressuring tomato growers to pay higher wages per pound.

Farm work is seasonal, strenuous, and dangerous, and 70 percent of such workers are born outside the United States. "Job opportunities for agricultural worker occupations should be abundant, because large numbers of workers leave these jobs due to their low wages and physical demands," the Labor Department's Bureau of Labor Statistics reported.[3]

Farmworkers "are involved in the planting and the cultivation and the harvesting of the greatest abundance of food known in this society," Cesar Chavez said while organizing the United Farm Workers union in the 1960s. "They bring in so much food to feed you and me and the whole country and enough food to export to other places. The ironic thing and the tragic thing is that after they make this tremendous contribution, they don't have any money or any food left for themselves."[4]

Farmworkers still have the lowest annual family incomes of any U.S. wage and salary workers, according to the Labor Department's most recent National Agricultural Workers Survey (NAWS). They work 42 hours per week and earn $7.25 per hour on average, but this "average" varies greatly.[5] For example, workers who have labored for the same employer for multiple years earn more than other workers. Those who have been with an employer for a year or less earn an average of $6.76 per hour, and those who have been with the same employer for at least six years earn an average of $8.05 per hour. Annually, the average income of crop workers is $10,000 to $12,499 for individuals and $15,000 to $17,499 for a family. Thus, 30 percent of all farmworkers had total family incomes below the poverty line.

Most farmworkers are paid based how many buckets or bags they pick of whatever crop they harvest—a practice known as the "piece rate." Payment in this format has some drawbacks, says the National Farm Worker Ministry. "First of all, if workers are being paid by how much they pick, this acts as a disincentive to take breaks for water or shade, as taking breaks would cut into their productivity and thus cut into their pay.

"Additionally, it's possible for a farm worker being paid by piece rate to make less than the minimum wage. For instance, the piece rate for oranges in Florida is 85 cents per 90-pound box of oranges. Average productivity for a worker is eight boxes per hour, which means that, during an eight-hour workday, a worker will produce 64 boxes of oranges (or 5,760 pounds of oranges!). According to the 85 cents piece rate, a worker would receive only $6.80 an hour, which is significantly less than Florida's $7.31 minimum wage for farm work (as of 2011)."

Food Industry Seeks Immigration Reform

There are about one million farmworkers in the United States, most of whom are undocumented, living in fear of deportation, and isolated from the wider community. Comprehensive immigration reform has been out of reach in Congress.

President Obama, on November 14, 2014, stepped into the gap through executive action, providing administrative relief to millions of undocumented immigrants. An estimated one in six beneficiaries of this administrative relief would be a farmworker or immediate family member—more than 700,000 individuals. However, Obama's executive action met a legal challenge, and a federal appeals court ruled his action illegal in November 2015. The case was then forwarded to the Supreme Court for a final decision.

Meanwhile, Republican candidates for president sparred over immigration policy in a televised debate on November 10, 2015. Donald Trump and Sen. Ted Cruz (R-Texas) claimed then that they would deport millions of undocumented immigrants living in the country, while other candidates provided a pathway to legal status and possibly citizenship.

Immigration reform has strong support from the food industry, especially produce, meat, and poultry companies eager to maintain a reliable workforce. Gregory Bloom, an industry consultant who worked in six meat-processing plants for two decades, worried about a labor shortage in the food industry.[6]

"The only reasonable fix to the labor crisis is immigration reform," Bloom said in a *Meatingplace* blog. "We've known this for years, but as we've seen in Washington, our elected leaders are so polarized on the issues that they can't agree to much more than what to name bridges and post offices.

"As I met with my two senators and two of my congressmen last week on the Hill, all their staffers agreed that we are not likely to see any real progress on immigration reform until after 2017, when a new resident moves into the White House," he added. "This is a shame, and it's going to hurt us where it hurts most, putting three [square meals] on the table each day to feed our families. Food is going to cost more than it should because of the worker shortage. . . .

"It's a matter of food security for the U.S. As unthinkable as it seems, America could be food insecure soon because of the labor problem. . . . [I]f we don't fix our labor problem soon, no food on the shelves could be a reality at a grocery store near you."

Low Wages and Safety Issues Plague Food Industry

Immigration isn't the only labor problem plaguing the food industry. Low wages and safety and health problems give prospective workers reason to pause before taking jobs in meat- and poultry-processing plants.

The National Chicken Council reports that Americans consume 30 percent more chicken today than they did two decades ago, and consumption is expected to keep growing. The demand for affordable food is greater than ever.

In a report released in October 2015, Oxfam America said the chicken industry "really treats its workers like shit."[7]

Oliver Gottfried, senior advocacy and collaborations advisor, told a Food Tank webinar on "The Human Cost of Cheap Chicken" that Oxfam America spent two years putting together its report, which looked at the lives of 250,000 poultry-processing workers. The investigators found "incredibly high rates of injury and illness, low wages of declining value, and vulnerable populations working in a climate of fear," he said.[8]

Gottfried noted that chicken processing has skyrocketed to 8.6 billion pounds annually, with consumers eating an average 89 pounds each year. He said the top 10 poultry companies control 78 percent of the market, adding, "They have tremendous control over production and hope to sell as much as they can."

"The industry taps into marginalized and vulnerable populations," the Oxfam report said. "Of roughly 250,000 poultry workers, most are people of color, immigrants, or refugees" from countries such as Myanmar, Sudan, and Somalia and were employed through resettlement programs. A former worker interviewed by Oxfam estimated that well over half of his coworkers at the processing plant didn't have documentation.

As an example of mistreatment, Oxfam America featured Bacilio Castro, a worker who began a 10-hour shift at 8 a.m. and cut wings from at least 45 chickens every minute—some 2,700 chickens per hour and 27,000 chickens per shift. He said 45 chickens per minute was the expected rate at the Case Farms poultry-processing plant in Morganton, North Carolina, where he worked.

Castro said his supervisor sometimes pushed for more chickens per minute. The plant offered cash bonuses to supervisors whose line workers were particularly productive, providing an incentive to keep the pressure on them.

"They didn't care about our health," Castro is quoted as saying. By the end of the day, he couldn't move his hands. His shoulders and back ached badly, and the line's overpowering smell of ammonia—used for refrigeration—lingered even when he was in his own home, giving him a constant, terrible headache.

Castro's job also brought considerable risk of neurological damage, Oxfam reported. The National Institute for Occupational Safety and Health found in April 2015 that 76 percent of tested poultry-processing employees had abnormal results in nerve conduction exams, while 34 percent showed signs of carpal tunnel syndrome.

Another chicken plant worker explained to Oxfam how she and many of her coworkers started wearing diapers to work because they were constantly denied bathroom breaks during their shifts. A male worker said he developed a prostate problem as a result of infrequent urination.

Oxfam commented, "The growing demand for cheap poultry is squeezing the industry, and giants such as Tyson Foods or Perdue Farms have made quantity the bottom line. Those most feeling the squeeze are people who work long shifts at breakneck speed with a single half-hour break while earning less than $10 an hour, often with little compensation for injuries incurred on the job."

Oxfam noted that most of the chicken sold in the United States is processed into parts and specially packaged: breasts, tenders, thighs, legs, strips, skinless, breaded, glazed, sliced, spiced, and shaped. In the vertically integrated system of the modern poultry industry, there is now a range of jobs along the factory assembly line that didn't exist 50 years ago.

New jobs include "line loaders" who place the chickens on conveyor belts, "hangers" who insert the chicken's feet into overhead shackles, back/breast separators, shoulder cutters, wing cutters, de-boners, and a host of others. "These workers are widely exposed to chemicals like ammonia and chlorine, which is often used to disinfect chicken carcasses. The industry's pervasive use of antibiotics in chicken can also affect workers, who have been known to build up antibiotic resistance that complicates their recovery from infection," said Oxfam.

Since the 1970s, the Occupational Safety and Health Administration (OSHA) has been the primary monitor of meat-processing workers' safety in the country, developing standardized workplace regulations and conducting inspections to ensure that they are met.

"But it is understaffed and underfunded: OSHA inspected less than 1 percent of the country's workplaces in 2013," reported Oxfam. "When it does inspect plants, penalties for violations don't pack a punch. In 2014, the average federal penalty issued by OSHA for a 'serious violation'—health and safety hazards that pose significant risk of injury or death—was just $1,972.

OSHA in November 2015 announced immediate implementation of a Regional Emphasis Program that would target poultry processing plants in Arkansas, Louisiana, Oklahoma, Texas, Florida, Georgia, Alabama, and Mississippi, focusing on "musculoskeletal disorders and ergonomic stressors affecting industry workers."[9]

"The pace today churns out a lot of chicken, but it also churns through a lot of human beings," Oxfam concluded. "A quarter of a million people work in a profitable industry that provides the most popular meat in the country to millions of consumers. . . . It's time for industry, the government, and consumers to take action for vital change."

Worker Advocates Reach Out to Poultry CEOs

On November 20, 2015, worker advocacy groups sent a letter to CEOs of three of the so-called Big Four poultry companies, demanding "immediate action to raise wages, improve safety conditions and guarantee fair treatment" for workers who process turkeys as well as chicken. The letter was delivered to Jim Perdue, CEO of Perdue Farms; Bill Lovette, president and CEO of Pilgrim's Pride; and Joe Sanderson Jr., CEO of Sanderson Farms.[10]

The CEO of Tyson Foods, which controls about a quarter of the market, didn't receive a letter because that company has committed to raising wages of some plant workers. "When we campaign, we engage firms to respond," Oxfam's Gottfried told the Food Tank webinar. "There's a little bit of movement with Tyson. They're going to raise pay and start a safety pilot."[11]

Responding to the Oxfam report, the poultry industry stressed the progress it had achieved over the years and promised to continue seeking innovative ways to protect its workforce. "It is unfortunate that Oxfam portrays an undeserved negative image of the entire poultry industry despite our outstanding record of improvement in employee health and safety, particularly over the past three decades," the National Chicken Council and U.S. Poultry and Egg Association said in a joint statement. They also issued a lengthy paper outlining their member companies' approach to worker safety, noting that occupational injuries and illnesses had fallen 80 percent over the past two decades.[12]

However, OSHA is "concerned that the extent of poultry workers' injuries may be far greater than the elevated risks reported by employers and seen in Bureau of Labor Statistics data," an agency spokesperson wrote in an email to *Meatingplace*.[13]

The poultry industry isn't the only meat-processing industry affected by work injuries and animal welfare. In January 2016, some 60 Democratic members of Congress urged the USDA to delay publishing a proposed

HACCP-based Inspection Model Project (HIMP) hog inspection rule, which they said could result in adding "thousands of debilitating injuries [to workers], including: cuts, lacerations, and musculoskeletal disorders." They said that rapid HIMP line speeds "present one of the greatest risks of inhumane treatment of animals, as workers are often pressured to take violent shortcuts to maintain speed."[14]

Cities, States, and Companies Move to Raise Minimum Wage

The U.S. economy hasn't worked for the average family since the end of the Clinton administration, commented Mortimer Zuckerman, chairman and editor-in-chief of *U.S. News & World Report*. Adjusted for inflation, median earnings of men working full-time year-round are where they were in 1980.

"That's unfair because productivity has been rising for two decades but the benefit has been confined to the already well-off," he continued. "Today, income inequality in the U.S. exceeds [that in] any other democracy in the developed world. Two-thirds of American families earning less than $30,000 a year are often in crisis mode when the bills come in, but the misery is conspicuously not shared. In 1944 the top 1 percent earned 11 percent of all income. By 2012, it was 23 percent of the nation's income. The mismatch between reward and effort makes a mockery of the American dream."[15]

In our disappointing new century, real output per person from 2000 to 2011 rose nearly 2.5 percent a year, but real pay increased less than 1 percent over the same period, according to the Bureau of Labor Statistics. Adjusted for inflation, incomes in 2014 were still roughly $2,100 lower than when President Obama took office in 2009 and $3,600 lower than when President George W. Bush took office in 2000.[16]

The U.S. federal minimum wage was first established during the Depression in 1938 and has risen from 25 cents to $7.25 per hour. Despite the increases, inflation has eroded its value. Returning the minimum wage to the value it held in 1968 would require an increase to nearly $10 per hour.

In his 2013 State of the Union address, President Obama called for raising the minimum wage to $9 per hour, which in adjusted terms would put it back to its early 1980s level. According to White House estimates, this increase would boost the wages of some 15 million people, especially women.[17]

Critics, such as the Washington, D.C.–based American Enterprise Institute, assert that the real effects of minimum-wage increases hurt businesses, raise prices, and are counterproductive in the long run for the working poor, as increases can lead to unemployment. At the macro level, a substantial increase in the federal minimum wage is likely to have broad effects, with some studies predicting that it could "ripple" across the economy, boosting the wages of nearly 30 percent of the American workforce.[18]

Yet the current low minimum wage has more effects than sustaining poverty. The growing consumption of increasingly less expensive food, notably fast food, is a potential cause of the alarming increase in obesity over the past several decades. With higher wages, poor people could work shorter days (for example, not take two jobs) and find time to prepare healthier food that is even cheaper than fast food.[19]

A working paper published in 2009 by the National Bureau of Economic Research, "The Impact of Minimum Wage Rates on Body Weight in the United States," concluded that increases in body mass index (BMI) between 1968 and 2007 could be blamed on the decline of the real minimum wage during that same period.[20]

"We find that a $1 decrease in the real minimum wage was associated with a 0.06 increase in BMI," the authors reported. "This relationship was significant across gender and income groups and largest among the highest percentiles of the BMI distribution. Real minimum wage decreases can explain 10 percent of the change in BMI since 1970. We conclude that the declining real minimum wage rates [have] contributed to the increasing rate of overweight and obesity in the United States. Studies to clarify the mechanism by which minimum wages may affect obesity might help determine appropriate policy responses."

The Harvard Kennedy School of Government's Journalist's Resource pointed to the huge research literature on the minimum wage, recommending a 2014 book, *What Does the Minimum Wage Do?* by economists Dale Belman of Michigan State University and Paul Wolfson of the Tuck School of Business at Dartmouth College. Synthesizing some 200 papers, the book's authors wrote, "Evidence leads us to conclude that moderate increases in the minimum wage are a useful means of raising wages in the lower part of the wage distribution that has little or no effect on employment and hours. This is what one seeks in a policy tool, solid benefits with small costs. That said, current research does not speak to whether the same results would hold for large increases in the minimum wage."[21]

In 1994, Alan Krueger—a Princeton economist who later became chairman of President Obama's Council of Economic Advisers—and his colleague David Card published a seminal paper, "Minimum Wages and Employment: A Case Study of the Fast-Food Industry in New Jersey and Pennsylvania," which framed much of the subsequent debate.[22] The two scholars examined the results of a 1992 New Jersey law that raised the minimum wage, comparing the outcomes in the fast-food industry to those in the bordering state of Pennsylvania, where wage laws remained the same. Their study, using data, called into question textbook assumptions about how labor markets might work. The findings included the following:

- "No evidence that the rise in New Jersey's minimum wage reduced employment at fast-food restaurants in the state."
- "Prices of fast-food meals increased in New Jersey relative to Pennsylvania, suggesting that much of the burden of the minimum-wage rise was passed on to consumers."

That Krueger-Card paper implied that the neoclassical models, which suggest an increase in the minimum wage would result in fewer jobs and higher prices, didn't comport with reality—data triumphed over theory. Over the next decade, economics scholars debated whether the paper's fundamental insights were right and could support policy.

The National Employment Law Project cited recent polls showing overwhelming public support for higher minimum wages, especially among the 42 percent of American workers who are paid less than $15 an hour. A growing number of employers, including some large corporations, are recognizing that the low-wage business model is actually not good for business and have been raising base pay for their lowest-paid workers, with some adopting at least a $15 minimum wage.[23]

The nationwide *Fight for $15* strikes and protests on November 10, 2015 may have prompted the first question at the Republican presidential debate the same day. Front-runners Donald Trump and Ben Carson both said they opposed raising the minimum wage, as did Sen. Marco Rubio (R-Fla.). Trump commented that U.S. workers' wages are too high, and none of the other seven Republican candidates voiced disagreement.

Just two days later, Popeyes' CEO Cheryl Bachelder, a representative of an increasing number of business executives and other employers, told *CNN Money*, "Everybody in retail is dealing with an increase in minimum wage. We will adjust to increased costs just like we have before. Life will go on. . . . Labor costs are going up. When Target, Walmart and McDonald's moved wages higher, the marketplace moved with them."[24]

Other employers have been raising minimum pay rates even higher, with nearly two dozen adopting base hourly wages of $15 or more over the past two years. Those $15-plus companies include Ben & Jerry's and Moo Cluck Moo, a fast-casual restaurant chain in the Detroit area.

"As even more states and cities, as well as public and private employers raise minimum wages and increase base pay for workers, those politicians who stand in the way and oppose higher minimum wages look increasingly out of touch," said the National Employment Law Project.[25]

In the absence of a federal minimum wage increase for restaurant workers and other low-wage employees, some cities and states have decided to take matters into their own hands. Some 14 states and the District of Columbia decided to raise their minimum wage in 2014. Some cities are raising their minimum wage to as much as $15 an hour.

Several large low-wage companies have also pledged to give raises. Walmart in February 2015 said it would increase wages for a half-million workers to at least $9 an hour. McDonald's followed suit, at least for the 90,000 workers employed at corporate-owned locations, if not those employed by franchisees.

"To some extent, these announcements may be driven by a desire to cultivate goodwill in the face of much bad PR about treatment and compensation of low-wage workers," wrote *Washington Post* columnist Catherine Rampell. "But the primary motivation for these firms . . . is likely the bottom line: To attract and retain talent, especially in a tightening labor market, employers know they need to start offering better pay."[26]

CHAPTER TWELVE

Treatment of Food Animals

The meat and poultry industry is in the business of killing livestock, which isn't a pretty picture under the best of circumstances. While most Americans expect our laws to protect food animals before slaughter, the reality falls far short. Animals raised for food are among the least protected class of animals in our nation. The United States has no federal laws protecting food animals while they're raised on farms.

"In the absence of laws, there's a moral race to the bottom by meat companies as they try to outcompete one another," Paul Shapiro, vice president for farm animal protection at the Humane Society of the United States (HSUS), told a Food Tank luncheon seminar at American University in Washington, D.C.[1]

Like state and federal prisons, concentrated animal feeding operations (CAFOs) are usually located far from towns and cities, where the sight of confined animals and foul smells are repellent to onlookers. In numerous states, the meat and poultry industries have sought legislation, dubbed "ag-gag" bills, that would prohibit undercover investigations revealing these unpleasantries.

The Harris Ranch Beef Company feedlot, located halfway between Los Angeles and San Francisco, was dubbed "Cowschwitz" by critics. As many as 100,000 cattle at a time are crowded atop their excrement on one square mile of land. "From the highway, the stench wallops you like a punch in the face and lingers in your car and clothing for miles—and in your memory forever," wrote Barry Estabrook in a blog post in January 2012.[2]

After journalist Michael Pollan criticized the foul-smelling feedlot in his best-selling book, *The Omnivore's Dilemma*, David Wood, chairman of Harris Ranch Beef, wrote a letter to the president of California Polytechnic State University threatening to withdraw financial support if Pollan gave a lecture at the university. As a result, Pollan was downgraded to speaking in a panel discussion.

Animal welfare advocates argue that food animals should be treated humanely before slaughter. This issue pits the HSUS and its allies against an industry that insists it's already handling its livestock without cruelty.

Temple Grandin, an animal scientist who teaches at Colorado State University and serves as a consultant to the meat and poultry industry, raised her bar for animal welfare in 2015. In an interview with *Grist* magazine, she revised her view that food animals need a "decent life" and instead require "a life worth living."[3]

Asked about specific things she'd like to change, she replied, "We have this abstractification, with activists attacking things they don't even know anything about. And ag has responded poorly. Ag-gag laws: dumbest thing they could have ever done. That just makes you look guilty. Why are they passing a law to make it a crime to video something?"

Appealing to Voters at the State Level

In the absence of federal laws, the HSUS has adopted strategies that appeal to voters at the state level. HSUS president and CEO Wayne Pacelle said he came to believe that the ballot initiative is "a democratic safety valve to allow for policies to be adopted that were popular with the public but that had been unfairly thwarted by a small number of state legislators." In legislatures across the country, he said, bills related to wildlife or farm animal welfare often get assigned to committees typically filled with lawmakers with ties to the industries the bills are "trying to reform—and thus go nowhere."[4]

Despite strong political and legal opposition, animal welfare advocates succeeded in passing legislation in California forbidding the sale of eggs from laying hens confined in battery cages, including sale of eggs from other states. Voters approved Proposition 2 on the state ballot in 2008.

Six egg-producing states challenged the California law in federal courts in 2014, charging violation of the Constitution's commerce clause. Judge Kimberly Mueller of the U.S. District Court for the Eastern District of California dismissed their case (*State of Missouri et al. v. Kamala D. Davis et al.*), ruling that the plaintiffs representing the states of Missouri, Nebraska, Oklahoma, Alabama, Kentucky, and Iowa didn't have standing to file their case. The court's ruling included a final judgment favoring the State of California, the HSUS, and the Association of California Egg Farmers.[5]

However, in an 80-page brief to the Ninth Circuit Court of Appeals, the six states argued that the California law violates interstate commerce by forcing other states to comply with its rigid standards, which have no basis in food safety. The state of Utah filed an *amicus* brief in support of the other states' appeal.[6]

Meanwhile, California's cage-free law has gained support from numerous companies and consumers. Aramark, the largest U.S.-based food service company, agreed to expand its battery cage-free commitment to include all company purchases of liquid, precracked eggs in the United States by 2020.

Aramark, which runs dining operations in thousands of institutions across the nation, unveiled a comprehensive animal welfare policy with HSUS in 2015 that "will address a broad spectrum of issues impacting the treatment of animals for pork, veal, beef, poultry and dairy production."[7]

In 2012, Aramark also committed to purchasing only gestation crate-free pork by 2017. "Responsible purchasing has always been core to Aramark's mission to 'Enrich and Nourish Lives,'" the company said, adding that it "looks forward to advancing animal welfare as part of its overall corporate responsibility commitment."

Consumers have become aware of where and how laying hens live, thanks to undercover videos by animal welfare advocates and photos of tons of dead birds thrown out of mammoth barns after outbreaks of avian flu.

"The egg market for probably the last 30 years has been a very sleepy category," Betsy Babcock, a proprietor of Handsome Brook Farm, a pastured egg business with operations in 41 states, told *The New York Times*. "What we've seen over the last year or so, though, is a revolution, with pastured eggs going from being a niche-y segment in the natural food market and Whole Foods to being a thriving business in places like Kroger [supermarkets]."[8]

Yvonne Vizzier Thazton, director of the University of Arkansas's Center for Food Animal Wellbeing, said animal agriculture scientists are confused these days, because laying hens living in outdoor free-range settings are subject to more negatives than in conventional cage systems. However, in today's markets, animal welfare "is a driving force in advertising and apparently sales."[9]

Massachusetts Is New State Ballot Battleground

A closely linked HSUS strategy is persuading major corporations to change policies or else risk embarrassment by reports they buy meat from processors who are cruel to animals. For example, animal welfare groups proposed a cage-free ballot initiative in Massachusetts for the 2016 statewide election, but it wasn't going anywhere until McDonald's announced in September 2015 that it plans to source eggs from cage-free laying hens within 10 years.[10]

The "admirable move" by McDonald's makes clear that the future of egg production is cage-free, the HSUS said, noting that Burger King, Nestlé,

Sodexo, Aramark, Heinz, Starbucks, Compass Group, and numerous other companies had also committed to 100 percent cage-free eggs. "We're heartened that McDonald's policy comes with a timeline," said HSUS president Pacelle. The fast-food giant said it would source cage-free eggs for all restaurants in the United States and Canada by 2025.

The Massachusetts Society for the Prevention of Cruelty to Animals and its allies proposed a ballot item "to curb extreme confinement and lifelong immobilization of animals at industrial-style factory farms" in that state. The coalition aimed to collect more than 90,000 signatures in order to qualify this animal welfare proposal for the 2016 statewide ballot.[11] Among others, the coalition included HSUS, Massachusetts Society for the Prevention of Cruelty to Animals, Animal Rescue League of Boston, American Society for the Prevention of Cruelty to Animals, United Farm Workers, Center for Food Safety, family farmers, veterinarians, and public health professionals.

Massachusetts' highest court ruled in early July 2016 that an initiative to ban sales of meat produced from tightly confined animals would be included on ballots in November. If the ballot initiative passes, Massachusetts farms and businesses in 2022 would have to sell only eggs from cage-free hens, pork from pigs not born or raised in gestation crates, and veal from calves not raised in a tight enclosure. Advocates said the rules would simply ensure hens, pigs, and calves have enough room to stand up, lie down, turn around, and extend their limbs.

McDonald's Decision seen as "Tipping Point"

As might be expected, the animal agriculture industry warned that the Massachusetts initiative would raise prices and hurt family farmers. Chad Gregory, president and CEO of United Egg Producers (UEP), commented, "UEP has always supported customer and consumer choice in the types of eggs they buy, and the McDonald's decision is an example of that process working as it should. The ballot proposal in Massachusetts effectively takes away that choice by mandating the sale of a certain type of egg."[12]

The Massachusetts ballot initiative caught the attention of major agriculture lobbies in Washington, D.C., which deliberated how to campaign against the proposal.

Ken Klippen, president of the National Association of Egg Farmers, saw McDonald's decision as a "tipping point" that would raise production costs by 36 percent, which would be passed on to consumers. He cited a recent statistic that 14 percent of the U.S. population is food insecure, noting that many poor people rely on eggs for protein.[13]

Klippen reported that the National Pork Producers Council and a sheep industry lobby were interested in opposing the proposed ballot initiative in Massachusetts. The National Cattlemen's Beef Association and the American Farm Bureau Federation also showed interest, he said.

"They see what's happening as 'the thin edge of the wedge,' with HSUS trying to reduce the supply of animal foods by increasing the cost. I'm trying to strategize for a course of action. What happened in California [with its cage-free law] will happen in Massachusetts," Klippen said.

Dave Warner, spokesperson for the National Pork Producers Council, said the end goal of the HSUS is "to significantly reduce the consumption of meat because they don't want animals being raised and turned into food." He said the Massachusetts ballot question, if made law, would raise the cost of producing meat and thus the cost of the meat for consumers.

As prices go up, consumption would go down, Warner said, and could create a cycle of higher prices begetting lower demand begetting still higher prices. "It's basic economics," he said. "If they can affect basic economics, they can reduce consumption of meat."

The Boston Globe said the ballot initiative is likely to bring a raging debate to a state with relatively little egg and meat production and not known for divisive battles over agricultural issues. The Massachusetts ballot initiative could pose the biggest test yet for animal welfare groups to move their cause forward.[14]

On other fronts, the HSUS has succeeded in persuading several large food corporations to reject suppliers who confine pregnant hogs in gestation crates. In a joint announcement with the animal welfare group, Hilton Worldwide announced in April 2015 a phased commitment to stop buying eggs from chickens confined in cages and pork from pigs raised in gestation crates. The changes would initially apply in 19 countries where products are currently available and will be adopted in other markets as supply becomes available, Hilton said.[15]

Suppliers to hotels owned by Hilton Worldwide—including Hilton, Waldorf Astoria, Conrad, Canopy, and DoubleTree—would be required to provide pork from pigs bred in groups rather than gestation crates. "With more than 2,000 restaurants in our global footprint, our goal is to have a considerable impact on sustainable sourcing in our industry as well as drive humane treatment of animals throughout our supply chain," said Jennifer Silberman, vice president, corporate responsibility for Hilton Worldwide.[16]

Regarding gestation stalls for pregnant sows, prominent industry consultant Temple Grandin commented, "Confining an animal for most of its life in a box in which it is not able to turn around does not provide a decent life . . . We've got to treat animals right, and gestation stalls have got to go."[17]

Undercover Videos Expose Animal Cruelty

In 2015, an investigator for Mercy for Animals worked under cover for six weeks at a Tyson Food's facility outside of Carthage, Mississippi, producing a candid video in October showing poultry abuse.[18] The video findings include the following:

- "Workers punching, throwing, beating, pushing, and otherwise tormenting frightened animals for fun;
- "Birds painfully shocked with electricity but remaining fully conscious when their throats are cut open;
- "Improperly shackled birds getting their heads ripped off while they are still alive and conscious; and
- "Chickens dumped on top of one another on a conveyor belt, causing many to suffocate under the weight of other birds."

Mercy for Animals brought as many as 33 misdemeanor criminal counts against the company and its employees. A Mississippi Justice Court was scheduled to review the affidavits and decide whether summons would be issued.

Responding to the video, Tyson reported it had fired two of the workers and affirmed it views proper animal handling as "an important moral and ethical obligation." It said all Tyson workers, including the person who shot the video, are trained in proper animal handling. The statement added that any Tyson employee who observes "bad behavior" should contact a supervisor or use the company's compliance and ethics hotline.[19]

HSUS Battles "Ag-Gag" Bills in State Legislatures

In defense of whistleblowers, the HSUS opposed in state legislatures numerous "ag-gag" bills that would criminalize investigators who seek to expose animal cruelty.

A U.S. District Court in August 2015 ruled that Idaho's new ag-gag law is unconstitutional, because it was motivated by "animus towards animal welfare groups, and because it impinges on free speech, a fundamental right." In the first-ever federal court decision to strike down an ag-gag statute, Judge Lynn Winmill said Idaho's law violates both the First Amendment right to free speech and the Equal Protection Clause.[20]

"Audio and visual evidence is a uniquely persuasive means of conveying a message, and it can vindicate an undercover investigator or whistleblower who is otherwise disbelieved or ignored," Judge Winmill wrote in a 28-page decision on the Idaho case, adding, "Prohibiting undercover investigators or whistleblowers from recording an agricultural facility's operations inevitably suppresses a key type of speech because it limits the information that might later be published or broadcast."

Idaho's ag-gag law would have made it a crime for a journalist or animal rights investigator not to disclose media or political affiliations when requesting a tour of an industrial feedlot or applying for employment at a dairy farm. The law would also have allowed an employee to be convicted for videotaping animal abuse or life-threatening safety violations at an agricultural facility without first obtaining the owner's permission. Any person who violated the law faced up to a year in jail, and could be forced to pay twice the "economic loss" a business suffers as a result of an exposé revealing animal abuse or unsafe working conditions.

Idaho attorney general Lawrence Wasden in December 2015 asked the U.S. Appeals Court in San Francisco to review the district court's opinion that the state's new ag-gag law is unconstitutional.[21]

Idaho is one of eight states in the past few years to have adopted bills banning or restricting undercover investigations on the abuse of farmed animals. However, nearly 30 states introduced bills banning or restricting undercover investigations surrounding the abuse of farmed animals since ag-gag was conceived in the early 1990s.

Idaho was the only state to pass an ag-gag bill in 2014, but several more states introduced such bills in 2015. In North Carolina, legislators overrode their governor's veto to pass an ag-gag law. They nullified Gov. Pat McCrory's veto of the Property Protection Act (House Bill 405), which allows businesses to sue employees who document wrongdoing inside their facilities.

In his veto message, McCrory said he vetoed HB 405 because it doesn't "adequately protect or give clear guidance to honest employees who uncover criminal activity. I am concerned that subjecting these employees to potential civil penalties will create an environment that discourages them from reporting illegal activities" in other settings, such as nursing homes and day care centers.[22]

Opponents called HB 405 an ag-gag bill because the principal target is undercover animal welfare advocates who take jobs to document alleged abuses to farm animals. The state's major newspapers in Raleigh, Charlotte, Fayetteville, and Greensboro ran editorials favoring a veto.

The HSUS described HB 405 as "a dangerous ag-gag bill that would have punished whistleblowers who report abuse at any workplace in the state, including factory farms, nursing homes and day care centers." Journalism groups and the AARP warned that the bill would apply to all employers, not just those in food and agriculture. Industry workers could be discouraged from coming forward with evidence of elder abuse.[23]

During debate over the veto, the bill's Republican supporters concluded that the bill is important to protect businesses from bad actors and voted to override Gov. McCrory's objections. "We need to vote for this [bill] because it has gotten out of control what some so-called employees have done to businesses," one was quoted as saying.[24]

In January 2016, Mercy for Animals' efforts led to the conviction of chicken farm worker Danny Miranda on three counts of misdemeanor animal cruelty, based on an undercover video taken on a farm in North Carolina. That seemed to be the last of such videos in North Carolina, because the state's ag-gag law went into effect on January 1, 2016, with penalties up to $5,000 per day for anyone who conducted an undercover investigation of animal agriculture.

However, six advocacy groups filed a lawsuit against North Carolina's ag-gag law on January 13, 2016. The groups said they were confident the law would be found unconstitutional and "a victory in North Carolina will deter other state legislatures from repeating North Carolina's mistake."[25] Also opposing the North Carolina law, *The New York Times* editorial board declared that "the secrecy permitted by ag-gag laws should have no place in American society."[26]

The meat industry itself has some reservations about ag-gag laws. Richard Raymond, former USDA undersecretary for food safety, told *Meatingplace* magazine, "The industry needs to stop defending the bad actors that are in their business, and it needs to stop clamoring for 'ag-gag' laws that seem to shout out that you have something to hide."[27]

Candace Croney, director of Purdue University's Center for Animal Welfare Sciences, agreed, "No matter what the intention, [ag gag laws make it look] like the industry has something to hide."[28]

Industry Lobby Sees Veganism in Disguise

As a fallback against animal welfare victories, the industry-supported Animal Agriculture Alliance (AAA) charged that the HSUS and its allies are wolves in sheep clothing. They're out to reduce availability of meat, milk, and eggs so that many more consumers will become vegans, AAA said.

Hannah Thompson, AAA communications director, covered an Animal Rights National Conference in September 2015 and issued a report describing her findings. She said the speakers stressed the importance of focusing on "incremental changes" toward veganism by running pressure campaigns against food companies and convincing consumers to go vegan gradually.[29]

She said David Coman-Hidy, executive director at The Humane League, noted that activists need to scale back their demands to achieve small victories. "You need to look at everything as stepping stones," he is quoted as saying. He encouraged activists to start small with their demands in order to seem rational, but always pressure companies to move toward eliminating meat, milk, and eggs from their menus.

Alex Hershaft, founder of the Farm Animal Rights Movement (FARM), reportedly stated that activists should gradually convince consumers to go vegan by saying, "We are trying to reduce the number of animals used for food. We aren't trying to make everyone vegan." By just getting their foot in the door, they are more likely to keep the attention of the specific individual or audience. He said, "Take them one step at a time or you will lose them."[30]

"Sending eyes and ears to events like the Animal Rights Conference to gather information about what activist groups are planning and saying behind closed doors is very important in order for the industry to better understand the animal rights movement and how it affects their businesses," commented AAA president and CEO Kay Johnson Smith. "By attending these events we can more effectively counter their misleading campaigns against animal agriculture."[31]

Thompson acknowledged that animal welfare groups have clever political strategies, such as reaching out to financial and investment companies. "If we aren't at the table in these discussions, we will surely be on the menu," she warned.[32]

Asked about accusations that the HSUS has a "vegan agenda," Pacelle told *The Boston Globe* that adversaries want to shift the debate away from the group's focus on better animal welfare. Pressed on whether he wants more U.S. consumers to adopt a vegan diet, he said he doesn't.[33]

"We, as a nation, have very high consumption rates for animal products," he added. "Higher than the Argentineans or the French or the Italians or the Japanese or the Germans. And I think that there are a host of problems associated with large-scale animal agriculture. But our primary focus is to improve the living conditions of animals in agriculture."

Industry Told to Get Out of Defensive Crouch

In a lengthy interview published in *Meatingplace* magazine, Candace Croney, director of Purdue University's Center for Animal Welfare Science, said the meat and poultry industry's message has gone wrong. "Oftentimes when we talk about animal welfare, it is in the context of how it pertains to production and economics," she said, adding, "For example, responding to questions about the ethics and behavioral restriction involved in continuous confinement of animals with answers about food safety and economics infuriates people who think the respondent is tone deaf to the problem or ignoring or dodging the question."[34]

Croney noted that industry is "operating in a dynamic where the animal protection groups are very, very active. They have adopted new public outreach strategies that influence retailer groups with very media-friendly stories, which get a lot of attention, creating a paradigm where people feel there is a lot of bad stuff happening. In fairness, there are operations shown in these undercover videos where bad things are happening. So, the idea that it's just one bad apple does not ring true for the average person.

"Far too often the industry seems defensive because they are being criticized, but rather than focusing on the welfare problems, they are focusing on the people who are drawing attention to the welfare problems. And I think that is a huge problem."

The Purdue professor said the best a processor can do is "be really consistent and clear about the expectations of the quality of product and the conditions and the quality of life offered to the animals they're sourcing from.

"Some packers have done some pretty extraordinary things, including putting together animal welfare advisory groups and setting pretty stringent standards. . . . I think once you get into processing, the best that you can do is send a really clear message that animal welfare is important to everybody along the food chain."

Mark Graves, a meat industry consultant, agreed. He noted that "new purchasing influences such as health and wellness, safety, social impact, experience and transparency are motivating consumers. The old traditional factors such as price, taste and convenience less so." To ignore "pesky millennials [or] patronize them is also a peril we don't need. We need to respond positively. . . . We have a lot of 'splainin' to do."[35]

The USDA's Agricultural Marketing Service led the way in April 2016 by proposing organic livestock and poultry production rules to include specific guidance on animal welfare. The provisions include (1) requiring producers and handlers to ensure animals' health and well-being throughout life, including transport and slaughter; (2) specifying physical changes allowed and forbidden in organic livestock and poultry production; and (3) setting minimum indoor and outdoor space requirements for poultry.[36]

Given all the newly aroused public interest in animal welfare, the livestock industry is likely to modify its goal to produce cheap meat and instead treat its animals more kindly over the coming decades.

CHAPTER THIRTEEN

Food Advocacy Changes America

As discussed in Chapter 1, four leaders of the food movement in 2014 proposed a national food policy weaving universal access to healthful food with farm policies supporting environmental objectives. However, they failed to persuade President Obama to mention a national food policy in his State of the Union address in February 2015.

Refusing to give up, the Union of Concerned Scientists (UCS) in October 2015 launched a "Plate of the Union" campaign challenging presidential candidates to address the national food policy issues in 2016.[1] Joined by Food Policy Action and the HEAL Food Alliance, the UCS commissioned a survey of 1,000 voters that found the following:

- Some 81 percent of voters are very concerned that one-third of today's children will develop type 2 diabetes.
- Voters are also concerned regarding the gap between Dietary Guidelines and the policies to implement them.
- Voters believe special interests and money in politics influence the system. Some 75 percent are concerned that five of the eight worst-paying jobs in America are in the food system.

The survey also found "a strong appetite for change." By party, 85 percent of Democrats, 77 percent of independents, and 62 percent of Republicans favor incentives to encourage sustainable farming. Half (50 percent) of voters favored putting limits on government subsidies to the largest farm businesses.

Armed with survey results, Ricardo Salvador, director of the UCS food and environment program, told a Food Tank event in Washington, D.C., that the national food policy proposal is a challenge to the United States as a democracy. "Can citizens change food policy?" he asked.

"Do we live in a democratic nation?" he continued. "Economic elites have had independent influence on policy issues over 18 years. That's a hallmark of a plutocracy. The system is locked in. It's a ritualized system and an unrepresentative legislative body. . . . We need new executive leadership [from the next president]. Can we get food into the discourse?"[2]

Pursuing the Plate of the Union, Salvador and Mark Bittman, a former *New York Times* food columnist, met with presidential candidates' staffs in Iowa on January 21, 2016, in search of campaign commitments to food policy changes.[3] They asked the candidates to pay more attention to food issues and suggested "low-hanging fruit" that a president-elect could implement during his or her first year in office.

AGree, a similar nonpartisan group, tweeted the presidential candidates, urging them to address food and farming as they seek election. The group issued a call to action in a briefing paper: "Our food and agricultural system from 'farm to fork' is vital to the health of our nation, but facing a period of enormous transition. Presidential leadership is critical. The right policies can directly improve the health of America's farms, families, economy and the environment."[4]

At the National Food Policy Conference in April 2016, Bob Carpenter, a consultant to Republican politicians, reported that food policy and safety "aren't in the hearts of American voters. They're crowded out by other issues." Republican candidates want stability for farmers and sufficient funds for food safety, and they consider the food stamp program "horrible."[5] Journalist Jerry Hagstrom noted that Republican candidates, seeking to bond with likely voters, expressed love for fast food.[6]

On the other side, Celinda Lake, a political strategist for Democrats, called food safety "a huge hidden issue that can be extremely powerful," especially to women voters. "Food policy is a great issue for uniting, but candidates don't talk about it—yet!"[7]

Bring Stakeholders to the Table

When the four food advocates published their national policy manifesto in November 2014, David Festa, vice president of ecosystem programs at the Environmental Defense Fund, recommended that they bring stakeholders to the table and engage elected representatives. For the political system to act, stakeholders—in this case farmers, ranchers and food companies—need to know they are a part of the solution and have confidence in the alternatives, he said, adding, "Not only is this a political necessity, solutions are more likely to be robust if the people who know the most about our food system help inform policy choices.

"Instead of telling them what to do, work with them to create solutions," he continued. Food companies and farmers are already looking at ways to meet growing demands for food while shrinking their impact on the environment, he said.

"For the past decade, EDF has worked with grower networks in several states to test and prove sustainable methods that enable farmers to become more productive while minimizing nutrient losses to water and air that are costly to both the farmers' wallets and the environment. The good news is that they've managed to reduce nutrient losses by an average of 25 percent on half a million acres while increasing or maintaining yields. The challenge is figuring out how to scale up these practices."[8]

Festa pointed out that major brands such as General Mills were asking farmers in the Corn Belt and Southeast to grow the grains they use in their products in ways that decrease greenhouse gas emissions and reduce polluted fertilizer runoff. Their initiatives have prompted one large agribusiness, United Suppliers, to train their retailers to help farmers meet this growing demand. Festa wondered what we can we learn from them.

When United Suppliers caught wind of Walmart's pledge to reduce greenhouse gas emissions by, in part, asking its top suppliers to reduce fertilizer losses from cropping systems, they jumped at the chance to differentiate themselves in the marketplace.

"For us, it was a no brainer," Matt Carstens, United Suppliers vice president, told the EDF. "If Walmart and major food companies have identified fertilizer pollution as a business risk, it makes sense for us to help them address that risk. We want to be at the forefront of helping farmers meet these demands. It's a great business opportunity, not to mention the right thing to do. After all, farmers want the same thing. Reduced losses translate to increased profits and greater sustainability."

Festa said a second constructive step is to take a look at Congress: "Why not invite [members of Congress] to launch a serious discussion around one (if not all) of the nine points the co-authors list? Better yet, invite them to use their convening powers to focus attention on a solvable problem."

Festa said some critics would say the best thing Congress can do is shine a light on progress and stay out of the way, adding, "Others will point to specific interventions that could help scale up win-win practices. That is exactly the kind of debate that we need.

"There is a history of non-partisan debate on agricultural issues: Farm Bills usually pass Congress with large majorities," he concluded. "Let's call upon that tradition to figure out how we can meet human needs for food and water in ways that improve nature and the wellbeing of agricultural communities."

Addressing the National Food Policy Conference in April 2016, Sen. Debbie Stabenow (D-Mich.), the leading Democratic member on the Senate Agriculture Committee, stressed the importance of forming coalitions to get the right policies from Congress. She noted that obesity is a national security issue because military applicants are often too fat to fight.[9]

Translating Public Concern into Food Policy

Other food advocates have wondered how public concern could be translated into food policy. In an article in *The Nation*, author Michael Pollan speculated that states, territories and the health insurance industry would line up with the food movement. "When change depends on overcoming the influence of an entrenched power, it helps to have another powerful interest in your corner—an interest that stands to gain from reform," he wrote. "In the case of the tobacco industry, that turned out to be the states, which found themselves on the hook (largely because of Medicaid) for the soaring costs of smoking-related illnesses. So, under economic duress, states and territories joined to file suit against the tobacco companies to recover some of those costs, and eventually they prevailed."[10]

Pollan forecast that the food movement would find such allies, especially because the newly enacted Obamacare "put the government on the hook for the soaring costs of treating chronic illnesses—most of which are preventable and linked to diet. . . . The food movement is about to gain a powerful new partner, an industry that is beginning to recognize that it, too, has a compelling interest in issues like taxing soda, school lunch reform and even the Farm Bill."

Yet that alliance never came about. The United States has largely downplayed prevention of chronic illness and focused on treatment instead. Although diabetes cases more than tripled between 1990 and 2010, the health care industry responded by improving medical interventions to control blood sugar, serum cholesterol, and hypertension. Diabetics dying from the disease declined from about 41 percent to 17 percent.[11]

With most consumers opposed to warnings, taxation, and other regulations to discourage excess calorie consumption, the United States "has drifted toward a second-best policy of acceptance and treatment," wrote Robert Paarlberg, an adjunct professor at the Harvard Kennedy School of Government. "We try to live with that excess by providing physical accommodations and ramping up spending on medical treatments for the health risks associated with obesity."[12]

Industry Adjusts to Changes in Consumer Preferences

The food movement also faces an industry fearful of losing profits. In his book *Salt Sugar Fat: How the Food Giants Hooked Us*, Michael Moss, an investigative reporter for *The New York Times*, described a secret meeting in 1999 of the heads of America's 11 largest food companies. They gathered at Pillsbury headquarters in Minneapolis to discuss childhood obesity. Other companies represented included Nestlé, Kraft, Nabisco, General Mills, Procter & Gamble, Coca-Cola, Mars, Cargill, and Tate & Lyle.[13]

"What's driving the increase [in obesity]?" asked Michael Mudd, a Kraft vice president, in a slide presentation. He cited an abundance of "inexpensive, good-tasting, super-sized energy-dense foods." He urged his colleagues to pull back on their use of salt, sugar, and fat to reduce cravings for unhealthy foods.

But Stephen Sanger, head of General Mills, immediately challenged Mudd. "Don't talk to me about nutrition!" he declared, speaking on behalf of the typical American consumer. "Talk to me about taste. And if this stuff tastes better, don't run around trying to sell stuff that doesn't taste good."

Sanger's remarks carried the day, and the 11 CEOs decided to ride out the obesity crisis without making any changes.

Paul Marsden, a British writer, famously declared, "Business is all about solving people's problems—at a profit."[14] Consumer advocates have called attention to a variety of problems in the U.S. food system, and it's now up to the industry to solve them at a profit.

While receiving a leadership award from the James Beard Foundation in October 2015, Sam Kass, executive director of First Lady Michelle Obama's Let's Move! campaign, said food policy advocates are now insiders who will be more effective if they work within the food system and make compromises.

"One of the things about the White House is you get to see what is happening," Kass said in his acceptance speech. "What I am seeing is leadership of all kinds. I've seen it in regular families. We are in every single boardroom of every single food company for sure. Five years ago, that was not the case. Leadership needs to evolve. We are inside now. We don't have to throw stones. We are shaping policy."

Kass said he learned in the White House that successful advocates "have a clear and thought-out strategy, a strategy that must be rooted in pragmatism."[15]

Both the meat industry and the soda industry are adjusting their products to meet changes in consumer preferences. A *Packaged Facts* consumer survey in 2015 found about a third of respondents reported they were eating more meatless meals than in the past, and 15 percent said they avoid red meat completely. Some 70 percent of those surveyed said they still prefer to obtain their protein from animal sources.[16]

The survey found that 25 percent of consumers switched to healthier meat and poultry products in 2015, and over half were willing to spend more for better-for-you meat and poultry products. "These consumers are seeking out alternative shopping venues, such as farmers markets and natural food stores, as well as purchasing organic and natural meat and poultry products," according to the report.

Meatingplace editor Lisa Keefe suggested that the industry consider "going beyond meat—to look at Beyond Meat, the Bill Gates–backed (among other investors) maker of plant-based meat analogs in Manhattan Beach, Calif.; and Modern Meadow (lab-grown meat, based in Brooklyn); Gardein (also plant-based meat analogs, in Vancouver); Impossible Foods (plant-based analogs for meat, cheese and eggs, in Redwood City, Calif.); and Mark Post's cultured meat lab at Maastricht [Netherlands] University.

"The rest of the consumer packaged goods world has managed to shift the perception of dietary protein in consumers' minds from primarily animal-based products to, well, just about anything," she added. "Rather than try to shift it back, meat companies might consider going along for the ride. Rather than make and distribute only animal-derived, meat-based products, processors might redefine themselves as makers and distributors of protein products, then create or acquire companies and brands related to protein, regardless of origin."[17]

Keefe's suggestions foreshadowed launch of the Plant-Based Foods Association, whose mission is "to ensure a fair and competitive marketplace for businesses selling plant-based food intended to *replace* animal products such as meats, dairy and eggs . . . and educating consumers about the benefits of plant-based foods [emphasis added]." Veteran consumer advocate Michele Simon served as the group's part-time executive director.[18]

The plant-based group gave the heebie-jeebies to Hannah Thompson, communications director for the Animal Agriculture Alliance. She warned that Simon "is no stranger to anti-animal agriculture activism . . . [Simon] frequently refers to animal rights extremist groups HSUS [Humane Society of the United States] and Mercy for Animals as reliable sources on animal care. Her writing about animal agriculture is not exactly fair or balanced."[19]

In the soda industry, Coca-Cola bought the coconut water company ZICO, increased its ownership in Keurig coffee, and purchased a 30 percent stake in organic, cold-pressed-juice company Suja, according to *Business*

Insider. The company also launched new products, such as lower-calorie Coke Life and carbonated SmartWater.

Coke now claims more than 1,000 reduced-, low-, and no-calorie options, accounting for more than 25 percent of the beverages the company offers worldwide. Nearly half of Pepsi's beverage sales are now in low- or zero-calorie drinks, juice, or sports drinks.[20]

"We've been future-proofing our product portfolio, reshaping it to capitalize on consumers' increasing interest in health and wellness," PepsiCo CEO Indra Nooyi told reporters in April 2016. "Guilt-free products account for approximately 45 percent of our portfolio by revenue. The growth of our everyday nutrition products, which accounts for a quarter of our global net revenue, is outpacing the growth of the balance of the portfolio. And we've had a significant amount of activity underway to transform our portfolio."[21]

However, the CSPI later reported the Coca-Cola and PepsiCo are "borrowing a page from the tobacco industry playbook and investing heavily to boost consumption in low- and middle-income countries" such as Brazil, China, India, and Mexico, even though the incidence of obesity and diabetes is increasing rapidly in those countries.[22]

Grassroots Efforts Are Foundation of Change

Marion Nestle, the high-profile nutrition professor profiled in Chapter 9, sees the food movement gradually fixing the food system. At the close of the 2013 edition of her book *Food Politics*, she painstakingly reviewed the efforts of food advocates to reform current industry practices. She lamented that such efforts are frustrated at every turn by individual companies, trade associations, Congress, and federal agencies.

"I am often asked how I remain optimistic in light of the food industry's power to control and corrupt government," she reported. "That's easy: the food movement. Everywhere I look, I see positive signs of change. Healthier foods are more widely available than they were when *Food Politics* first appeared [in 2002]. Vast numbers of people, old and young, are interested in food and food issues and want to do something to improve food access and health."[23]

Nestle noted that more schools are serving healthier meals, more farmers markets are springing up, and more consumers care about humane farm animal production. When NYU started its food studies program in 1996, it was virtually alone, but many colleges and universities are now teaching students to think critically about the food system.

"Food issues are high on the agendas of local, state, national and international governments," she added. "The media cover such issues extensively and, as one reporter told me, so many food issues demand national attention that they constitute a Full Employment Act for the reporters assigned to cover them."

Nestle suggested that local efforts at food reform may succeed in countering industry public relations: "I see grassroots community efforts to create better and more equitable food systems as the best expression of democracy in action—of the people, by the people, for the people."

Grassroots efforts alone are unlikely to bring about a national food policy, but they are the foundation of such change. A generation ago, no one would have expected long-distance running to become mainstream or same-sex marriage to become acceptable. It took paradigm shifts to bring new perceptions.

With the advent of social media, advocates can speak directly to the public and urge changes from farm to fork. Tweeting and blogging keep the advocates in constant communication with millions of people. The cheap food policy that drove Congress and the industry for many years is losing ground to consumers who want fresh and nutritious food and kind treatment of animals.

Washington Post columnist Tamar Haspel lamented "a misguided, unconstructive discussion about several hot-button food-related issues, GMOs first among them," and then sought opinions from eight prominent food and agriculture experts. In a puzzling move, she dismissed food safety as an issue, declaring, "Our food is extremely safe." "Pretty much everybody I've talked with concedes that there are problems, . . . it's hard to find a villain," she wrote. "A complex set of interacting players and factors drives these problems, and solutions tend to be commensurately complex."[24]

Haspel interviewed UCS executive Ricardo Salvador; Agriculture Secretary Tom Vilsack; former Agriculture Secretary Dan Glickman; Bob Stallman, president of the American Farm Bureau Federation; Tom Colicchio, chef and cofounder of Food Policy Action; CSPI director Michael Jacobson; Laura Batcha, executive director of the Organic Trade Association; and Hugh Grant, CEO of Monsanto Company.

The food leaders' responses were all over the map, although several appealed for more dialogue on food policy. Vilsack said he was fed up with divisive conversations on food policy, and food should be a unifying issue. Glickman agreed that producers, processors, retailers, and consumers should be talking to one another. The Farm Bureau's Stallman said farmers and ranchers must be more engaged in the public debate.

Emphasizing the need to feed two billion more people by 2050, Monsanto's Grant opposed "needless friction" in the food policy debate. He cited conventional agriculture versus organic agriculture and other useless fights. OTA's Batcha warned against downplaying organic, opposing government favoring one production system over another.

Consumer advocates made strong proposals. The UCS's Salvador said government should invest in supporting the foods it recommends that we eat, such as fruits and vegetables. Food Policy Action's Colicchio urged that the ties between subsidies, conservation, and crop insurance be stronger. The CSPI's Jacobson recommended soda taxes and FDA limits or warning labels on the calorie content of drinks.

In a later *Washington Post* column looking forward to the 2016 New Year, Haspel said, "making the changes necessary to fix the problems in both our agriculture (pollution, greenhouse gases, soil erosion) and in our diets (too few vegetables, too many calories) requires a fundamental shift in attitude. We all have to pay attention to things that haven't been on the radar. . . . I'm focusing on [changes] that have a ripple effect: changes that, with luck, will beget other changes that, ultimately, can change the zeitgeist."[25]

Good Food Campaign by Arabella Advisors

Meanwhile, Arabella Advisors, a philanthropic consulting firm in Washington, D.C., launched a Good Food campaign in December 2015, proposing a list of 12 policy practices, some aligned with policies proposed by the four Berkeley movement leaders in 2014. The firm was founded by Eric Kessler, whose claim to fame includes persuading Tom Vilsack to become agriculture secretary in the Obama administration.

"The time to fix our food system has come," Kessler wrote in a blog. "We hope you will join us as we help to grow Good Food—a new system that produces delicious, nutritious, sustainable food that is accessible for all. . . . We believe that a unique opportunity has arrived to change America's food system for the better. The potential impacts are huge."[26]

"All of us believe that a policy environment that better supports Good Food is both possible and essential," said Kessler in a later blog. "A better policy environment can produce Good Food jobs, spur needed innovation and remove barriers to business expansion in our food system, and increase access to good food in communities across America . . .

"We hope our list will help drive a discussion about building a shared, ambitious, yet realistic Good Food policy strategy—one that enables funders, investors, advocates, and other stakeholders to effectively coordinate efforts, leverage one another's resources, and extend the impact of the food movement," he continued. "The forces that work counter to a Good Food system have a policy strategy, and they execute against it well. To counter their influence, we need a strategy of our own."[27]

The Arabella list includes the following:

- Private sector participation in new farmer initiatives that reward permanent job creation
- "Good Food Practitioner" (GFP) certification under USDA's Agriculture Marketing Service
- A path for citizenship for GFP-credentialed workers by reforming the current visa program
- A network of Regional Food Innovation Hubs within Farm Bill Title VII
- A competitive grant program for states that use federal funds to create conditions for Good Food innovation
- Passage of the PRIME Act (a bill to extend the exemption of custom-slaughtered animals from federal inspection requirements) to help address negative impacts of supply-chain consolidation and enable the sale of more regionally raised meat
- Encouragement of local food purchases within SNAP, aka food stamps, child nutrition, and other feeding programs
- Data for best practices in SNAP, streamlining access to benefits and improving nutrition criteria
- A tax incentive for businesses in food deserts that could produce healthy food, sell at least 50 percent of it locally. and employ a workforce that is at least 50 percent local
- An executive order mandating Ecosystem Service Restoration standards
- Incentives for small farms to transition to USDA Organic
- A food waste reduction program under USDA's Agricultural Marketing Service to encourage markets for imperfect produce and promote food waste recycling

Kessler said the Good Food initiative is likely aligned with Berkeley group's year-old proposal and not meant to be competitive: "It's some initial ideas to get the conversation going. It's far from final, but it's inclusive and realistic.

"Everything on the list we mention needs to happen and could potentially happen. It's policy, not politics. Both are critical. That's where we are now. There seems to be significant support. Funders and investors are putting money into the Good Food supply chain."[28]

National Strategy Needed to Combat Obesity/Diabetes

However, a bottom-up political movement influencing food companies isn't enough to combat the obesity/diabetes epidemic. A research article published in *The Lancet* forecast more than 40 percent of U.S. men and women will be obese by 2025.[29]

James Levine, codirector of the Mayo Clinic and Arizona State University Obesity Solutions, urged "a very clearly defined national strategy . . . that deals with the spectrum of the social challenges, the medical challenges and thinking it through a structure." Addressing a National Press Foundation event in February 2016, Levine pointed out the NIH and other leading organizations seek to combat the health crisis but too often ignore the politics. He stressed that food companies first and foremost respond to their shareholders.

"[Food companies'] job is to sell product, whatever that product might be," said Levine. "The sophistication that they operate at, in terms of their corporate strategies, in terms of their lobbying capabilities, in terms of their organization, in terms of responding to media reports on this or that, whatever it might be within the industry . . . is highly orchestrated and very, very well organized. I think at that the very least, in the scientific and public health quarters, we need to have a level of organization and sophistication that is certainly equal if not better."[30]

The next president should appoint a commission to address the obesity/diabetes crisis by recommending food policies, such as controlling advertising to children, much as the government fought to reduce tobacco smoking. We need to move ahead to fix the food system!

Notes

Foreword

1. M. Nestle, P. R. Lee, and R. B. Baron, "Nutrition Policy Update," in *Nutrition Update*, Vol. 1, ed. J. Weininger and G. M. Briggs (New York: Wiley, 1983), 285–313.

2. National Nutrition Consortium, "Guidelines for a National Nutrition Policy," *Nutrition Reviews* 32, no. 5 (1974): 153–157. The consortium included the American Institute of Nutrition, the American Society for Clinical Nutrition, the American Dietetic Association, and the Institute of Food Technology.

3. Michael Pollan, *In Defense of Food: An Eater's Manifesto. Food Rules: An Eater's Manual* (New York: Penguin Books, 2008).

Chapter One

1. Steven Perlberg, "Tom Brady Calls Coca-Cola 'Poison for Kids,'" *Wall Street Journal*, Oct. 12, 2015.

2. Interview and follow-up e-mail with Ricardo Salvador, Union of Concerned Scientists, Feb. 2, 2015.

3. Michael Pollan, Mark Bittman, Ricardo Salvador, and Olivier de Schutter, "How a National Food Policy Could Save Millions of American Lives," *Washington Post*, Nov. 7, 2014.

4. Interview with Ricardo Salvador, Feb. 2, 2015.

5. Pamela Hess, Arcadia Center for Sustainable Food and Agriculture, remarks at the USDA's Agriculture Outlook Forum, Feb. 25, 2016.

6. François Zeller, "Food Policy on New Federal Government Agenda," Food Secure Canada, Jan. 19, 2016.

7. "IDFA to Sponsor National Food Policy Conference," International Dairy Food Association, April 8, 2015.

8. "The Post's Sweet Talk, Circa 1978," *Washington Post*, May 19, 2008.

9. Michael Pertschuck, "Stoning the National Nanny: Congress and the FTC in the Late 70's," lecture to University of California School of Business Administration, Nov. 11, 1981.

10. Steve Clapp and Ellen Haas, "Empty Calories: The Reagan Record on Food Policy," Public Voice for Food and Health Policy, Oct. 1988.

11. "Tell President Obama: It's Time for a National Food Policy," Union of Concerned Scientists, Nov. 2014.

12. David Festa, "A National Food Policy? What the Bittman-Pollan Op-ed Missed," *Growing Returns*, Environmental Defense Fund, Nov. 18, 2014.

13. Twitter chat by Sen. Cory Booker (R-N.J.) and Reps. Rosa DeLauro (D-Conn.) and Chellie Pingree (R-Me.), Nov. 7, 2014.

14. Interview with David Acheson, The Acheson Group, Feb. 27, 2015.

15. Ibid.

16. Pollan et al., "How a National Food Policy Could Save Millions of American Lives."

17. Interview with Jenn Yates, Union of Concerned Scientists, March 2015.

Chapter Two

1. "Percent of Consumer Expenditures Spent on Food, Alcoholic Beverages and Tobacco That Were Consumed at Home, by Selected Countries, 2013," USDA Economic Research Service.

2. Danielle Nierenberg, "There Is No Such Thing as Cheap Food," *Food Tank* blog, April 7, 2015.

3. "Pathogens Causing US Foodborne Illnesses, Hospitalizations, and Deaths, 2000–2008," Centers for Disease Control and Prevention.

4. Kimberly Kindy and Brady Dennis, "*Salmonella* Outbreaks Expose Weaknesses in USDA Oversight of Chicken Parts," *Washington Post*, Feb. 6, 2014.

5. Sandra Hoffmann, Bryan Maculloch, and Michael Batz, "Economic Burden of Major Foodborne Illnesses Acquired in the United States," USDA Economic Research Service, May 2015.

6. Stephen Clapp, "Denmark Embarrasses U.S. When It Comes to *Salmonella*," *Food Chemical News*, April 23, 2015.

7. Rep. Rosa DeLauro (D-Conn.), "Statement on New Standards for Poultry Parts and Ground Poultry," Jan. 21, 2015.

8. Lynne Terry, "A Game of Chicken," *The Oregonian*, May 1, 2015.

9. Ibid.

10. "The Trouble with Chicken," PBS television broadcast, May 11, 2015.

11. "USDA Staff Urged Foster Farms Recall Almost Nine Months before It Took Effect," Food & Water Watch, June 4, 2015.

12. "Foster Farms Recognized for 75 Years of Leadership by Federal, State and Local Leaders," Foster Farms news release, June 16, 2015.

13. Ibid.

14. Ibid.
15. Ibid.
16. J. Cawley and C. Meyerhoefer, "The Medical Care Costs of Obesity: An Instrumental Variables Approach," *Journal of Health Economics* 31, no. 1 (2012): 219–230.
17. Uri Ladabaum, Ajitha Mannalithara, Parvathi A. Myer, and Gurkirpal Singhm, "Obesity, Abdominal Obesity, Physical Activity and Caloric Intake in US Adults: 1988 to 2010," *American Journal of Medicine*, March 12, 2014.
18. Ibid.
19. Ibid.
20. Anahad O'Connor, "Coca-Cola Funds Scientists Who Shift Blame for Obesity Away from Bad Diets," *New York Times*, Aug. 9, 2015.
21. Marion Nestle, "Let's Ask Marion: Can Exercise Balance Out Soda Drinking?" *Food Politics* blog, Aug. 14, 2015.
22. Anahad O'Connor, "Coke's Chief Scientist, Who Orchestrated Obesity Research, Is Leaving," *New York Times*, Nov. 24, 2015.
23. "United States Leads World Diabetes League among Developed Nations, While UK, Ireland and Australia among Those with Lowest Rates," International Diabetes Federation news release, Dec. 1, 2015.
24. W. Marder and S. Chang, "Childhood Obesity: Costs, Treatment Patterns, Disparities in Care, and Prevalent Medical Conditions," Thomson Medstat Research Brief, 2006.
25. "The Cost of Obesity to US Cities," *Gallup Business Journal*, Gallup-Healthways Well-Being Index 2012–2013, June 1, 2012.
26. Ibid.
27. L. Y. Wang, D. Chyen, S. Lee, et al., "The Association between Body Mass Index in Adolescence and Obesity in Adulthood," *Journal of Adolescent Health* 42, no. 5 (2008): 512–518.
28. Ibid.
29. E. A. Finkelstein et al., "Obesity and Severe Obesity Forecasts through 2030," *American Journal of Preventive Medicine* 42, no. 6 (2012): 563–570.
30. Hodan F. Wells and Jean C. Buzby, "Dietary Assessment of Major Trends in U.S. Food Consumption, 1970–2005," Economic Information Bulletin No. 33, USDA Economic Research Service, March 2008.
31. J. Foscolo, "CAFOs vs. Pasture and the Food Laws That Affect Meat Price," www.foodlawfirm.com, Jan. 5, 2012.
32. Ibid.
33. Ibid.
34. Ibid.
35. "Factory Farms Continue to Dominate U.S. Livestock Industry," Food & Water Watch, May 27, 2015.
36. Ibid.
37. "Animal Agriculture: Waste Management Practices," U.S. General Accounting Office, July 1999.

38. Testimony of Tom Elam, FarmEcon LLC, at Senate Agriculture Committee hearing, July 7, 2015.

39. Erika Fry, "What the Worst Bird Flu Epidemic in U.S. History Means for Farms," *Fortune*, June 25, 2015.

40. "What Are the Hidden Costs of Industrial Agriculture?" Union of Concerned Scientists, April 25, 2015.

Chapter Three

1. Wil S. Hylton, "A Bug in the System," *New Yorker*, Feb. 2, 2015.

2. Chuck Jolley, "Food Safety: An Interview with Nancy Donley," *Food Safety News*, April 8, 2011.

3. Barbara Kowalcyk, "Kevin's Story," Center for Foodborne Illness Research and Prevention website.

4. Tanya Roberts, "'Free Riders' and Weak Economic Incentives to Control Foodborne Pathogens," Center for Foodborne Illness Research & Prevention, July 2015.

5. "New Report: Food Industry's Drive for Profits over Safety Has Fueled Series of Illness Outbreaks, Puts Public at Risk," American Association for Justice, Sept. 16, 2015.

6. Marion Nestle, *Safe Food: The Politics of Food Safety* (Berkeley: University of California Press, 2003), 111.

7. Amber Healy, "FSIS: Baseline Study Not Necessary to Implement Non-O157 Testing," *Food Chemical News*, June 1, 2012.

8. Lydia Zuraw, "Mechanically Tenderized Beef Label Goes into Effect May 2016," *Food Safety News*, May 13, 2015.

9. Stephen Clapp, "DeLauro Urges OMB, USDA to Finalize Mechanically Tenderized Beef Rule," *Food Chemical News*, Feb. 19, 2015.

10. USDA Food Safety and Inspection Service, "USDA Finalizes Rule to Enhance Consumer Protection, Ensure Retailers Can Track Sources of Ground Meats," Dec. 11, 2015.

11. Stephen Clapp, "Denmark Embarrasses U.S. When It Comes to *Salmonella*," *Food Chemical News*, April 23, 2015.

12. Ibid.

13. William James, "FSIS' *Salmonella* Policies: Actions vs. Accomplishments," *Meatingplace*, Sept. 16, 2015.

14. "Consumer Federation of America Issues Analysis of USDA Meat and Poultry Inspection Program, Recommendations for Improvement," CFA report, April 28, 2015.

15. "Outbreaks of Antibiotic-Resistant *Salmonella* Require Urgent USDA Action, Says CSPI," Center for Science in the Public Interest news release, Oct. 1, 2014.

16. Stephen Clapp, "CFA Study Finds USDA Falling Short on Meat and Poultry Safety Oversight," *Food Chemical News*, April 28, 2015.

17. Ibid.

18. "Foodborne Illness Source Attribution Estimates for *Salmonella*, *Escherichia coli* O157 (*E. coli* O157), *Listeria monocytogenes (Lm)* and *Campylobacter* Using Outbreak Surveillance Data," Interagency Food Safety Analytics Collaboration (IFSAC) Project, Feb. 2015.

19. Stephen Clapp, "Regulatory Outlook: FSIS Focuses on *Salmonella* in Poultry Again This Year," *Food Chemical News*, Feb. 3, 2015.

20. Ingrid Mezo, "FSIS Releases Final Pathogen Standards for Chicken Parts, Ground Chicken and Turkey," *Food Chemical News*, Feb. 4, 2016.

21. Ibid.

22. Gardiner Harris, "President Promises to Bolster Food Safety," *New York Times*, March 14, 2009.

23. Dan Flynn, "All Five Convicted Former PCA Managers Now in Federal Custody," *Food Safety News*, Nov. 19, 2015.

24. Rick Schmitt, "As More Imported Foods Reach the Dinner Table, Holes Remain in FDA Safety Net," *Fair Warning*, June 26, 2014.

25. "DeLauro Urges Release of TPP Text on Sanitary and Phytosanitary Measures," Beltway Notebook, *Food Chemical News*, Oct. 22, 2015.

26. Lydia Zuraw, "Food Safety Groups Oppose Trans-Pacific Trade Partnership," *Food Safety News*, Nov. 10, 2015.

27. Lydia Zuraw, "FDA Finalizes FSMA Preventive Controls Rules for Human, Animal Foods," *Food Safety News*, Sept. 10, 2015.

28. Rep. Louise Slaughter (D-N.Y.), "Slaughter Blasts FDA for Failure to Act as Report Shows Large Increase in Antibiotic Use," Dec. 10, 2015.

29. Centers for Disease Control and Prevention, "Untreatable: Report by CDC Details Today's Drug-resistant Health Threats," Sept. 16, 2013.

30. Ibid.

31. Lydia Zuraw, "White House Calls for Action Plan to Address Antibiotic Resistance," *Food Safety News*, Sept. 18, 2014.

32. Ibid.

33. "FDA Proposes Rule to Collect Antimicrobial Sales and Distribution Data by Animal Species," Food and Drug Administration, May 19, 2015.

34. Stephen Clapp, "Antibiotic Resistance Council to Face Challenges in Fulfilling Obama's Mission," *Food Chemical News*, Sept. 30, 2015.

35. "AHI Statement on FDA Proposed Rule on Antibiotic Sales Data," Animal Health Institute, May 19, 2015.

36. "California Governor Signs Bill Regulating Animal Antibiotics," *Food Safety News*, Oct. 10, 2015.

37. "Progress on Antibiotics: California Leads the Way with a Tough New Law," *Washington Post* editorial, Oct. 26, 2015.

38. "Pew, Others Urge Increased Funding to Combat Superbugs," Pew Charitable Trusts, March 16, 2016.

39. Interview with Ron Phillips, vice president for legislation and public affairs, Animal Health Institute, Aug. 17, 2015.

40. "Letter to the US Chain Restaurant Industry: Prohibit the Routine Use of Antibiotics in Your Meat Supply," National Resources Defense Council, Sept. 15, 2015.

41. "SUBWAY® Restaurants Elevates Current Antibiotic-Free Policy," Subway Restaurants, Oct. 20, 2015.

42. Mark Graves, "Who Is Winning on Antibiotics and Branding: Beef, Pork or Chicken?" *Meatingplace* blog, July 17, 2015.

43. "The 2015 Food & Health Survey: Consumer Attitudes toward Food Safety, Nutrition & Health," Food Insight, International Food Information Council, May 8, 2015.

44. "EWG's Dirty Dozen Guide to Food Additives," Environmental Working Group, Nov. 12, 2014.

45. Tom Neltner and Maricel Maffini, "Generally Recognized as Secret: Chemicals Added to Food in the United States," National Resources Defense Council, April 2014.

46. Lydia Zuraw, "Settlement Reached in GRAS Lawsuit against FDA," *Food Safety News*, Oct. 21, 2014.

47. "Paper Box Chemicals No Longer Considered Safe by FDA for Contact with Food," *Food Safety News*, Jan. 5, 2016.

48. Michael Jacobson, Lisa Lefferts, and Laura MacCleerly, "Re: The Urgent Need for Warning Label on Synthetically Dyed Foods to Highlight Risks to Children's Health," letter to FDA officials from Center for Science in the Public Interest, March 15, 2016.

49. Lisa Lefferts, "Seeing Red: Time for Action on Food Dyes," Center for Science in the Public Interest, Jan. 19, 2016.

50. Ingrid Mezo, "Panera Pledges to Ditch Additives and Preservatives," *Food Chemical News*, May 5, 2015.

51. David Acheson, "A Single Food Safety Administration: Good, Bad or Impossible?" *The Acheson Group* blog, Feb. 5, 2015.

52. Declan Conroy, "CDC Official Says 2016 May Be 'a Tipping Point' in Foodborne Illness Prevention," *Food Chemical News*, Feb. 26, 2016.

Chapter Four

1. "Scientific Report of the 2015 Dietary Guidelines Advisory Committee," Feb. 19, 2015.

2. Amber Healy, "2010 Dietary Guidelines Not as Tough as Recommendations, but Food Industry and Nutrition Experts Pleased," *Food Chemical News*, Feb. 4, 2011.

3. Marion Nestle, "The 2015 Dietary Guidelines, at Long Last," *Food Politics* blog, Jan. 7, 2016.

4. Frank Hu, "Assessing the New U.S. Dietary Guidelines," *Harvard Gazette*, Jan. 11, 2016.

5. David L. Katz, "Change the Name of 'Dietary Guidelines for Americans'—It Is False Advertising," Change.org petition to the USDA, Jan. 10, 2016.

6. Joan Murphy, "FSMA Receives $104.5 Million Boost in FY 2016 Omnibus Bill," *Food Chemical News*, Dec. 16, 2015.

7. "Meat and Poultry Play Role in Healthy Diet, New Dietary Guidelines Affirm," North American Meat Institute, Jan. 7, 2016.

8. "2015 Dietary Guidelines for Americans Recommendation for Added Sugars Intake: Agenda Based, Not Science Based," Sugar Association, Jan. 7, 2016.

9. "Grocery Manufacturers Association Responds to Release of 2015 Dietary Guidelines for Americans," Jan. 7, 2016.

10. "New 'Dietary Guidelines' Recommends Eating Less Sugar & Meat," Center for Science in the Public Interest, Jan. 7, 2016.

11. "Dietary Guidelines Fail to Recommend Less Meat Consumption," Environmental Working Group, Jan. 7 2016.

12. "United Fresh Statement on Release of the 2015–2020 Dietary Guidelines for Americans," United Fresh Produce Association, Jan. 7, 2016.

13. Rep. Rosa DeLauro (D-Conn.), "DeLauro Statement on the New Dietary Guidelines," Jan. 7, 2016.

14. "Scientific Report of the 2015 Dietary Guidelines Advisory Committee," Feb. 19, 2015.

15. Dariush Mozaffarian and David Ludwig, "Viewpoint," *Journal of the American Medical Association*, June 23/30, 2015.

16. Ashley Welch, "'Ultra-Processed' Foods a Huge Chunk of American Diet," *CBS News*, March 10, 2016.

17. Stephen Clapp, "Meat Industry Questions 'Sustainability' in Dietary Guidelines Discussion," *Food Chemical News*, Oct. 23, 2014.

18. Glenn Lammi, "Advisory Committee's Violations of Federal Law Threaten Credibility of 2015 Dietary Guidelines," *Legal Pulse*, Washington Legal Foundation, Dec. 3, 2015.

19. "Scientific Report of the 2015 Dietary Guidelines Advisory Committee," Feb. 19, 2015.

20. Stephen Clapp, "NAMI criticizes Dietary Guidelines Advice on Red and Processed Meat," *Food Chemical News*, Feb. 19, 2015.

21. "Vilsack Promises Dietary Guidelines 'within the Lines,'" Beltway Notebook, *Food Chemical News*, March 5, 2015.

22. Stephen Clapp, "Vilsack and Merrigan Seek Support for SNAP and School Meal Standards," *Food Chemical News*, April 23, 2015

23. Kathleen Merrigan et al., "Designing a Sustainable Diet," *Science*, Oct. 1, 2015.

24. Clapp, "Vilsack and Merrigan."

25. Nina Teicholz, "The Scientific Report Guiding the US Dietary Guidelines: Is It Scientific?" *BMJ*, Sept. 23, 2015.

26. Bonnie Liebman, "BMJ Publishes Error-Laden Attack on Dietary Guidelines Report," Center for Science in the Public Interest, Sept. 23, 2015.

27. Stephen Clapp, "Food Industry and Health Advocates Clash in Dietary Guidelines Comments," *Food Chemical News*, May 12, 2015.

28. Ibid.

29. Ibid.

30. Ibid.

31. Lisa M. Keefe, "October's Gonna Be Scary: NAMI's Betsy Booren on Upcoming IARC Review," *Meatingplace*, July 27, 2015.

32. "Protein: It's What's for Breakfast, Lunch and Dinner," Beltway Notebook, *Food Chemical News*, April 20, 2015.

33. Clapp, "Food Industry and Health Advocates Clash."

34. "House Agriculture Committee Leaders Want Answers on DGAC Comment Review Process," Beltway Notebook, *Food Chemical News*, May 15, 2015.

35. Ibid.

36. Joan Murphy, "DGAC, Health Groups Attack Riders for 'Gutting' Dietary Guidelines," *Food Chemical News*, June 24, 2015.

37. "Beef and Other Food Business Donations Funding Congressional Meddling on Nutrition," Center for Science in the Public Interest, June 25, 2015.

38. Stephen Clapp, "Consumer Advocates and Industry Representatives Spar over DGAC Report," *Food Chemical News*, March 24, 2015.

39. Clapp, "Food Industry and Health Advocates Clash."

Chapter Five

1. "Healthy Food for a Healthy World: Limit Food Marketing to Children," Chicago Council for Global Affairs, June 17, 2015.

2. Michael Pertschuck, "Stoning the National Nanny: Congress and the FTC in the Late 70's," lecture to University of California School of Business Administration, Nov. 11, 1981.

3. "Tootsie Roll Urged to Stop Marketing Junk Food Directly to Children," Center for Science in the Public Interest, Dec. 4, 2014.

4. Rebecca M. Schermbeck and Lisa M. Powell, "Nutrition Recommendations and the Children's Food and Beverage Advertising Initiative's 2014 Approved Food and Beverage Product List," *Preventing Chronic Disease*, Centers for Disease Control and Prevention, April 23, 2015.

5. Dale L. Kunkel, Jessica S. Castonguay, and Christine R. Filer, "Evaluating Industry Self-Regulation of Food Marketing to Children," *American Journal of Preventive Medicine*, Aug. 2015.

6. Roberto A. Ferdman, "Why Parents Should Be Worried about the Types of Food Their Kids Are Seeing on TV," *Washington Post*, May 11, 2015.

7. Jennifer L. Harris, Megan LoDolce, Cathryn Dembek, and Marlene B. Schwartz, "Sweet Promises: Candy Advertising to Children and Implications for Industry Self-Regulation," *Appetite*, Rudd Center for Food Policy & Obesity, Sept. 2015.

8. Ibid.

9. Stephen Clapp, "Child Advertising Restrictions Seen Failing to Meet Health Standards," *Food Chemical News*, April 27, 2015.

10. Elaine D. Kolish, "It's Time to Can the 'We Can: Go, Slow, Whoa' Categories: CFBAI Refutes Article in *American Journal of Preventative Medicine*," Children's Food and Beverage Advertising Initiative, May 18, 2015.

11. "Statement of Elaine Kolish, VP and Director, BBB's Children's Food and Beverage Advertising Initiative (CFBAI) on the Report on Candy Advertising Published in the Journal *Appetite*," Sept. 10, 2015.

12. "Cereals Advertised to Children Are Improving under Self-Regulation," Children's Food and Beverage Advertising Initiative, Nov. 5, 2015.

13. "Voluntary Nutrition Criteria Mean Children See Ads for Healthier Foods," Children's Food and Beverage Advertising Initiative, Dec. 21, 2015.

14. Stephen Clapp, "Burger King Joins Other Big Three in Dropping Soda from Kids' Meals," *Food Chemical News*, March 10, 2015.

15. "Jack in the Box Removes Soda from Its Kids' Menus," Center for Science in the Public Interest, Feb. 10, 2016.

16. Michael Moss, *Salt Sugar Fat: How the Food Giants Hooked Us* (New York: Random House, 2013).

17. "[End to Child Obesity] Commission Presents Its Final Report, Calling for High-Level Action to Address Major Health Challenge," World Health Organization, Jan. 25, 2016.

18. Steven L. Gortmaker et al., "Three Interventions That Reduce Childhood Obesity Are Projected to Save More Than They Cost to Implement," *Health Affairs*, Nov. 2015.

19. Chase Purdy, "American Beverage Association Bristles at Soda Tax Study," *ProPolitico Morning Agriculture*, Nov. 4, 2015.

20. "Soda Industry Spending against Public Health Tops $100 Million," Center for Science in the Public Interest, Aug. 25, 2015.

21. "Junk Food at Checkout Aisles Promotes Overeating, Says CSPI Report," Center for Science in the Public Interest, Aug. 3, 2015.

22. "Healthier Checkout Lanes Coming to Aldi Supermarkets," Center for Science in the Public Interest, Jan. 12, 2016.

23. Stephen Clapp, "School Nutrition Association Accused of Neglecting Child Obesity Problems," *Food Chemical News*, July 12, 2013.

24. Ibid.

25. Ibid.

26. Stephen Clapp, "School Nutrition Association Fails to Penalize Its Former Lobbyists," *Food Chemical News*, March 26, 2015.

27. Ibid.

28. Stephen Clapp, "School Food Fight Heats Up with Proposal to Ditch Fruit and Veggie Requirement," *Food Chemical News*, Jan. 30, 2015.

29. Ibid.

30. Ibid.

31. Sen. John Hoeven (R-N.D.), "Hoeven Introduces Legislation to Provide Permanent Flexibility for Sodium and Grain Requirements in School Meal Programs," March 2, 2015.

32. "Food Industry Evolves to Meet School Lunch Challenges," *ProPolitico Morning Agriculture*, Aug. 10, 2015.

33. "The Urban School Food Alliance and the Alliance for a Healthier Generation Leverage $3 Billion in Purchasing Power for Market-Driven Change in School Meals," Oct. 21, 2015.

34. "A Matter of National Security," Beltway Notebook, *Food Chemical News*, Sept. 27, 2010.

35. Stephen Clapp, "Vilsack Enlists Medical Experts to Defend Current School Meal Standards," *Food Chemical News*, March 19, 2015.

36. Ibid.

37. "SNA Releases 2016 Position Paper Calling for Increased Funding for School Meal Programs," School Nutrition Association, Feb. 9, 2016.

38. Bettina Elias Siegel, "The Real Problem with Lunch," *New York Times*, Jan. 15, 2016.

Chapter Six

1. Nick Kotz, *Let Them Eat Promises* (New York: Doubleday Anchor Books, 1971), 198.

2. Interview with Robert Greenstein, Center on Budget and Policy Priorities, Oct. 18, 2013.

3. Hilary Mantel, *Bring Up the Bodies: A Novel* (New York: Holt, 2012).

4. "Pass the Plate," Beltway Notebook, *Food Chemical News*, April 27, 2012.

5. "Hunger in America: The Definitions, Scope, Causes, History and Status of the Problem of Hunger in the United States," America's Second Harvest, 2004.

6. Ibid.

7. National Commission on Hunger, "Freedom from Hunger: An Achievable Goal for the United States of America," 2015.

8. Ibid.

9. "FRAC Launches the Campaign to End Childhood Hunger," FRAC History, Food Research and Action Center website, 1991.

10. "Effects of Poverty, Hunger and Homelessness on Children and Youth," American Psychological Association, 2015.

11. "Hunger in America," America's Second Harvest, 2004.

12. Ibid.

13. Ibid.

14. Stephen Clapp, "House Votes 216–208 to Approve Farm Programs-Only Farm Bill," *Food Chemical News*, July 12, 2013.

15. "Farm Bill's Fate Unclear as House Republicans Seek to Split Off Food Stamps," *Food Chemical News*, July 10, 2013.

16. Daren Bakst and Rachel Sheffield, "Six Reforms for the House Farm Bill," Heritage Foundation, June 27, 2013.

17. Ibid.

18. "How Hungry Is America?" Food Research and Action Center (FRAC), April 2015.

19. Chairman Paul Ryan (R-Wis.), "Expanding Opportunity in America: A Discussion Draft from the House Budget Committee," July 24, 2014.

20. Robert Greenstein, "Commentary: Ryan 'Opportunity Grant' Proposal Would Likely Increase Poverty and Shrink Resources for Poverty Programs over Time," Center on Budget and Policy Priorities, July 25, 2014.

21. Scott Winship, "Would a Block-Granted Safety Net Mean Less Aid to Families?" *Forbes*, July 31, 2014.

22. Robert Greenstein, "Commentary: The Ryan 'Opportunity Grant' Proposal—A Reply to Scott Winship," Center on Budget and Policy Priorities, Sept. 9, 2014.

23. Susan Cornwell, "House Speaker Ryan Wants Obamacare Replacement, Welfare Cuts," Reuters, Dec. 4, 2015.

24. "The Effects of Potential Cuts in SNAP Spending on Households with Different Amounts of Income," Congressional Budget Office, March 16, 2015.

25. Stephen Clapp, "Vilsack and Merrigan Seek Support for SNAP and School Meal Standards," *Food Chemical News*, April 23, 2015.

26. National Commission on Hunger, "Freedom from Hunger: An Achievable Goal for the United States of America," 2015.

27. Jenny Hopkinson, "Landmark Hunger Report Stirs Pot on SNAP Limits," *ProPolitico Morning Agriculture*, Jan. 5, 2016.

28. National Commission on Hunger, "Freedom from Hunger."

29. Ed Bolen et al., "More Than 500,000 Adults Will Lose SNAP Benefits in 2016 as Waivers Expire," Center on Budget and Policy Priorities, Jan. 5, 2016.

Chapter Seven

1. Nick Kotz, *Let Them Eat Promises: The Politics of Hunger in America* (Upper Saddle River, N.J.: Prentice Hall, 1970), 1.

2. Ibid., 2.

3. Ibid., 2.

4. Ibid., 3.

5. Ibid., 8.

6. Ibid., 18.

7. Ibid., 19.

8. Ibid., 107.

9. Ibid., 50.

10. Ibid., 172.

11. Ibid., *Washington Post* blurb on back cover.

12. Interview with Nick Kotz, March 6, 2014.

13. Kotz, *Let Them Eat Promises*, 123.
14. Ibid., 130.
15. Interview with Nick Kotz.
16. Kotz, *Let Them Eat Promises*, 181.
17. Ibid., 234.
18. Ibid.
19. Interview with Richard W. Boone, Jan. 24, 2014.
20. Interview with Nick Kotz.
21. E-mail from Nancy Amidei, University of Washington, June 20, 2015.
22. Interview with Michael Jacobson, Dec. 19, 2013.
23. *Center for Science in the Public Interest Newsletter*, April 1971.
24. Interview with Michael Jacobson.
25. CSPI 40th anniversary report, 2011.
26. CSPI entry, in *Encyclopedia of the Consumer Movement* (Santa Barbara, Calif.: ABC-CLIO, 1997), 90.
27. Kotz, *Let Them Eat Promises*, 187.
28. Ibid., 184.
29. Author Steve Clapp's personal recollections.
30. Interview with Rodney Leonard, July 5, 2013.
31. Ibid.
32. Kris Shepard, *Rationing Justice: Poverty Lawyers and Poor People in the Deep South* (Baton Rouge: Louisiana State University Press, 2009), 104.
33. Community Nutrition Institute (CNI) entry, in *Encyclopedia of the Consumer Movement*, 118.
34. Interview with Ron Pollack and follow-up e-mail, Dec. 2, 2013.
35. Recorded phone call between Pres. Lyndon Johnson and Sen. James O. Eastland (D-Miss.), University of Virginia Miller Center, June 23, 1964.
36. Interview with Ron Pollack.
37. "FRAC History," Food Research and Action Center website, www.frac.org.
38. "About FRAC," www.frac.org.

Chapter Eight

1. Interview with Carol Tucker-Foreman, Oct. 8, 2013.
2. Candy Arthur, "At Agriculture, Carol Foreman Fights for Consumers—No Ifs, Ands or Earls Butz about It," *People*, Nov. 28, 1977.
3. Interview with Carol Tucker-Foreman.
4. Ibid.
5. James Kilpatrick, "USDA's 'Dragon Lady' Is Busy Breathing Fire Again," *Washington Star*, Jan. 8, 1979.
6. Interview with Carol Tucker-Foreman.
7. "Mark Hegsted's Personal Account of the Dietary Goals," written in the early 1990s, *Food Politics* blog, Aug. 18, 2009.
8. Interview with Carol Tucker-Foreman.

9. Stephen Clapp, "Dietary Guidelines Advisory Panel Fights Back on Saturated Fat Issue," *Food Chemical News*, Sept. 17, 2014.

10. Elizabeth Becker, "Agriculture Chief Disavows Plan to Eliminate Test on School Beef," *New York Times*, April 6, 2001.

11. Interview with Robert Greenstein, Center on Budget and Policy Priorities, Oct. 18, 2013.

12. Ibid.

13. Ibid.

14. Interview with Carol Tucker-Foreman.

15. Ibid.

16. Interview with Robert Greenstein.

17. Interview with Richard W. Boone, Jan. 24, 2014.

18. Interview with Robert Greenstein.

19. Ibid.

20. Interview with former senator Robert Dole (R-Kans.), Nov. 12, 2013.

21. Interview with Ellen Haas, Oct. 2, 2013.

22. Susan Levine, *School Lunch Politics: The Surprising History of America's Favorite Welfare Program* (Princeton, NJ: Princeton University Press, 2008).

23. Rep. Pat Roberts (R-Kan.), "Healthy Meals for Healthy Children," *capitolwords*, Sunlight Foundation, May 16, 1996.

24. Sara Fritz, "Controversies Crop Up around Agriculture Official," *Los Angeles Times*, Oct. 5, 1996.

25. Interview with Ellen Haas.

26. E-mail from Ed Clooney, Congressional Hunger Center, Jan. 2, 2014.

Chapter Nine

1. Paul Simon, *The Politics of World Hunger* (New York: Harper's Magazine Press, 1973).

2. Arthur Simon, *The Rising of Bread for the World: An Outcry of Citizens against Hunger* (Costa Mesa, Calif.: Paulist Press, 2009), 74.

3. Ibid., 81.

4. Ibid., 92.

5. Ibid., 96.

6. David Beckmann and Arthur Simon, *Grace at the Table: Ending Hunger in God's World* (Washington, D.C.: Bread for the World Institute 1999), 201.

7. Beckmann and Luck, 2010 laureates, the World Food Prize (www.worldfoodprize.org).

8. "Freedom from Hunger: An Achievable Goal for the United States of America," National Commission on Hunger, 2015.

9. Letterhead, Interfaith Action for Economic Justice, Oct. 18, 1983.

10. Steven Tipton, *Public Pulpits: Methodists and Mainline Churches in the Moral Argument of Public Life* (Chicago: University of Chicago Press 2008), 283.

11. Ibid., 285.

12. Ibid., 287.
13. Ibid., 289.
14. Ibid., 291.
15. Ibid., 293.
16. Ibid., chap. 8.
17. Ibid., chap. 8.
18. Interview with Marian Burros, *New York Times*, Dec. 3, 2013.
19. Interview with Carol Tucker-Foreman, Oct. 8, 2013.
20. Interview with Marian Burros.
21. Matthew Benson, "La Vida Locavore: Food Revolutionary Joan Dye Gussow," *Organic Gardening*, Nov. 15, 2011.
22. Michael Pollan, *In Defense of Food: An Eater's Manifesto* (New York: Penguin, 2008), 26.
23. Interview with Joan Dye Gussow, Nov. 29, 2013.
24. Joan Dye Gussow, "Children's Television Commercials: A Content Analysis," *Journal of Nutrition Education*, April 1974.
25. Interview with Joan Gussow.
26. Paula Brookmire, "The Great Food Debate: He Says Fortify, She Says Educate," *Milwaukee Journal*, July 5, 1973.
27. Interview with Joan Gussow.
28. Ibid.
29. Joan Gussow, "Realism Is Not a Realistic Option," keynote address, Marion Institute, May 8, 2013.
30. Marian Burros, "A New View on Training Food Experts," *New York Times*, June 19, 1996.
31. Marion Nestle, *Food Politics: How the Food Industry Influences Nutrition and Health* (Berkeley: University of California Press, 2002).
32. Ibid.
33. Ibid.
34. Ibid.
35. Steven Milloy, "New Nutrition Book Choking on Bad Science," *Fox News*, Feb. 22, 2002.
36. Mary Grabar, "Food Fetish on Campus," John William Pope Center, March 12, 2014.
37. Marion Nestle, "Is Food Studies the End of Civilization? Really?" *Food Politics* blog, March 21, 2014.

Chapter Ten

1. Howard Buffett, farmer and conservationist, remarks at the USDA's Agricultural Outlook Forum, Feb. 25, 2016.
2. Laura Batcha, Organic Trade Association, remarks at the USDA's Agricultural Outlook Forum, Feb. 25, 2016.

3. Chris Clayton, *The Elephant in the Cornfield: The Politics of Agriculture and Climate Change* (n.p.: Amazon Digital, 2015).

4. Ibid.

5. "Climate Change, Global Food Security and the U.S. Food System," U.S. Global Change Research Program, Dec. 2015.

6. Letter to global leaders from food companies, organized by Ceres nonprofit organization, Oct. 1, 2015.

7. Joel K. Bourne, *The End of Plenty: The Race to Feed a Crowded World* (New York: Norton, 2015), 147.

8. Ibid., 148.

9. Ibid., 142.

10. Secretary of State John Kerry, speech in Milan, Oct. 17, 2015.

11. Bourne, *The End of Plenty*, 148.

12. Ibid., 316.

13. "Global Food Security," Office of the Director of National Intelligence, Sept. 22, 2015.

14. "Cultivating Equality: Delivering Just and Sustainable Food Systems in a Changing Climate," Food Tank, CARE, CGIAR, and Climate Change, Agriculture and Food Security; Oct. 2015.

15. Kathleen Merrigan, "Redesigning Food Policy in and Outside of Our Nation's Capital," speech at University of Maryland College of Agriculture and Natural Resources, May 20, 2014.

16. "FAO Launches Digital Platform on Family Farming," UN Food and Agriculture Organization, June 16, 2015.

17. "Family Farmers Feed the World," Food Tank, Oct. 26, 2015.

18. "Healthy Food for a Healthy World: Leveraging Agriculture and Food to Improve Global Nutrition," Chicago Council on Global Affairs, April 16, 2015.

19. Marco Springmann, "Impact of Climate Change on Food Production Could Cause over 500,000 Extra Deaths in 2050," *The Lancet*, March 2, 2016.

20. "USDA and EPA Join with Private Sector, Charitable Organizations to Set Nation's First Food Waste Reduction Goals," USDA news release, Sept. 16, 2015.

21. "GMA Applauds National Food Waste Reduction Goals," Grocery Manufacturers Association, Sept. 16, 2015.

22. Chris Arsenault, "Rich Nations Spend $250 Billion on Farm Subsidies, Hurting Poor Growers—Study," Reuters, Oct. 16, 2015.

23. Clayton, *The Elephant in the Cornfield.*

24. Carter Brace, "Ricardo Salvador Criticizes Farming Industry as Part of Food Day Programming," *The Dartmouth* (Hanover, N.H.), Oct. 27, 2015.

25. Jerry Hatfield, USDA soil scientist, in Clayton, *The Elephant in the Cornfield*, 180.

26. Clayton, *The Elephant in the Cornfield*, 181.

Chapter Eleven

1. Marion Nestle, *Safe Food: The Politics of Food Safety* (Berkeley: University of California Press, 2003), 110.

2. Ken Jacobs, Ian Perry, and Jenifer MacGillvary, "The High Public Cost of Low Wages," University of California Berkeley's Center for Labor Research and Education, April 13, 2015.

3. Eve Tahmincioglu, "The 8 Lowest-Paying Jobs in America," *NBC Nightly News*, July 12, 2010.

4. "Cesar Chavez: An American Hero," Food Tank, March 29, 2014.

5. "Low Wages," National Farm Worker Ministry website, 2016.

6. Gregory Bloom, "Help Wanted: Will Train. No Experience Necessary. $15 per Hour with Benefits. Start Tomorrow," *Meatingplace*, Nov. 19, 2015.

7. Tess Owen, "The Big Chicken Industry Really Treats Its Workers Like Shit," Oxfam America, Oct. 27, 2015.

8. Oliver Gottfried, speech delivered to Food Tank webinar, "The Human Cost of Cheap Chicken," Nov. 12, 2015.

9. "Worker Advocates Demand Poultry CEOs Hike Wages, Improve Safety," *Meatingplace*, Nov. 20, 2015.

10. Oliver Gottfried remarks at Food Tank webinar, Nov. 12, 2015.

11. Steve Sayer, "OSHA Zeroing In on Poultry Establishments—and Then Some . . . ," *Meatingplace*, Nov. 6, 2015.

12. "Poultry Industry Cites Continuous Progress on Worker Safety Record, Responds to Oxfam Report," National Chicken Council and U.S. Poultry and Egg Association, Oct. 26, 2015.

13. Lisa Keefe, "Stepped-Up Scrutiny Puts Poultry under a Spotlight," *Meatingplace*, Feb. 12, 2016.

14. Letter to Agriculture Secretary Tom Vilsack on HIMP hog inspection from 60 Members of Congress, Jan. 19, 2016.

15. Mortimer B. Zuckerman, "Income Inequality Makes a Mockery of the American Dream," *U.S. News & World Report*, March 27, 2015.

16. Ibid.

17. "Remarks of the President in the State of the Union Address," White House Office of the Press Secretary, Feb. 12, 2013.

18. Richard Ghiselli and Jing Ma, "Study: Raising Wages to $15 an Hour for Limited-Service Restaurant Employees Would Raise Prices 4.3 Percent," Purdue University, July 27, 2015.

19. DaeHwan Kim and John Paul Leigh, "Estimating the Effects of Wages on Obesity," *Journal of Occupational and Environmental Medicine*, May 2010.

20. David O. Meltzer and Zhuo Chen, "The Impact of Minimum Wage Rates on Body Weight in the United States," National Bureau of Economic Research, April 2011.

21. Dale Belman and Paul Wolfson, *What Does the Minimum Wage Do?* (Kalamazoo, Mich.: W. E. Upjohn Institute for Employment Research, 2014), 401.

22. David Card and Alan B. Krueger, "Minimum Wages and Employment: A Case Study of the Fast Food Industry in New Jersey and Pennsylvania," National Bureau of Economic Research, Oct. 1993.

23. "It's Time to Raise the Minimum Wage," Economic Policy Institute and National Employment Law Project, April 23, 2015.

24. Paul R. La Monica, "Popeye's CEO on Fast Food Wage Hikes: 'Life Will Go On,'" *CNN Money*, Nov. 12, 2015.

25. "It's Time to Raise the Minimum Wage."

26. Catherine Rampell, "Moving the Needle on Pay," *Washington Post* Writers Group, April 7, 2015.

Chapter Twelve

1. Paul Shapiro, Humane Society of the United States, remarks to a Food Tank luncheon, Nov. 12, 2015.

2. Barry Estabrook, "Meet Your Meat: Feedlot vs. Free-Range," *Politics of the Plate* blog, Jan. 2, 2012.

3. Nathanael Johnson, "Temple Grandin Digs In on the Practical Side of What Animals Want," *Grist*, July 22, 2015.

4. Joshua Miller, "Animal-Welfare Vote May Break New Ground," *Boston Globe*, Nov. 1, 2015.

5. Stephen Clapp, "Six Egg-Producing States Back in Court to Challenge California's Hen Cage Ban," *Food Chemical News*, Nov. 10, 2014.

6. Stephen Clapp, "Six States Challenge California's New Egg Law on Food Safety Grounds," *Food Chemical News*, March 9, 2015.

7. "Aramark Establishes Animal Welfare Policy," Aramark, April 30, 2015.

8. Stephanie Strom, "Putting the Chicken before the Egg," *New York Times*, Nov. 23, 2015.

9. Yvonne Vizzier Thaxton, "Cage-Free Marketing vs. Science vs. Public Opinion," *Meatingplace* blog, Feb. 16, 2016.

10. Stephen Clapp, "Massachusetts Is New Cage-Free Eggs Battleground, Thanks to McDonald's," *Food Chemical News*, Sept. 23, 2015.

11. Miller, "Animal-Welfare Vote."

12. Joshua Miller, "Amid Push for Cage-Free Eggs in Mass., Advocates Laud McDonald's," *Boston Globe*, Sept. 9, 2015.

13. Joshua Miller, "Egg Industry to Fight Ballot Initiative," *Boston Globe*, Sept. 30, 2015.

14. Clapp, "Massachusetts Is New Cage-Free Eggs Battleground."

15. Joshua Miller, "Animal-Welfare Vote."

16. Declan Conroy, "Hilton Commits to Cage-Free Eggs, Gestation Crate-Free Pork," *Food Chemical News*, April 6, 2015.

17. "Crammed into Gestation Crates," Humane Society of the United States, Feb. 19, 2015.

18. "Criminal Charges Filed against Tyson Foods and Six Slaughterhouse Workers Caught on Hidden Camera Torturing Animals," Mercy for Animals news release, Oct. 28, 2015.

19. "Animal Rights Group Files Criminal Misdemeanor Affidavits against Tyson and Six Employees," *Food Safety News*, Oct. 28, 2015.

20. Dan Flynn, "Federal Judge in Boise Strikes Down Idaho's New 'Ag-Gag' Law," *Food Safety News*, Aug. 4, 2015.

21. Dan Flynn, "Idaho Appeals Federal Court Decision Overturning State's Ag-Gag Law," *Food Safety News*, Dec. 17, 2015.

22. Stephen Clapp, "North Carolina Legislature Overturns Governor's 'Ag-Gag' Bill Veto," *Food Chemical News*, June 8, 2015.

23. Ibid.

24. Ibid.

25. Declan Conroy, "Advocacy Groups Sue North Carolina over 'Ag Gag' Law," *Food Chemical News*, Jan. 13, 2016.

26. *New York Times* editorial board, "No More Exposés in North Carolina," Feb. 1, 2016.

27. Richard Raymond, "Welfare for Animals and Cull Cows," *Meatingplace*, Oct. 6, 2014.

28. Rita Jane Gabbett, "Leading with the Science Isn't Always the Best Way to Approach Consumers about Animal Welfare," *Meatingplace*, Oct. 2014.

29. Hannah Thompson, "In Their Words: What Animal Rights Organizations Say behind Closed Doors," *Meatingplace*, Sept. 22, 2015.

30. Ibid.

31. Ibid.

32. Hannah Thompson, "Animal Rights Groups Eyeing Investors," *Meatingplace*, Feb. 9, 2016.

33. Miller, "Animal-Welfare Vote."

34. Gabbett, "Leading with the Science."

35. Mark Graves, "Consumer Confusion?" *Meatingplace*, Feb. 4, 2016.

36. "Organic Livestock and Poultry Practices," USDA's Agricultural Marketing Service proposed rule, AMS website, April 7, 2016.

Chapter Thirteen

1. Declan Conroy, "Beltway Notebook: Presidential Candidates Asked to Commit to Food Policy Changes," *Food Chemical News*, Jan. 20, 2016.

2. Ricardo Salvador, Union of Concerned Scientists, speaking at Food Tank luncheon, Nov. 12, 2015.

3. "Plate of the Union Campaign in Des Moines Jan. 21 to Meet with Presidential Campaigns," Food Policy Action, Jan. 20, 2016.

4. "A Call to Presidential Action: Elevating Food and Agriculture as a National Priority," AGree, Jan. 2016.

5. Bob Carpenter, consultant to Republican politicians, remarks at National Food Policy Conference, April 6, 2016.

6. Jerry Hagstrom, *The Hagstrom Report*, remarks at National Food Policy Conference, April 6, 2016.

7. Celinda Lake, political strategist for Democrats, remarks at National Food Policy Conference, April 6, 2016.

8. David Festa, "A National Food Policy? What the Bittman-Pollan Op-ed Missed," *Growing Returns*, Environmental Defense Fund, Nov. 18, 2014.

9. Sen. Debbie Stabenow (D-Mich.), remarks at National Food Policy Conference, April 7, 2016.

10. Michael Pollan, "How Change Is Going to Come in the Food System," *Nation*, Sept. 14, 2011.

11. Robert Paarlberg, "Why We Can't Get Obesity under Control," *Washington Post*, Dec. 25, 2015.

12. Ibid.

13. Michael Moss, *Salt Sugar Fat: How the Food Giants Hooked Us* (New York: Random House, 2013), 1–3.

14. Paul Marsden, *SmartBrief*, Nov. 2015.

15. Sam Kass, acceptance speech at James Beard Foundation awards, *The Hagstrom Report,* Oct. 23, 2015.

16. "Meat and Poultry: U.S. Retail Market Trends and Opportunities," *Packaged Facts*, Dec. 24, 2015.

17. Lisa M. Keefe, "The Center of My Plate: The Editor's Blog—Hormel's Next Acquisition," *Meatingplace*, Jan. 18, 2016.

18. Michele Simon, "Our Mission," Plant-Based Foods Association website, March 22, 2016.

19. Hannah Thompson, "Meat Alternative Groups Upping Their Game and Look Who Is Leading Them," *Meatingplace* blog, March 22, 2016.

20. Kate Taylor, "Longtime Staples of the American Diet Are in Danger of Going Extinct," *Business Insider*, Dec. 12, 2015.

21. "PepsiCo to Move Focus Away from Colas, CEO Indra Nooyi says," *FoodBev Media*, April 20, 2016.

22. "'Carbonating the World' Tracks Soda Industry in Big Tobacco's Global Footprints," Center for Science in the Public Interest, Feb. 9, 2016.

23. Marion Nestle, *Food Politics: How the Food Industry Influences Nutrition and Health* (Berkeley: University of California Press, 2013).

24. Tamar Haspel, "If GMOs Aren't the Problem with Our Food System, Then What Is?" *Washington Post*, Nov. 8, 2015.

25. Tamar Haspel, "10 Things We Should Do to Fix Our Broken Food System," *Washington Post*, Dec. 23, 2015.

26. Eric Kessler, "Arabella's Recipe for Good Food," Arabella Advisors, Dec. 3, 2015.

27. Eric Kessler, "12 Good Food Policy Priorities," Arabella Advisors, Dec. 9, 2015.

28. Interview with Eric Kessler, Arabella Advisors, Jan. 19, 2016.

29. Majid Ezzati et al., "Trends in Adult Body-Mass Index in 200 Countries from 1975 to 2014: A Pooled Analysis of 1698 Population-Based Measurement Studies with 19.2 Million Participants," *The Lancet*, April 2, 2016.

30. Jenny Hopkinson, "A Call for a National Obesity Strategy," *ProPolitico Morning Agriculture*, Feb. 23, 2016.

Index

ABOUT THE AUTHOR

Steve Clapp has covered food policy in Washington, D.C., for more than 40 years. Formerly, he served as a Peace Corps volunteer in northern Nigeria and worked as a field program evaluator ("inspector") for the U.S. Office of Economic Opportunity. His published works include *Africa Remembered: Adventures in Post-Colonial Nigeria and Beyond* as well as many articles for *The Washington Post* and *Washingtonian* magazine. Clapp earned a magna cum laude degree in English from Harvard College and a magna cum laude master's degree from the Columbia Graduate School of Journalism.